Shere Hite **Sex & Business**

FINANCIAL TIMES

Prentice Hall

In an increasingly competitive world, it is quality
of thinking that gives an edge. An idea that opens new
doors, a technique that solves a problem, or an insight
that simply helps make sense of it all.

We work with leading authors in the fields of
management and finance to bring cutting-edge thinking
and best learning practice to a global market.

Under a range of leading imprints, including
Financial Times Prentice Hall, we create world-class
print publications and electronic products giving readers
knowledge and understanding which can then be
applied, whether studying or at work.

To find out more about our business and professional
products, you can visit us at www.business-minds.com

For other Pearson Education publications, visit
www.pearsoned-ema.com

Pearson
Education

Shere Hite **Sex & Business**

FINANCIAL TIMES
Prentice Hall

London – New York · San Franciso · Toronto · Sydney
Tokyo · Singapore · Hong kong · Cape Town · Madrid
Paris · Milan · Munich · Amsterdam

PEARSON EDUCATION LIMITED

Head Office:
Edinburgh Gate
Harlow CM20 2JE
Tel: +44 (0)1279 623623
Fax: +44 (0)1279 431059

London Office:
128 Long Acre
London WC2E 9AN
Tel: +44 (0)207 447 2000
Fax: +44 (0)207 240 5771
Website: www.business-minds.com

First published in Great Britain in 2000

© Pearson Education Limited 2000

The right of Shere Hite to be identified as Author
of this Work has been asserted by her in accordance
with the Copyright, Designs and Patents Act 1988.

ISBN 0 273 64198 0

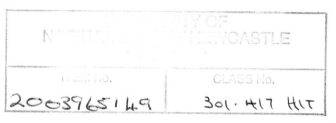

British Library Cataloguing in Publication Data
A CIP catalogue record for this book can be obtained from the British Library

This publication is designed to provide accurate and authoritative information
in regard to the subject matter covered. It is sold with the understanding that
neither the author nor the publisher is engaged in rendering legal, investing,
or any other professional service. If legal advice or other expert assistance is
required, the service of a competent professional person should be sought.

The publisher and contributors make no representation, express or implied,
with regard to the accuracy of the information contained in this book and
cannot accept any responsibility or liability for any errors or omissions
that it may contain.

10 9 8 7 6 5 4 3 2 1

Typeset by Pantek Arts, Maidstone, Kent.
Printed and bound in Great Britain by Biddles Ltd, Guildford and King's Lynn.

The Publishers' policy is to use paper manufactured from sustainable forests.

Contents

Chapter 5

How to Work with Men: Everything Women Should Know About Working with Men...

Chapter 6

How are Women Working with Other Women?

Introduction
A New Psychology at Work

Can men and women really work together?

Women and men at work are developing new kinds of relationships with each other – despite a bumpy road strewn with 'sexual harassment

How good is your mental software? Are you 'programmed' to stick your head in the sand and hope change is not 'too swift or painful' – or with an updated positive outlook?

lawsuits' and other landmines. These new relationships can fundamentally change the nature of society: new kinds of relationships

New kinds of relationships between the sexes, pioneered in the workplace, will spread to the rest of society and 'private life', as more people fundamentally change how they relate to one another at work.

between the sexes, pioneered in the workplace, will spread to the rest of society and 'private life', as more people fundamentally change how they relate to one another at work and how they see themselves. A more diverse emotional landscape is emerging, one with better concepts of 'masculine' dignity (less linked to money/career) and 'female' strength, plus other positive values. This improved software (for emotions and minds) will enhance daily life, make it richer and more profound.

Men have just begun to make apparent their inner changes.

How good is your mental software? Are you 'programmed' to stick your head in the sand and hope change is not 'too swift or painful' – or with an updated positive outlook?

The long-heralded 'Big Changes of the 21st Century' are here: at work, if we bother to look closely,.'new relationships' are springing up everywhere. There is a new scene at work. I hope here to provide a new take on some avoidable dilemmas, and offer a new software package, ready to install, for status quo addicts, mental slouches and other laggards – anyone who wants to know how to use the new situation at work for his/her own advantage. Men, as well as women, will profit enormously from the new work dynamics possible.

This doesn't have to be complicated or take forever. It can even be fun. You'll see.

PS: If you think this book and these issues are mostly about women, you are wrong: a major focus of this analysis of relationships at work is on men and 'male psychology'. The question of who men are, who men have been, and who men are becoming, is just as important as the question of who women are and will become. In fact, men have just begun to make apparent their inner changes.

Shere Hite

Preface
A New Emotional Landscape

Underwater Frescoes of the Mind

Some say 'human nature' is a fixed phenomenon, that a new psychological-emotional landscape cannot be possible. They point to the Athenian playwright Sophocles, or to Shakespeare, saying that their plays prove that 'human nature has always been the same; civilizations have always been the same, humans love, hate, are jealous, greedy and fear each other...'

> Some say 'human nature' is a fixed phenomenon, that a new psychological-emotional landscape cannot be possible.

Yet isn't this merely lazy justification of the status quo? Think of the antique (pre-6th-century) Greek myths and how hard it is for us to understand some of the myths' stories in their original form. The archaeologist Marija Gimbutas[1] has proposed a worldview for this period, pre-history, that is quite different from the standard view 'real-history-starts-with-the-Greeks-and-Egyptians' – a history that extends 20,000 years further into the past with a complex, sophisticated and lively artistic tradition – and most probably a different psychological and emotional landscape.

A new emotional landscape is possible, even if one never existed before.

How can we make a new psychological-emotional landscape?

People often prefer to claim that they have no myths, that myths are for 'stupid' or 'primitive' people. Yet underlying the social system studied by sociologists, and the emotions studied by psychologists, lie myths of creation, myths of family and myths of heroic behaviour. These archetypes, currently unacknowledged or called 'instinct', form the backdrop of our psyches and beliefs.

At present, the myths are undergoing change, a new psychological landscape is struggling to come into existence. In order for this to happen, and to take part in defining the new landscape, it is important to understand these myths.

Slowly, my work has been endeavouring to discover the identity of some of these underwater 'unconscious' frescoes in our minds – the backdrop to our psyches and emotions.

1 Gimbutas, M., *The Language of the Goddess*, Harper, San Francisco, 1995.

Naming this terrain will allow a new landscape to emerge.

As a result of my research, I believe that a completely different emotional-psychological landscape is now trying to emerge. Part of our psychology has been resistant to change because a hidden layer in the psyche, an identity behind our psychologies (often mistakenly called 'human nature') has not been analyzed. Undercovering this buried underwater layer is one of the goals of my work. This hidden layer is composed of all the myths and stories that create the human emotional spectrum as we know it. This is the terrain we meet when we are born, that we learn to take as 'inevitably' our own.

Naming this terrain will allow a new landscape to emerge.

Myth-Psychology: A New Field

When you are born, you are offered a variety of mythologies with which to write the scenario of your life. Which you choose depends on various psychological factors built into your individual situation and family (read Freud and other psychologists).

My work is trying to redesign the entire package of available choices or mythologies on offer – not to rewrite psychology (although it does that, too, in part). Is a completely different set of scenarios possible? Are the subconscious myths we live by changeable? Yes.

The five Hite reports and this book try to question and re-imagine (on the basis of measuring the counterpoint between what people say they experience and what society says they should be experiencing, how society says they should interpret their experiences), the repertoire of lives we can have: there are new ways to interpret our experiences and emotions.

Inside most of us an intense battle is raging between 'traditional values' and new beliefs. These beliefs as yet have unclear shapes and names, but here we try to name some of them, turn on a few sources of light in this new landscape.

Just as the early Greeks and Romans saw themselves differently from the later Christians, we now are beginning to see ourselves differently yet again.

Inside most of us an intense battle is raging between 'traditional values' and new beliefs.

Overview
A Brief Guide to this Book

What Men and Women Should Know about Doing Business with Each Other

Can men and women really work together?
It may be uncomfortable to admit, but, however liberated we are, deep within us, lingering in the corners of the subconscious are involuntary stereotypes to which we probably conform when dealing with other people. We almost can't help it; they come from generations of entrenched social behaviour supported by our friends, family and the media.

Lingering in the corners of the subconscious are involuntary stereotypes to which we probably conform when dealing with other people.

While we may understand in part the complex father–daughter, mother–son, wife–husband (or lovers) or brother–sister relationships, there is no training ground in most people's lives for

Banging the drum of the gender wars is no longer the point.

learning how to work or do business with the opposite sex.

Banging the drum of the gender wars is no longer the point. What is? If we can get to the root of the problem and discover the real nature of our thoughts and motivations, throw out the counterproductive attitudes and keep the good, then we can harness the diverse skills that men and women possess and combine them in a new way, to change the atmosphere and maybe even the nature of 'work'.

Today's work and business environments are a quantum leap from those of a mere generation ago. The proliferation of women in executive and management positions, the evolution of the personal assistant, the number of men entering secretarial roles and the increase in numbers of female entrepreneurs represent just some of the factors that contribute to a major realignment of gender positions. And yet, although the old rules no longer apply, there is widespread confusion across both sexes as to what, if any, new rules do apply. So people fall back on stereotypes.

The Trouble with Society...

The world seems unprepared (still...) to accept that both men and women can be great (or, indeed, terrible) leaders. Old stereotypes pervade the media, where females leaders are portrayed as monstrous Titans like Margaret Thatcher (the Iron Lady), or dangerous, seductive predators such as the character portrayed by Demi Moore in *Disclosure*, while male leaders are heroic figures like Tony Blair, or benevolent founding fathers like Gandhi...

Our whole social system is built around reinforcing the gender roles that have been set in stone for generations.

Who is to blame? Well, who has not laughed at jokes depicting women as flippant, indecisive and useless beings, only interested in marriage and beautification? Or jokes about a true man being a hunter, provider and DIY man extraordinaire?

Our whole social system is built around reinforcing the gender roles that have been set in stone for generations.

The Trouble with Women...

Even today, many families are still run on the old patriarchal system, the man king of his household, the woman brought up to defer or 'face the consequences'. An associated belief is that, as the man is the provider, he is thus entitled to more money and power. It is difficult psychologically to break out of this system.

Since women are taught that they should be the nurturers and supporters of life, when trying to take the reins of power themselves, they often fear they are breaking a dangerous taboo, and will be punished – rejected, seen as unfeminine, ruthless, aggressive or dominating. This is a fear that their male counterparts don't generally have to deal with.

When we are adolescents, society still dictates that it is the man who should initiate the chase during courtship. Although this is changing, many women are still nervous or uncomfortable asking for a date, let alone a promotion or pay rise.

Transferring this to the workplace, one notices a similar confusion of roles: labelling women as 'flirts' or docile, hard-working daughters, men as father or authority figures, etc. What women achieve at work seems, in this context, almost invisible.

In addition, women working with other women as colleagues, or as female bosses or secretaries, find that a new dynamic is going on, vying with the (still partially in place) 'females as competitors or best friends' software.

The Trouble with Men...

Men have an 'opposite problem': conditioned to become providers and protectors of 'the family', they have to fight assuming that women should not be colleagues or competitors. Men (like women) seek the approbation of other men – their male peers are still basically 'the people who matter'. After all, men too grew up in the father-on-top-is-best (or should be) family.

There is enormous pressure for men to get ahead, climb the career ladder and become overlord. They are usually introduced to the idea of working with women in an arena that traditionally belonged to them as something to worry about. Thus, when a woman is promoted over a man, it can lead to his feeling disenfranchised and socially embarrassed, his pride hurt.

Mix these 'male' and 'female' cocktails together, shake – and you can come up with a foamy mixture ready to explode: resentment and lack of understanding can run rampant. Some men (although a declining number) see women as interlopers deserving whatever treatment they get, from sexual harassment to ridicule, to having to prove themselves twice as much as men, to even deserving lesser pay (because, after all, 'they have babies and take their careers less seriously'). They say things like 'If a woman can't take the heat, she should stay at home.'

Mix these 'male' and 'female' cocktails together, shake – and you can come up with a foamy mixture ready to explode: resentment and lack of understanding can run rampant.

In contrast to this, men who believe women do have a rightful place in the corporate world and who like working with women face the problem of how to promote a woman without sparking rumours they are having some form of 'inappropriate relationship'. Many people still fall back on the old cliché that men and women cannot be friends: if any promotion of a woman takes place, there must have been a motive other than genuine respect and belief in that person's abilities.

Throw Out the Rulebook

So what now? Some of the Fortune 500 CEOs quoted in this book offer answers to these conundrums in corporate life; others offer a route back to past mistakes and dead-ends.

Men and women today are already in a new time and space, but sometimes habitual attitudes can be hard to change – they cling stubbornly like old coffee stains. Yet people can move beyond clichés, and see each other as individuals and professionals in a new way, for mutual reward and a more progressive way of working and interacting.

Throughout this book are a series of software commands for your brain – speedy ways to breeze through this information, including theories from my earlier research – arriving at the office on a Monday with a New You on view...

After researching and interviewing business men and women around the globe, CEOs from Fortune 500 companies, I offer here keys to understanding the conundrums and dynamics going on now in offices, my own theories and solutions for overcoming outdated (embarrassing) gender clichés, quickly.

Men and women today are already in a new time and space, but sometimes habitual attitudes can be hard to change – they cling stubbornly like old coffee stains.

Instead of burying gender differences and being paranoid about each other, men and women can embrace their different strengths, and be proud of them. Both bring something valuable to work. The differences we can have in approach are some of the most energizing and productive forces in action today, if those differences are used creatively.

From love in the workplace to sexual harassment, from men managing women to women managing men – or in fact women managing women – this book endeavours to cover every aspect of corporate relationships between the genders – it seems the first book to tackle this topic, the only book of its kind.

I wrote it because I believe that through a deeper understanding of the motives, needs and attitudes we have, we can bulldoze over the walls we have built up and begin a new era of mutual understanding, respect and success.

The findings,

the facts,

the statistics

What is really happening at corporations? No formal study had been done, no statistics made. It seemed time for someone to undertake a sampling of the basic questions.

Corporations in conflict with women are more and more in the news: Texaco pays US$40 million to women for back pay and gender discrimination in a 1998 lawsuit; Toshiba pays US$5 million in a sexual harassment lawsuit (1999); 900 women at Merrill Lynch file claims of discrimination in a 1999 class action lawsuit; and Monica Lewinsky makes headlines: 'Was it sexual harassment or mutual consent?' What's going on?

These headline cases are the tip of the iceberg of unresolved issues between women and men, now making their presence felt in a big way at work.

Not only women have complaints. Corporations are also in conflict, with their male employees, including their executives. How many studies have we all read showing that men are working too hard, too many hours, too long, 'neglecting their children and families', having heart attacks too young, and so on? All of these studies are true. But *why* is this happening? Wasn't the new technology and changing global economic picture supposed to make people's lives easier, make it necessary for them to work less hard? Why, then, these studies and statistics about men's difficulties and dissatisfactions? Is there anything men themselves can do to change things?

A better way forward can be found.

Not only women have complaints. Corporations are also in conflict, with their male employees, including their executives.

I wanted to investigate today's office and corporate culture in more depth, discover whether the theoretical work I had done earlier was relevant to current corporate situations. After all, sexual harassment is a subject with direct connections to my work on sexuality and sexual identity, both male and female.

What I found – using a modest, relatively brief non-random sample questionnaire and conducting interviews in many countries – is that issues of identity and psychology come together now in office relationships in a way no one would have predicted even ten years ago – and with extremely positive possibilities.

Here are some of the results of my questionnaire for corporations; other results can be found throughout the book.

Findings and Facts

These statistics are based on a sample of ten corporations, all of which have asked to remain anonymous. I leave it to the reader to decide how representative they are based upon his or her own experience.

Do women like their jobs?
66% of executive women
53% of secretarial and clerical women
41% of middle management women
83% of professional women (doctors, attorneys, professors)

Do men like their jobs?
75% of executive men
22% of secretarial and clerical men
31% of middle management men
67% of professional men (doctors, attorneys, professors)

Why do executive women like their jobs?
72% because of the status, feeling of importance, worth
91% because of the challenge of the task
74% because of the interesting people worked with
82% because of the money received, benefits

Why do executive men like their jobs?
73% because of the status, feeling of importance, worth
69% because of the challenge of the task
66% because of the interesting people worked with
90% because of the money received, benefits

Do women in middle management believe they can progress to become a member of the board of directors, an executive or CEO?
41% yes, it's a question of working hard, harder than the men around me
22% no, the top of the company is all men; I don't see any breakthrough
37% I don't want to progress upwards in the corporation

Do men in middle management believe they can progress upwards?
59% yes, it's a question of working harder than the others and having good connections
23% no, there are others who are more favoured or fit the slot better
18% I don't want to move up

Do men like working on an equal footing with women on the job?
31% yes, it's more interesting
17% yes, if the woman is not aggressive
52% no, frankly I find it easier and prefer to work with men

Do women like working on an equal footing with men in the job?
41% yes, it's interesting and they accept me
45% yes, if the man is not negative and works as hard as I do
14% no, frankly I find it easier and prefer to work with women

Do you feel appreciated and paid what you are worth in your job?

Men:
32% yes
68% no

Women:
44% yes
56% no

Have you experienced sexual harassment at work, i.e. been pressured sexually in a situation that could affect your job?

Women:
38% seriously
21% slightly
41% repeatedly

Men:
14% seriously
68% slightly
18% repeatedly

Do you believe that some slight flirtation at the office is acceptable?
40% women
65% men

Should the CEO of your company be married or single?
33% married and stable
18% single, if he doesn't run around too much
49% it's his choice

Have you ever been involved in a love affair at work?
62% women
71% men

Was it a positive experience or more negative?

Men:
- 61% positive
- 39% negative

Women:
- 27% positive
- 73% negative

Do you think men at work bully the other men more or bully women more?

Men:
- 23% women are bullied more
- 77% men are bullied more

Women:
- 81% women are bullied more
- 19% men are bullied more

Do women bosses treat women employees differently from male employees?

Men:
- 91% yes
- 9% no

Women:
- 94% yes
- 6% no

Does your wife, husband or partner act jealous, at times, of people with whome you work at the corporation, especially people of the opposite sex?

Men:
- 61% yes
- 25% no
- 32% sometimes
- 64% depends on how I talk about it

Women:
- 39% yes
- 62% no
- 31% sometimes
- 43% depends on how I talk about it

How would you feel if your corporation had an all-women board of directors?
- 13% startled
- 16% pleased
- 38% worried
- 18% I would not like to work for such a corporation
- 15% I would like to work for such a corporation

These statistics tell a story, but not necessarily (as often assumed) a story of gloom and doom.

These trends can be used in a very positive way, leading to improved working and personal relationships, if we are not frightened by change, and follow this transition through in the correct way. This book is dedicated to helping achieve this goal.

These trends can be used in a very positive way, leading to improved working and personal relationships.

At work, should women and men relate the way they used to when they were 'at home' together or dating? Of course not. Should they relate as friends? Yes and no. Colleagues are not always friends, neither need they be; relationships at work are not by definition 'friendships'. Football, soccer and sports teams are one way in which men learn to compete and use teamwork with all types of other men, whether friends, enemies or rivals, yet there is no similar training ground for learning how to work or do business with the opposite sex. For the most part, we are only taught (somehow) to 'meet and mate'. These old lessons are inappropriate.

Everything you thought you knew,

but could be surprised to find

is now different

Everything You Thought You Knew, But Could Be Surprised to Find is Now Different

Can men and women really do business together?

Today's work and business environments are a quantum leap from those of a mere generation ago. The proliferation of women in executive and management positions, the evolution of the personal assistant, the number of men entering secretarial roles and the increase in numbers of female entrepreneurs – these represent just some of the factors that are contributing to a major realignment of gender positions.

Although the old rules no longer apply, there is widespread confusion across both sexes as to what, if any, new rules do apply.

Although the old rules no longer apply, there is widespread confusion across both sexes as to what, if any, new rules do apply.

To understand today's business environment demands a radical reassessment of gender roles and the rules of engagement. Questions of ethics and behaviour are too often left to the vagaries of supposed common sense and conventional wisdom; we allow ourselves to stumble through an ethical minefield of sexual morality that may lead to entrusting final judgement to the courts.

A better idea: implement new strategies and tools for establishing effective cross-gender channels of communication – do ourselves, the world, and business, a favour.

As things stand, the atmosphere at work is poisoned by ridiculous semi-conscious assumptions and ideas. For example, Billy Graham, one of the US's most popular and well-known preachers speaking to Larry King on CNN Television, autumn 1998, re the Clinton impeachment trial, stated: 'I have never in all my 40 years of the ministry, been alone with my secretary in a room with the door closed. (She) has been my secretary for many years, but I always keep the door open.' Is this idea the old cliché, 'Women are the gateway to sin, the devil's invitation to men'???

With so many more women than ever working in business, a clearing of the air is needed. Sexual harassment lawsuits, increasingly in the news, could become unnecessary (as well as the pain, hurt feelings and damaged pride they involve, not to mention money they cost) if the simple guidelines and training techniques given here are employed.

With so many more women than ever working in business, a clearing of the air is needed.

It is not surprising that relationships between women and men encounter rough sailing or trouble spots. Ancient clichés cause much of the friction. If people can remove such clichés from their minds, productivity and morale will be much higher.

A quick way to grasp the depth of the problem in your own mental software is to consider the following…!

Men and women both bring something valuable to work. The difference they can have in approach may be one of the most energizing and productive forces in action today – if the differences are understood and used creatively. What we are trying to create is not a unisex world, but a world with varied individuals flourishing – technicolour. As anyone working in a modern, mixed-gender, corporate environment will tell you, the important challenge is to get a new kind of office interaction up and running.

At work, should women and men relate the way they used to when they were 'at home' together or dating? Of course not. Should they relate as friends? Yes and no. Colleagues are not always friends, neither need they be; relationships at work are not by definition 'friendships'. Football, soccer and sports teams are one way in which men learn to compete and use teamwork with all types of other men, whether friends, enemies or rivals, yet there is no similar training ground for learning how to work or do business with the opposite sex. For the most part, we are only taught (somehow) to 'meet and mate'. These old lessons are inappropriate.

The culture has never really believed in male-female friendships, seeing the two sexes as inevitably doomed to feel the sexual tingle if alone in a room! Thus, for many people, developing work relationships with those of the opposite gender is not easy or comfortable. It can, however, become so.

We need to create a variety of new styles of workable relationships. So keep reading…

The Situation as Men See It

Most men now believe it is politically correct to welcome women into the workplace, but in fact have some reservations – even the most stalwart supporters of the 'new woman' – as these men comment:

'I guess it is inevitable that women are inside upper management of corporations – women are everywhere in business now – but I almost wish they weren't. I wonder if it's for the best. Weren't things better when women did not try to be tough and come out and compete with us at work? I like feminine women, and the pressures of equality make them tougher than I like them.'

'I have a daughter and I certainly plan to pay for a good university for her studies (when she gets that old, she's only six!). But I wonder what the future will hold for her – a nice home with children? A single life fighting with her boss? Will she be satisfied with the reward of work, coming home late at night, maybe to a husband, maybe not? Still, I'll do everything I can to teach her she's my equal.'

'I want women at work. I find that they make work more interesting, they bring another perspective to work projects, another energy – they have a lot of enthusiasm and are not afraid to show it. On the other hand, sometimes I get so fixated on not using my male status to block their careers, I'm so busy being a nice guy, that I mess up my own career.'

For the most part, we are only taught (somehow) to 'meet and mate'. These old lessons are inappropriate.

Of course there are men who do not want women at work at all, but these are a minority in my sample (see Chapter 5).

The Situation as Women See it

Women say that they are faced with various obstacles – the 'invisible' glass ceiling (you'll get pregnant, you'll stay at home, you'll fall in love, we already have one woman, two or three women will never get along, it will be a hen party...), outright discrimination (can't get an appointment, 'you can't be serious'), the perils of sexual harassment (to play along, run away or speak up and complain – all roads are hazardous and can lead to being tossed out!) and low pay (sex discrimination suits are now blazing ahead, Merrill Lynch, Texaco and Ford having made enormous settlements for back pay in class action discrimination lawsuits).

Naturally, women are not pleased about this situation, but optimistic about the future: if so much change has occurred in the last twenty years, which shouldn't more change be possible? Women will try for more change in the years ahead, because they like working (despite its problems), both for financial and quality-of-life rewards. A 1999 study showed that women say they like working not primarily because 'the couple today cannot afford only one income' (common wisdom before the study), but because the rewards at work are more tangible

It will require a change of attitude by women towards other women in order for the growing numbers of women at work to mean better pay and advancement for women.

(getting paid, getting sometimes appreciated) than the rewards at home, i.e. taking care of children can be wonderful but is usually unpaid and poorly appreciated – the children play games on the mother and mock her authority over them, while the father avoids it all by coming home late, etc. All in all, work seems a definite step up in status and finances to most women, and they like it.

Women's relationships with other women at work still lag behind. Most women still understandably see men as the real power centres, perhaps out of habit, but also because this is the reality at most corporations now. It will require a change of attitude by women towards other women in order for the growing numbers of women at work to mean better pay and advancement for women. It is difficult for women to start to take each other seriously, see each other as power centres, but this is coming, the next big step.

Although more and more women now find a solid footing inside Fortune 500 companies, the number of women at the top, statistically, remains stubbornly small, especially in upper management and on boards of directors. The reasons usually cited for this – i.e. 'we can't find qualified women', 'we are hiring young women now as trainees and hope they will work up to the top', or 'the problem for women is that they must interrupt their careers for childbearing' – are not the real reasons for this deficit. The situation has grown historically out of a culture that saw women as second-class, even going so far as saying women had no souls. Although many now praise women's intelligence and capacities, discrimination at work is still the order of the day – at least, if government figures and statistics are any guide. Saying that 'all is changing' may be premature, unless a new analysis of the way forward is found; one such analysis is offered here.

Quite a few male executives feel uncomfortable with the lack of women at the top, but, by the same token, many (understandably) don't want to face the clichés some of their colleagues may throw at them, i.e. 'He wants to promote her because he's got a girlfriend!' In short, one of the basic but hidden reasons so few women are at the top of corporations has to do with sexual politics: a male executive does not want to be pointed out as 'the one who wanted her here', to insist on promoting or hiring a female executive, as he may be accused of having a sexual affair with her (and 'this is why he promoted her') – or having poor judgement.

Working Closely with a Colleague of the Other Sex

'Be friendly, don't be friendly, never flirt, don't take it seriously, go out for coffee, don't go out for coffee'... what is right? If you're sometimes confused, you're not alone!

What are the new rules?

People now are in transition, making the rules up as they go along, as these women's remarks show:

'I met a man at the office, I like him. I'm not sure what this means. Can I just like him, or do I want to spend more time with him? I'd like to be friends, I guess. I'll be working with him on a project. I do have a boyfriend, I live with him and we're very happy. This man is also living with his new wife, I think he told me. He calls me several times a week to talk, and I feel we have a sort of special friendship. Wouldn't it be great if we could be friends and see each other every day? Still, I wonder about my motivations and where this could be leading. Then I think, don't be silly, it doesn't have to lead anywhere! You can be friends, that is colleagues, since what we talk about is our work and politics and so on, not private life or how we feel about each other, for the most part.

In short, one of the basic but hidden reasons so few women are at the top of corporations has to do with sexual politics.

'I catch myself thinking that the appropriate response to his friendliness is to be flirtatious sometimes, female, you know. It can be fun to flirt just a little bit, that is, flirt like a friend, joke around, playing with another friend, male or female, teases them and makes them feel special and funny. I think he understands that this is the idea, but then, I can't be sure. What if he misunderstands? What if a little part of me wants him to misunderstand? It would be flattering to my ego if he made a small overture of desire, it would make me feel I am irresistible or something, but would it really mean that? Or would it mean that he felt that he was doing the expected thing, in the situation? It could mean that he just did not know how to express his positive feelings for me, other than with the me–man, you–woman gestures. (Do I know how? Ha!)'

'It's hard to relate to any one of them, the guys at work, because they always seem to be part of a group of other guys. I can't be more nice to one than the other, or they close ranks. Naturally I like some of them more than others, I even imagine I'd like to be friends with one or two. I'm not sure how I would relate if there weren't the automatic block of the boy's brigade, plus the blinking sign "all sexual attractions and flirtations at work are illegitimate and off limits. You'll be considered a maverick and lose your job if you get out of line."'

'Do I flirt? Hell, I'm so confused I don't know how I really feel, I just know that the men seem very flirtatious to me (pretending not to be, but they hope I and the other women here think they are hunks, desirable). Anyway, they don't need to flirt with other guys to get ahead, why do they reproach us women for trying? It's about our only special weapon, we need it to make us equal with their special weapon, i.e. being "one of the boys". I can never be "one of the boys", so I have to flirt to get special privileges to even be on the same level of attention.'

A female receptionist describes how she thinks the men at her firm see her:

'I am a black woman working as a receptionist in an all-male insurance office. I don't let any of the men here give me a hard time. I know they hired me in part because I'm black, but, I've kept the job because I'm well-qualified and good at what I do. I see the men here like my sons, stray boys who need a helping hand. They get to see me as their "mom" but, at the same time, look down on me because I'm "just the receptionist" – so it works out fine. I guess I don't make their wives jealous either, because I'm black and I'm over 30. It's only lonely sometimes going out to have a bite for lunch, but there are one or two other secretaries I meet up with sometimes. Most of the time, though, I'm on my own.'

Men talking about their secretaries can be very revealing:

'With my secretaries, I wasn't very demanding. I guess I'm not typical. I fancied one or two for a short time, but they told me to fuck off, and that put me in my place. One of them in particular was fresh and young, and I was too – it was playtime!'

'My wife is a bore, I married her because my parents and her parents more or less insisted. I like the fun I have joking around with the girls at work, they talk about their boyfriends, going out to clubs and dancing, they smoke cigarettes and make jokes – a far cry from my wife who is constantly complaining about something the children did (that I should speak to them about), or needing more money for the house. Am I turned on sexually by the girls at work? Yeah, one or two especially, but so far I haven't invited them anywhere – just for a coffee at the office canteen. It was embarrassing once, we were standing there, waiting for our coffees, and I could feel myself getting an erection. There were quite a few senior colleagues around, and I was worried they would think I was not attending to my job. So I cut it short, and left her there to drink her coffee alone.'

'I had an idiot secretary, but I kept her because she was young and cute and looked good, to be frank – a decoration for my legal practice. I wasn't turned on by her in the slightest myself, but maybe some of my clients were. I don't know how she felt.'

'Are secretaries attractive? It depends on how hungry you are. Sometimes you feel like a predator, an animal on the prowl out to no good, you know you will hate yourself afterwards (and even have a problem getting rid of her) but on the other hand, it's fun and exciting. When I was transferred here from another town (I was 29, now I'm 33), I found myself eyeing all the secretaries and any woman in the office. I would work late and then go home to my newly rented flat where the furniture was not properly installed (I never had time) and the refrigerator empty – the place looked like a desert, still unpacked boxes on the floor. My girlfriend and I spoke on the telephone every day, planned weekends together, but with her work and mine, it didn't always happen. When she came to visit or I visited her, the time was so short that we didn't feel quite right and sometimes argued rather than enjoying ourselves and making love. I knew the writing was on the wall.'

'I found myself more and more eyeing the secretaries – cute, young, dressed great. This situation got out of hand, and once I had one over to my apartment and we made love on my kitchen table, in a very wild way. The problem was, I didn't want to see her again, but there she was, every day at the office. So I called my girlfriend and pleaded with her to leave her job and come and live with me, get a job in the town I was in. To help me out and live together. Fortunately, she came and we're together now for four years. This has helped me stabilize and get on with my career.'

These replies may make some women who hear them wonder if they as executive women get more respect than secretaries. Of course women hope they get more respect than 'the other women' at work, but at the same time feel like traitors to women who are spoken of disrespectfully: they suffer from torn loyalties. To which group at work should they give their allegiance – other women, or men in power? How should they deal with this situation?

Mini Hite Report: Statistics

How is it going between male and female colleagues? Is real equality between women and men 'the norm' now? How does this new 'equality', this situation, feel?

How is it going between male and female colleagues? Is real equality between women and men 'the norm' now? How does this new 'equality', this situation, feel?

Men:

26% we treat the women at work equally

13% we treat the women at work equally, but they probably do not get paid what we do

61% I have to admit that the women are just not seriously included or considered

Women:

15% I feel treated equally

22% I feel treated equally, but not paid equally

63% I feel discriminated against in most ways

New rules and regulations

Does this subject seem like we are opening a can of worms? Too much to deal with? Don't worry! The changes are coming anyway and will improve and benefit your life quickly. Understand them to maximize your benefit.

How to Play to Win at Work in the New Gender Sweepstakes!

There is a tendency to see women's continuing lack of integration into higher levels of corporate management as either a 'woman's problem' or a 'man's problem', i.e. how bad men are ('men are prejudiced, behaving badly'), or 'women aren't behaving right', or 'women get pregnant'.

I prefer to see it as a mutual problem, with both sides frequently playing out scenarios of old dynamics from 'the family' or clichés about personal life – even clichés from dating. Women at work can see 'the father' as a boss or CEO, and men can see women as daughters (good girls) or 'tough career women' (bad girls, the cliché about women who don't stay at home and behave like dutiful daughters or good mothers).

The danger: to project stereotypes of family onto women or men at work, i.e. see them through 'how people should behave in the family' (especially women) – the 'dutiful daughter', the all-suffering martyr mother 'who doesn't demand anything' or the 'tough career girl' who 'doesn't want a family' stereotype.

The future should see us invent new relationships. There has not been much room for men and women to be friends in society, and now – with so many women and men working together – they are expected to suddenly know how to treat each other, how to behave and think in new ways.

But do we? We can profit from a few simple exercises... perhaps by simply giving a few commands to our brains (like we command our computers), we can make changes.

The future should see us invent new relationships.

This doesn't have to be complicated or take forever. It can even be easy...

The New Relationships

New male-female relationships: teammates and office buddies

I believe that more relationships than need to go down the road of 'we're attracted, we like each other, therefore since we're of the opposite sex, sex must be what we're after'.

Many people feel a spark of attraction for another person, but is it best expressed by having sex? (What do you do after? The next day? Next week? Maybe you won't want to have sex a second time, 'again'.) OK, but then where does the relationship go? Usually one person decides to dislike the other, or one person gets angry because the other seems to have wanted a 'one night stand'. That scenario doesn't have to take place anymore: the relationship that was trying to happen does not have to be expressed sexually; it can find new forms, not yet invented, so it can flourish through work and friendship.

When people at work feel a warm attraction, a spark of sympathy for each other, they can decide to use this energy in a variety of directions. Usually such a spark is interpreted as a danger signal, a signal that sexual desire is lurking in the background, but it doesn't have to be interpreted in this way. Now, we only see that direction because the culture says that is the only direction that is possible. The two people may think: 'It does seem a shame just to stop here, let this new potential friendship go at that. I'd like to know him/her better.' But this would seem to imply 'illicit dating' or 'sex'; they don't know what else to do. It would be nice to know that there are at least two or three types of long-term relationships that can be developed (and that are publicly, socially accepted) between the sexes, not just one (a sexual one).

Many people feel a spark of attraction for another person, but is it best expressed by having sex?

There should be various socially condoned ways men and women can be friends, and share time, without making others 'talk'. It is good to know another person and be around a person who brings energy and a sense of happiness to your day. Actually, when two men meet at work and 'hit it off', they do not have to think: 'Well, I'd like to work with him, I'd like to hire him as my second in command, but if I do it will cause waves at home with my wife, and I will constantly have to be telling myself to "watch it!". It could be rewarding, but it's too complicated.'

As long as the repertoire of relationships considered 'normal' between women and men is not expanded, women will be blocked by the 'glass ceiling' at work. And men will remain isolated in predictable scenarios.

As long as the repertoire of relationships considered 'normal' between women and men is not expanded, women will be blocked by the 'glass ceiling' at work.

Was there a time in which the situation we have (male-female relationship limited to being either spouses, parent–child or sister–brother) truly made sense and carried society forward? Perhaps in ancient times, when more reproduction of the species was the main goal – men the 'providers' for the family (women, children) while women were occupied with pregnancy and nursing young children? It may have made sense to focus all male-female interaction in reproductive activities; today, however, most people want to use birth control during their sexual relations; most do not want more than one or two children.[1]

In fact, society might always have been better off with more choices of ways for women and men to relate. We cannot change the past, it is useless to debate "what if...".

What is clear now is that a diversity of possible relationships is needed, and will benefit us. We are not using our energies productively at present, we are spending too much energy fighting each other. These male-female fights are non-productive and must end.

Basic dilemmas would still occur – people would have children together but not want to live together, or fall in love 'innapropriately' at work, for example – but they would not be so prevalent as now, since two people meeting and hitting it off would, even though of the opposite sex, be able to find socially acceptable structures in which to express happiness at knowing one another. They would no longer be forced to express their liking or closeness by becoming a couple. After all, two men can 'hang out' together (otherwise known as 'hanging out with the boys' or 'a business engagement'); women and men should be able to do this too.

'But', you say, 'they would just be playing a game. Wouldn't they really want to go to bed together, eventually, so wouldn't the situation be dishonest?' I ask you: would they really want to go to bed together? Two men don't incessantly ask themselves if they are gay, just because they are not expressing their friendship with sex. Neither must a man and woman ask themselves this question, if there are social structures that accept friendship between men and women. They would accept liking each other within the confines of friendship or a new institution I am proposing here: teammates.

1 Why do some cry that 'a depressed birth rate' is leading to the 'collapse of the West' – especially in light of the high birth rates of 'other cultures'? So-called civilization is not created by superior numbers; if so, how could England have dominated the world during parts of the 19th century? (Note: birth rates in other parts of the world will also lower as more women escape from illiteracy, separate sexual expression and love from fear of pregnancy or forced reproduction, to have time to go to school. See United Nations Declaration on the Rights of Women, 1995, Beijing, summary statement.)

Teammates would focus on work, but have a good time doing it together.

Two people would see a bright future ahead for themselves as teammates. This relationship would not be hidden from colleagues, spouses or loved ones. Teammates would focus on work, but have a good time doing it together.

You can make a difference

Men and women today are already in a new time and space, but sometimes habitual attitudes can be hard to change – they cling stubbornly like old coffee stains. Yet people can move beyond clichés, and see each other as individuals and professionals in a new way, for mutual reward and a more progressive way of working.

People in corporations, by imagining new ways of looking at things, can contribute importantly to structuring a new global culture – especially now that corporations are larger and more important than ever before. Perhaps corporate cultures are evolving to become a new global culture. If so, individuals now, by their choices and ways of relating to each other, can contribute importantly to structuring this new global culture, the 'cosmopolitan global society' of the future as Anthony Giddens, Director of the London School of Economics, refers to it.

This new collegiality between women and men will create enormous energy for the good and make a big difference – in the corporation, in the individuals involved, and in the world, as all our actions have ripple effects...

Brain Software Commands

Note: Throughout this book, software commands are offered as a short cut to making rapid changes in your behaviour and perceptions at work. They could even save your job! Of course, you can take the alternative route (also offered in this book) of understanding more in depth how some of the clichés and assumptions we all have in our mental software came about; however, it is also possible to change your thinking rapidly, simply by deciding to do so and making the noted software changes. Unbelievable, but true.

WORKING ON YOUR MENTAL SOFTWARE

- Ideas to forget.

+ New software to install (in your brain).

Steps and guidelines for women and men to work together:

● Appraise your working partner for his or her skills and assets, as well as weak points.

● Imagine the most productive way you could combine your talents for long-term and short-term goals.

● Speak to her or him about these goals and plans, and how to work on them together.

Result: Write the results of your partnership or working relationship in your diary at the end of each working week. (Keep a journal of the work and the relationship's development.)

Test yourself after one month of this approach at your office:

● Have I made a better team at work?

● Is my own reputation enhanced?

● How do I feel?

● Have I shared bits of information about this relationship with my significant others, whether friends, spouses or loved ones?

Fun games to play with your colleagues... try them out at home first!

Things don't always go smoothly, even though no outward conflict may be apparent. Consider this scene.

A woman and a man are talking in an office corridor. During the conversation, she falls silent looking depressed or irritated, not making eye contact, then leaves. Returning to her office area, she soon finds another woman to talk to (briefly), looking for understanding in this new conversation.

Did the man notice? As she walks off, what is he thinking?

a I was stupid

b She was stupid

c I am confused! What did I do wrong?

Now think of the situation with the man's and woman's position reversed, i.e. he falls silent and walks off, leaving her to wonder what he was thinking. Does she conclude a, b or c?

Most importantly, what action can either person take to get communication back on track?

Let's replay the situation. Instead of walking off, the two of them, or either of them, could follow the Basic Communication Procedure of Hite Research: The Four Ss.

The Four Ss

1. **S**mile.

2. **S**low down and listen carefully; ask the other person to repeat her/his idea or comment if necessary – no matter how seemingly insignificant or casual the remark.

3. **S**ummarize your understanding of the other person by repeating briefly what you heard, then...

4. **S**peak about your reaction, respond.

Brain Game 2.1

Imagine you have an appointment for a job interview with someone of the opposite sex who is in the decision-maker's seat.

Next, imagine you are going on a job interview with someone of the same sex in the decision-maker's seat.

Notice the difference between your reactions. Is there a difference? In which scenario were you more relaxed? More yourself? More confident? What was different about your body language in the two imagined situations? Would you prepare differently the night before, or have different worries?

If possible, play these situations out with a friend or colleague. Talk about them.

Brain Game 2.2

What if the other person at work is sexually flirtatious with you (or you think so): how do you turn this in the direction of friendship without offending the other person? Choose one of the following:

a) You act as if you are not aware of, or did not notice, the flirtatious behaviour and simply continue with the same courtesy you would have with a same-sex colleague.

b) You have a direct confrontation, saying, 'Please don't do (x) because this is a work situation, and I'm not interested.'

c) You acknowledge the difference of your relationship, and say, 'This is one of the first times I have worked directly with someone of the opposite sex, and I want to try in every way I can to make our relationship one of friendly collegiality. If I sometimes give signals that are confused, this is only because I am! (smile) Well, probably because I am not used to the situation. But my goal is to work together in a productive, professional way over the long term, and to get the best result possible.'

Play these situations out with a friend or colleague. Think about them.

Brain Software Commands

Brain Game 2.3

SOFTWARE TO DELETE

Is she or he date material?

SOFTWARE TO INSTALL

I'm in a new situation. Here's my chance to try something new!

What should you do when there are cross words?

Every real relationship hits rough patches. Here are some useful things to say when the other person (no matter which gender) gets upset:

- Ask 'What have I done wrong? Let me try to redo it and improve things.'

- Say 'Talk to me about what's on your mind. I'm listening.'

- Ask 'What disappointed you? What is missing in what I said, or not happening?'

This does not make you look like a wimp, or give the other person all the power (in a negative sense). It makes dialogue possible – although it might be painful for a few minutes. It's worth it.

Guidelines

The four most important signals to give, to make the working relationship go smoothly (on a one-to-one basis):

1. Ask questions, be interested, listen and share your ideas with another person on a one-to-one basis.

2. Smile, don't snarl or be negative during the exchange.

3. Show you know where you are going, let your enthusiasm for work show, create an atmosphere that includes the other person in that direction.

4. Don't be judgemental, but do disagree early on with directions which seem wrong to you. Then listen to the response, in case you're wrong. If you decide you're wrong, say so. Try to reach mutual decisions.

Your Opinion…

What is your opinion and experience? What do you think? What have been *your* experiences of what's been discussed in this chapter?

Please use this space to write your remarks, or alternatively you may e-mail comments to the *Sex and Business* website at www.sexandbusiness.com/myopinion. Naturally, you may express yourself anonymously.

_____

_____

_____

_____

_____

_____

Although CEOs and chairmen are so powerful, very little is known about most of them, not even their names, except to their peers in the insider business world. Less yet is known of their private lives and views on such matters as the new politics of the family, men's revolt against 'the family' and desire for 'freedom', promotion of women to executive positions, democratization of families, etc. Their views on these matters are important, since the corporations they run affect so many people's lives – thus their policies on 'the family' (male and female identity) continue to shape the world.

View from the top:

how the chairman

sees things

View from the Top: How the Chairman Sees Things

Every corporation has a top dog who influences the atmosphere, advertising and sales of the company, as well as its future direction (and your job).

If you work for a corporation, you live in a land ruled by the equivalent of a president of a country, i.e. the CEO or chairman of the board of your company dictates the culture of your working day. Few corporations have constitutions that spell out the aims of the corporation (Bertelsmann, the global media firm, does have a constitution); thus who a CEO is and what he thinks is the key to understanding the scene at work.

If you work for a corporation, you live in a land ruled by the equivalent of a president of a country.

In an effort to demystify the Land of Work, I present here interviews I conducted with some of the world's top CEOs to help understand the human issues behind the 'mask of power'.

CEOs and top corporate executives are some of the most powerful people on earth today, but are often unknown. More powerful than many presidents and prime ministers, they frequently cultivate a low profile, so that their company will have more freedom, less media scrutiny; others simply have no reason to be in the limelight. However, with the business press increasingly popular – as the importance of businesses so large as to rival countries in population and power becomes clearer, i.e. global businesses are almost the new nation-states – more and more CEOs are being profiled and listened to.

Top Brass: Who Should They be in Private?

How do male[1] CEOs see their role: who must a man be to lead a firm? Must male executives be married with children, 'good, stable family men', considered morally privately 'perfect'? In the 1998–99 trial of President Clinton, such issues were the subject of extended public debate. Will this kind of scrutiny come to the heads of corporations, as they too are powerful leaders expected to comport themselves in a 'certain way'?

Whereas CEOs used to be thought of as 'the men in grey suits', listless and colourless conformists who did little that was dynamic or interesting, today they seem more like the glamour men of the 21st century. Like the corporations of the Industrial Revolution of the 19th century, carving out new fortunes from new industries, today's merger-fat corporate entities are making quite a splash as they become bigger and bigger, control more and more of the earth's surface and the people on it who depend on them for employment, goods and services. They organize life.

1 As there is only one female CEO of a top Fortune 100 company (at Hewlett-Packard, appointed July 1999) and in the top 300 FTSE index, the subject of CEOs is here addressed as male.

Today's merger-fat corporate entities are making quite a splash as they become bigger and bigger, control more and more of the earth's surface and the people on it who depend on them for employment, goods and services. They organize life.

Although CEOs and chairmen are so powerful, very little is known about most of them, not even their names, except to their peers in the insider business world. Less yet is known of their private lives and views on such matters as the new politics of the family, men's revolt against 'the family' and desire for 'freedom', promotion of women to executive positions, democratization of families, etc. Their views on these matters are important, since the corporations they run affect so many people's lives – thus their policies on 'the family' (male and female identity) continue to shape the world.

International corporations are not required by any international or enforceable law to follow moral or 'human rights' practices (either within their companies or in their practices around the world). Governments have signed the United Nations Charter promising to uphold certain principles, including 'human rights', but corporations have signed no such charter. If they feel compelled to hire women or 'minorities' and not discriminate, this is only because of public opinion or national laws.

Although corporations have not signed the United Nations Charter, they are subject to national laws, the laws of countries in which they operate or sell their merchandise, i.e. Toshiba was sued in a US court, etc.

In the UK, the Sex Discrimination Act was passed in 1975. Corporations must, therefore, follow its guidelines. It states that direct discrimination occurs when a person is treated less favourably on the grounds of their own sex. The Race Relations Act (RRA) was passed one year later in 1976, and so had the benefit of hindsight; the RRA also makes clear that an employer's or manager's intentions or motivation are relevant in deciding whether or not discrimination has taken place.

A company's policy on 'human rights' and 'the family' also depends on whether it is a private or public company. A public company may feel more pressure to 'act right' because it is owned by the public, bought and traded on the stock exchange, whereas a private company is privately held by several individuals or companies, and therefore answers only to them.

Interviewing CEOs in various countries, I was astounded to find out how very different they are in philosophy, private ethics, and understanding of the situation regarding male psychology and women at work. Once in a while, CEOs, or their PAs, outspokenly voiced a desire to distance themselves from these issues – women at work or how men feel about work and themselves. The PA for Unilever, for example, told me, 'He says he has nothing to do with these kinds of issues, these issues have nothing to do with our company!' This is a short-sighted view, as will be seen.

Must Male Executives be Married with Children?

Must a chief executive or chairman be a 'good, stable family man'? Do people respect their chiefs more when they have a family and seem to lead a 'complete' life, play their 'proper role' in society – display the symbols of power, i.e. an office, a staff, a car and a family?

Is a chairman or CEO allowed to separate or divorce?

In a survey of Fortune 500 top companies, only 5 per cent of CEOs are not married, and few are in their second or third marriages, or divorced. Alhough this may be changing, it seems necessary for most top politicians in every country to be married with children, to have the 'perfect family'. (Is this to show their capacity to reproduce?? No, because then all that would be necessary would be to have children, even out of wedlock.) It seems that a 'leader' must fulfil the social mandate of respecting traditional social codes of 'good comportment', fulfilling the reproductive and patriarchal duty of heading a family.

The rule seems to be, in other words, if you want to be promoted or elected, you must get married, have children – and stay married, no matter what.

The rule seems to be, in other words, if you want to be promoted or elected, you must get married, have children – and stay married, no matter what.

Is this fair? Will this continue? In a world in which 50 per cent of people are single, as they are now, perhaps not. Some would argue that 'more successful people' are married, but I would say something quite different: that we are, as a society, in the midst of a social revolution that is changing the way we live, changing the rules of private life for the better (see page 51, Democratization of the Family). People today are no longer willing to live in a reproductive unit simply because this is their duty, people now believe it is their duty to be as honest and genuine with others as they can be, that private life should be based on true love, and that seeking to found a relationship is a more ethical procedure than merely fitting an approved social model.

A particularly troubling social dilemma for many executives is: what if an individual is successfully married for many years, then meets someone new and falls in love? Is it more moral and ethical for him to remain with the person he married, to uphold duty, or to follow his 'true love' and be 'honest with the world'? Does he have a choice? Questions like this challenge the common wisdom that a leader should 'show stability and be married'. Is a leader more moral if he stays married, or if he follows his heart, in this scenario? This may have been partly the issue in the Clinton trial vis-à-vis Monica Lewinsky, i.e. were there pressures on him as 'the leader of the free world' to remain married and not to show any doubt or 'lack of stability' in his family duties?

Will Executives Begin to Reflect the New Family Demographics?

If 50 per cent of the population of the West today is 'single', can 50 per cent of a company's management and workforce be single – or would this be destabilizing? (Should corporations prefer 'married men' to 'single men'? Divorced women or men to never-married people? People with children or without? Lesbians or heterosexuals?)

Demographics indicate that now or in future, half of a company's workforce will not be married (either deciding to remain single, divorced or separated, or live with a partner of the same or opposite sex but not marry). In the past, corporations were structured as if they expected their employees to be married men, probably with children. This is less and less likely to be the case, yet the head of a corporation is almost always expected to be married with children. Although gay men represent around 10 per cent of the population, is this 10 per cent represented in most groups of men inside corporations? Usually, being gay is hidden at executive-level jobs. Will it continue to be?

Usually, being gay is hidden at executive-level jobs. Will it continue to be?

Although some say that if 50 per cent of people at work are single, this will cause instability inside a corporation (is this why CEOs or executives 'must be married', to set an

Mini Hite Report: Statistics

90% of the CEOs say that yes, women should be promoted to management level, although they are not there now (in 99% of cases).

75% say that women score better on their tests, whether at school or for entering the job, than men.

However, the reasons they give why women are not there now vary:

30% – 'The tragedy for women is that childbearing and mothering interrupts their careers, and then they cannot really make up the time, get back the years of experience they missed...'

30% – 'The problem has been discrimination, but we are now hiring (or have been hiring for the last ten years) bright young women MBAs who are moving up in the corporation, and in another twenty years, they will be at the top.'

20% – 'Men just do not feel as comfortable with women around, and at that level, to make the tough decisions necessary, you need an extremely good working atmosphere. Maybe in the future things will change, but for now, we have to do what works for the corporation and the shareholders.'

10% – No reason given ('none needed'?).

example?), this conclusion is inaccurate. The new social trends, people living with new kinds of families and relationships (even single), as well as in 'traditional families', are not by any means necessarily a threat to corporations' health. Such trends can actually be used to a corporation's advantage.

Conversations with CEOs: A State of Transition

What do CEOs think about the 'new social values'? Do they believe in 'traditional family values' or a variation of them? Must CEOs and other executives be 'good family men and women', or can they lead with other personal values, live 'alternate private lifestyles'? Are the 'new values' (the Spice Girls, single mothers and women CEOs, dads at home) beneficial for the world? The changes in women's position in society?

How will corporations function in the future to incorporate the 'new family politics', or the changes people have been and are making in their lives?

The questions
The questions I asked the CEOs include:

● What do you think of family values?

● What are the new 'rules' emerging in corporate management now with so many women working side by side with men?

● Is it good to have women at work? In management? What is your company's policy?

● How does your company deal with cases of sexual harassment? What is the new comportment or etiquette necessary now to make men and women work well together as friends, protégés and mentors?

● What do you think of the Clinton sex scandals?

● Must executives today present themselves as 'good family men', keep a tight rein on their private lives? Can an executive be single and date various people? Risk falling in love (and perhaps being emotional or 'out of control')?

● Can an executive woman be single, e.g. could Thatcher have been single?

● Do the media have the right to know about you?

● Should executives be 'good family men'?

● How are executives now handling their personal lives? Do they feel a lack of freedom or pressure to make their home life work, no matter what?

● How will corporations function in the future to incorporate the 'new family politics', or the changes people have been and are making in their lives?

Juan Villalonga, CEO, Telefonica, Madrid

What do you think of 'family values'?

This is an abstraction. The reality is: the world is changing.

How is your company trying to integrate the new situation of the 'family' and women's and men's work needs?

Our company is in the process of a huge cultural change, like the rest of Spanish society. Our objective is to create value for our shareholders: customers come first. Therefore we need a highly motivated group of people to work here, not bureaucrats – we want results. In this context, the changes in family structure and composition, and especially the changes in women's place in society, play a crucial part in our decisions about hiring.

Telefonica, Spanish Telecom, is recently totally privatised. It was always a private company, despite the government, operating as a monopoly. But now we have competition – whereas French or Dutch telecom don't have competition, they are part of government ministries and have more of a civil service mentality.

What is women's situation within Telefonica – especially in upper management?

We are hiring a lot of young women with MBAs. More than 50 per cent of people leaving the universities with MBAs are women. Their performance, their grades at university, was better than the performance of the men. There is obviously a correlation between this and the performance a woman will have in her work life.

Getting women into the upper stages of management is very slow, progress is slow, because in Spain women have not been in these positions, and so we don't have an existing pool of talent at the executive level to recruit from. We are starting now, taking university graduates with MBAs, putting them into our executive training programmes. We hope that in a few years there will be many women at the top.

Is there a difference between married and single women in your workforce, does one work out better for your company than the other? Do you have more managers or executives in one category than the other?

As the women here are younger, because most MBAs are young, they tend to be unmarried. This is not because we want this, in particular, but because it reflects the state of society, a complicated situation. The state of marriage and personal life is changing.

When a man and a woman decide to live together and to share a project in life, this works for women. But as men, we don't know how to react to this world phenomenon, the change in women's status vis-à-vis us men. We are trying to come to terms with it. Generally, men are not yet ready to take an equal place with women at work, nor to have an equally important working wife, not yet in Spain. But this is coming.

I think traditional marriage developed through stages. First, there was polygamy (the woman at home, and the man with others), then 60s' free love, and now women have the possibility to share experience with other people at the workplace. This changes everything about the psychological arrangement within the couple.

Today, if a woman has a male friend with whom she wants to share her life, many times a man will have to adapt his career. (It's always better to live with someone, but to have your own objectives.) In an executive job, in some cases we send people abroad, and sometimes we send women. This can be married women too. Sometimes the wife comes to us and asks 'Could you also find a job for my husband here?' We try to do this, so they can stay together, we want them to be happy. It's hard to be happy when you have to figure out night by night who to spend time with, who to go out with, etc.

What about when women have children? Some corporations say that they cannot advance women into executive positions, because they take maternity leave.

More and more, the man can stay home, or it can be the man who has a part-time job. Just because a woman has a child, it isn't necessarily her who has to stay home. If a woman wants to develop her career, she can keep on working, like men always did.

In Spain, most of the companies quoted on the stock exchange still have a low participation of women. But this is changing dramatically. I believe that women's advancement is virtually unstoppable. The best we can do is use this talent, make it work for us. Women will be the ones running the world in 100 years.

'I believe that women's advancement is virtually unstoppable.'

How do you hire and promote within the company?

Amongst employees and graduates, we look for leadership, willingness to win, commitment, common sense, don't get lost in Kennedy and Heathrow airports (know your way around...), speak languages, openness, flexibility. We promote on these characteristics. We don't believe in quotas, we just want the best-qualified person for the job.

In our experience, the performance of women is superior to the performance of men. Women are less interested in office politics – like the amount of floor space they get, rising up, status symbols like belonging to clubs, what kind of cars they have, their business cards and titles – and more concerned with the self-satisfaction of the work they are doing.

I am totally devoted to the shareholders. I personally look around the company and try to see talent. I spend an important part of my time trying to identify talent. Our company needs human resources; it is up to our managers to see people, to recognize talent. The contribution women are making to the company now is huge, and will increase.

Laurenz Fritz, Generalsecretariat Industriellenvereinigung (Chairman, Ministry of Business) Austrian Ministry for Industry (former CEO and Chairman of Alcatel)

What is your opinion about the current slogan, 'return to family values'?

I'm not convinced that it is more than a slogan. If you look into the reality, the number of divorced couples and single mothers are increasing, etc. so there should be a rethink. This could have important consequences: more people would be employed. If the society is mostly 'single' then all individuals need to pay the rent... they need jobs.

Women are appreciated when they have a job, so 60 per cent of women in Austria work outside the home. 'Housewife' – what is that??!! This is the attitude in Austria. Europe has less women working than Japan or the US. 72 per cent of all women in the US have jobs, 62 per cent in Japan, and only 56.1 per cent in Europe. The percentage of women in the workforce in Europe is, on average, 66.7 per cent, though in Austria 71.9 per cent of women participate.

Many women in Europe are losing their jobs now. My experience at Alcatel, where I was Chairman, demonstrates this. Before, Alcatel produced hardware; now they only make software. When it made primarily hardware, there were a lot of unskilled women in the workforce, 2/3 of the workforce were women. This has changed: now there are only about 200 women, or 10 per cent women in a workforce of 2,000. Workers are mostly men now, the jobs for unskilled women have disappeared.

If there were a 'return to family values', would less women work, therefore creating more full employment?

This is not the way to approach the future. We must keep women's options to work open, just as we do men's. Anyway, the definition of work is changing. In the future, those with regular eight-hour employment will be in a minority (and they will not work for one firm for life); most others will work independently for various companies, or as part-time employees.

How can women better integrate themselves into upper management?

At Alcatel, there were no women in the upper ranks or on the board. I changed that, but it was a little complicated.

To start, I said I wanted a woman on the board.

When you say that, people ask you a lot of questions, like 'Why do you want a woman' etc. I said, as I was the Chairman anyway (!) I want to have a woman, period. Find the best you can, better than a man, for the job. In the end, we found a woman so good she had to be taken, no one could find a reason not to accept her. She knew exactly how to present herself to the board for approval, how to act in this performance environment set up by men. She did have something different, however: her way of thinking!

'Why did I want a woman? Because women have different brains than men . . . women think with both sides of their brains.'

Why did I want a woman? Because women have different brains than men. This is not sexual harassment; women think with both sides of their brains. Scientific research has demonstrated a link between both sides of the brain. If something happens to this link in women, it takes months or years for the person to function normally, because women are used to using both sides of their brains. If something happens to a man's brain link, nothing happens! The right brain is generally used for emotions and languages, while the left is used for maths and science, etc.

We literally suppress most of our brains, we only use a minute part of them, and this influences how dense the synapses are. Music gives brain food for building up the synapses.

Can a man have a woman protégée? Or will people say, 'Oh, it's a sex thing!'?

This is a leading question... I say, don't be afraid to try it! I experienced this. Yes, I had to live with the cliché and the accusations, but the woman and I overcame all this and today she is still with the company. It takes courage, but it's important to do it.

At my old corporation, Alcatel, where I was the boss, I said from the beginning, I want to have a woman on the board. To avoid any rumours, I left the job of finding one to a headhunter company. Then she had to prove that she was the right choice to the board of directors (six men, we were adding one woman). She was divorced, and well-qualified workwise.

It was not easy for her in the beginning: she had to prove she was not only different, but excellent. She was very exposed, everyone was looking at her, just watching for one slip, ready to judge her... and me!

Did she act especially nice to you, or just the reverse, to compensate for the 'natural expectation' from a woman, i.e. to be 'nice'? Must women in these positions act more tough than men? After all, a woman can feel grateful to get a position, and wind up feeling flirtatious and overly fond of someone, because of traditional sexual politics. Being 'nice' can even seem like flirtation. (It's hard to behave naturally in the situation.) The office pressures could even bring on sexual feelings...

It was funny for her because eventually she knew it was me who asked for a woman, and she felt probably a certain affinity towards me because of this. She was my protégée, and everybody knew it. We had to go out of our way to show that there was no special relationship between us, and eventually people accepted this.

She is still there in the company, and by the way, after me, the new head, a French man, brought with him a human resources manager – a woman again.

CEOs could be afraid to hire women, or have them as protégées, because they could wind up like Clinton – accused of a sexual affair, even having one. Some men need to rethink their options with women, there is not only one type of relationship a man and woman can have... I had a younger sister, so I know there can be more than one way to relate between men and women. How a man grows up could affect his policies about women in the

corporation. He can live with old patterns, i.e. a woman is there for sex and seduction only! Or he could understand that there can be many kinds of relationships between men and women.

Co-educational schools make a difference too: they mean more possibility of working together later, getting to know the opposite sex as other than sexual – just like with a black person, there is fear if kids don't learn to know them in school.

Men and women can be friends and colleagues. Many men like to relate to women, but don't know how except sexually. This can be true of women too, they don't know any other way, and so act flirtatious when all they really feel is friendship. At the end of the day, 'sexual harassment' is not only a European problem, but universal. However, in Europe, I believe we can deal with it in a better way.

Jean-Jacques Gauer, CEO, Leading Hotels of the World, Lausanne, Switzerland

What do you think of the slogan 'preservation of family values'?

What are 'family values' really? Many executives today have two families – a working family (where you spend eight–nine hours) and a private family (with whom you spend much less time!... one hour in the morning when you wake up and are in a bad mood anyway, and one hour at the end of the day when you are dead tired – this can make for a tumultuous day!).

[Laughter.]

There are many cycles and fads. We had sexual liberation, the Beatles, the sixties, drugs, etc. After all these experiences and waves of behaviour, it is only normal that some traditional values come back. (Especially with the appearance of AIDS, people think twice before going ahead sexually, they become more conservative.) In advertising, for example, the ads of Volvo or Holiday Maker companies now stress how their product suits the family, ads today focus less on singles that they did before. I'm not sure that this conservatism will be there forever, the ball will probably bounce back again.

Out of the two extremes, individual freedom and family values, which do you see as most important to take forward to the future?

Extremes on both sides, or any side, are not good – like the religious extremes we see today. Individual freedom to move, think for oneself, was the good we learned in the sixties and seventies, and is the positive value to take forward. The eighties' and nineties' focus on 'family values' can be good if we take this to mean values of actively caring for other people, thinking about others, not a focus on the only good way people can live is daddy– mummy–children. After all, a family can be two friends!

Must politicians and CEOs be 'good family men'?

Ridiculous! Especially in the US, to see this demonstrated. There is a difference between private life and public life, a person in public life shouldn't be expected to be a Superman or Superwoman.

It would seem that many people today live privately much differently than they want to appear publicly. They may not like the pretences, but they don't know what to do about the situation to make it any different. Under these conditions, will the world ever change? If leaders have to keep up a front of being 'good traditional family members', can others openly construct their lives differently?

Things will change because suddenly events make a change possible. Look at when Martin Luther King went to Washington: he suddenly got a much bigger audience than anybody had expected. This changed the atmosphere, so that other people were then able to speak out too, thoughts that had been growing inside people came out publicly, making way for a new consensus of what justice should be, how society should be carried on.

Do you have many female employees in your hotel? In the overall corporation? Are they in management? Do you agree with the CEO who said to me: 'We tried feminism but then we found out that it didn't work; it is better for everybody if women stay home and take care of the home and children'?

That is absurd. Let me answer you in two ways: I have two hats I wear at work. One is as CEO of Leading Hotels, and the other is as the manager of the Hotel Palace. Leading Hotels always tried to promote women in its hotels. Here at the Palace, half of senior management are women. They are heads of such departments as finance, sales and marketing, health, the front desk, and human resources (the department that hires and organizes the staff).

I usually work a lot with women, because they seem to have a better way to handle the service industry, our industry, than men. (Maybe women wouldn't sell car engines as well as men, but they do outperform men in the hotel business.) Women have different radar than men in this regard. I think, in the future, the business world will be more in the hands of females. The male-female debate will not be an issue anymore, it will be education and attitude that count.

'Women have different radar than men . . . I think, in the future, the business world will be more in the hands of females. The male-female debate will not be an issue anymore, it will be education and attitude that count.'

What about the famous glass ceiling so painfully evident in the statistics, i.e. there are very few women in top corporate management? And rarely any on boards of directors...?

Not promoting women is wrong, if they are qualified. And today almost any woman can become qualified! Any woman can have an MBA, even a mother at home, age 35 or more – it doesn't matter! The University of Geneva has an MBA that you can get just by taking its courses over the internet! These women become very well-qualified, this is a good MBA course.

For some, is there still a perception that putting a man at the reception desk of a hotel or restaurant makes the place look more prestigious?

People who think like this will have a problem in the future.

The experience of people who work with women is very good. For example, my director of finance is 27. She got the job over an ex-manager of a multi-national corporation, a very big shot. I am glad I chose her, because she does extraordinary things to improve her job performance. I've been in this business for 26 years and I've never seen anyone do what she did: she volunteered to come in on Saturdays and Sundays to help out in various departments, so she could see first hand how they work and what their needs are. Now, when she puts in the figures, she knows exactly what they are for. She regularly visits all the departments to learn what is really going on, and keep involved. Most men would say, 'The weekend? Hey, I'm outa here!'

Statistically, women are not being promoted, not integrated into corporate boards. Why? Does maternity interrupt women's careers, or cause problems in promoting them?

Schwarzenegger showed us all that men can have children! I thought that issue was settled...?! In the future, people will have multiple jobs and careers in their lifetimes, not like in the past when you learned one trade as a teenager or early adult, then followed it until retirement or death.

Today, a man can stay home with a child, especially as he's likely to change careers anyway one or more times. If you have a dual income, then one can stay at home. Maybe men will realise it's important to give some love to a kid before he or she is 18, that's when it really matters.

This is the real world, the world today means you have to change your job or profession at least once or twice, to adapt – so why not emphasize your private life more at certain points, then shift back to work, and so on?

Do you think many corporations prefer to believe this is not the real world, or are trapped in old corporate cultures with old structures they cannot get out of? Quite a few CEOs told me the reason they have no women at the top is only a matter of time (a problem of time): they like to hire graduates out of college with new MBAs and bring them along in the corporation. None of them have been around long enough yet to be CEOs...

But – the days when you had to sit in at (for example) Swissair for 40 years, then become the CEO, then the Chairman for four glorious years, then you retired and died... these are mostly over. (Along the way, you divorced your wife and married your secretary, saw your loved ones one hour a night...) Swissair, for example, for the first time hired someone to become the CEO straight out of another company. He put it back into profitability status after two years. The idea that it's better and a safer bet

('he'll be more stable') to hire a man with children is a falsehood – look at Prince Charles!

Sexual harassment is a current topic in the news. Is this one reason (fear of such problems) that corporations could avoid hiring and promoting women?

Of course, sexual harassment happens, it is real, but isn't the problem exaggerated, especially in the US? We have guidelines in the US division of Leading Hotels about this; these guidelines for employees discuss such things as how far can you go without being engaged in a problem? But here in Switzerland, I don't feel we really have this problem, honestly.

Just because something comes from the States doesn't mean the idea has to be applied automatically in the same way in Europe. The US has many good and important products and ideas, such as space technology (and equality in general), but we in Europe will find better ways to integrate women into work and upper management that will avoid these pitfalls. The Americans are funny. Even though they label things like diet Coke with every ingredient, mineral composition, etc., they're still fat and unhealthy! The most diet-conscious people on earth are the most out of shape. Americans don't walk anywhere, they take their car to the supermarket, and so on. Why is the US like this, why can they fly to the moon but the average guy is so uneducated?

Do corporations have an obligation or responsibility to follow a human rights agenda?

Not exactly, but there is something like etiquette in life, culture. A successful corporation today must try to conform to expectations that are out there, go along with the times. This is normal. The business culture I want is one in which performance is what counts. Salary should depend on performance, not on whether the employee is married, single, gay or lesbian – it doesn't interest me. It just doesn't matter.

Corporations in Europe today will be the most profitable when they find constructive ways to deal with the new needs of people, the new ways of life people have developed – taking the best of the two major movements of the last 40 years, i.e. individualism but still caring about others, equal rights, into the future – making them part of new corporate structures and solutions for the future.

Dr Mark Wössner, Chairman (1980–98), Bertelsmann Corp., Germany

Bertelsmann's Chairman of eighteen years, Mark Wössner – now head of the Bertelsmann Foundation that controls Bertelsmann Corporation – quadrupled his company's size and worth during the last ten years.

Bertelsmann, one of the world's two largest media conglomerates, owns major publishing houses on four continents, television stations, AOL in Germany, book clubs all over the world, and a host of magazines in various countries.

What do you think of the current slogan 'Let's return to family values'?

I agree with its idea. Historically, mankind has always had a system of values focused on the family, based on religious tradition. Today these values bring together the common sense of all the cultures in Europe. Unfortunately, after World War II these values were eroded (in fact, all during the century), except in Italy and Spain. I admire the Italians and Spaniards, the richness of their culture lies in their focus on old family values.

In Germany, values have totally changed: we have more and more single households, unmarried people with children, and no more the habit of taking care of older people. No longer do people live together with three generations under one roof.

When I was a child, I slept in a small room with my parents after the Second World War; we had to do this, we had no more room. Then I slept with my brother. (Today he is head of the book division here.) After I married, my children's rooms when they were small were not really separate either; they had the choice to be alone or together. We constructed a passageway between their rooms, so they could close the door or they could talk and share secrets deep into the night, when they wanted... I used to do this with my brother, it is a wonderful thing to talk in the night.

Are there new 'rules' emerging in your corporation's management related to social changes in women's and men's situation, people's changing personal values? Clearly, there is a revolution in personal values that has been taking place... What do you think of the women's movement, feminism?

It depends, there are various types of feminism. Some kinds of feminism have hurt family values, but other kinds have changed and are changing the family in the right way. If female emancipation means that women now are no longer ready to take care of families and bear children, this I would not agree with, this would be going too far. Women have the right to be educated and decide who they want to marry, but then they should return to family roles, build families in addition to working. Otherwise we will find we have caused the collapse of civilization.

Why collapse? Can't men stay home and build families, while women run things for a while? I say, men should get the opportunity to be more equal! In my opinion, it is false to believe that feminism alone caused the end of the traditional family (as we supposedly knew it). Men first attacked the family in the 1960s with *Playboy* magazine and single heroes like James Bond's agent 007; now for almost 40 years we have seen only movies that glorify single male heroes, men who want to avoid marriage, being 'tied down'. They don't think of marriage as a great adventure, an opportunity for a wonderful, special intimacy for them; rather this propaganda makes them believe that their real lives, adventures, will be in the business place, at work, or in sports, out with the guys. In many films, a woman is just a meaningless convenience, a necessity for a man to do his duty and have children. Rock stars also have marketed themselves as single, 'searching for freedom'. When John Lennon married Yoko Ono, some saw this as treason!

The role of Hollywood films is very important... Let me consider this point.

Does your corporation have a policy on women? Are there women on the Bertelsmann board?

Our top board has seven seats. There are no women. Our second management level (division boards) has 45 seats, and there is one woman. Why? It is difficult to find women with the right qualifications. They need to have an MBA from Harvard or the equivalent school, and professional experience on the same level.

Aren't there women anywhere like this?

Yes and no. We had a meeting one time with a women's group, who told us to take some of their members. I told them, 'But you don't have the experience of the men on the board.' It's a problem, women just have not had enough time to develop the same background of experience that men have. Of course, it's true that women have experience in other ways, experience that is valuable. I admire women I see on airplanes, for example, who are struggling with children, and also managing to deal with a difficult husband, a complicated man. To manage a household and a complicated man shows great intelligence! Corporations should perhaps take these mothers with great experience.

But if you want to hire women who have learned how to take care of children, and husbands, like those you see on planes struggling with children, when their children are a little bit older and they are not so busy, then you may consider them 'too old' or they won't have the experience you require, so it seems

that this really means they will never be hired, doesn't it? Statistically, women seem to repeatedly hit a glass ceiling at a certain age and stage of work.

There are very few women on corporate boards in Germany. But we are planning to take women into our management. Right now they are just in the editorial positions and administration.

Will you and Bertelsmann lead in this area, will you be one of the first in Germany to put women on the board?

I will further female participation in the Bertelsmann Foundation that I head starting this year. We have a lot to do!

Can a man have a woman as a protégée? Would this cause gossip or discomfort?

I have several. I had one once who was head of our Department for Strategic Planning. This was a department I founded of about 20 or 30 people, that has developed our young tigers; it is like an intelligence service, our in-house consulting group. Now there are several women 'protégées', whom I will help in the Bertelsmann Foundation, my new big project.

Don't believe I'm a typical 'old family guy'. I think women should have careers. My daughter is a professional woman. She has just gotten married. But when she has her children she will not be able to work fifteen hours a day (like you have to, like I do, if you really want to have a remarkable or substantial career). Females don't have equal opportunity simply because their lives are complicated by having children. It takes ten years out of their lives to have children and it's difficult. How can a woman do both? She can't. After her children, she can go back to work, of course, but meanwhile she has lost five or ten years of professional experience.

My history, personally... well, I am married, this is my second marriage. My wife is a professional woman. Since she has a little more time than I do, she manages the household. She helps me with my business, hosting dinners for me. I regret that my first marriage didn't work out, but you understand how it is: if a woman devotes herself to helping a man, then after twenty years of this, you develop into having completely different worlds. She knows all about children and the house, and you know all about your business and the world outside. I grew to have less and less time, the more I took on responsibilities at work, then I spent the time I did have with my children, so my wife and I spent less and less time together...

The solution to the question of how women can work and be integrated, advanced, is to have new and different, very tolerant constructions of life – some women work, some men work.

'The solution to the question of how women can work and be integrated, advanced, is to have new and different, very tolerant constructions of life – some women work, some men work.'

How women and men work together at top levels of corporations is recently an area of broad interest. What are your experiences as to how these relationships work?

When I had an important female assistant (the one I mentioned, head of the Department of Strategic Planning), we were day and night in airplanes together, we travelled to New York, all over Germany, everywhere. Our relationship worked well. Then one day she went ahead of me to greet people before me. I guess she thought because she was a woman, even though she was my junior, she would do the 'woman's thing', smile and say hello first. I took her by the back of the collar, pulled her to her proper place behind me, and began to greet them first.

There should be no gender in corporations. I might be slightly nicer in small ways to a female colleague, but a colleague is a colleague. If you are in a company, you are neutral – neither male or female. A junior is a junior, male or female. I don't open a door for a woman, if she is a colleague. If I am her superior, she should hold the door for me. A man must behave like a colleague to women at work, not be either a macho or a softie.

Has Bertelsmann had cases reported of sexual harassment?

No, I never heard about anything like that.

In the giant empire of Bertelsmann, there has never been one case, not even an unofficial complaint?

A company culture should respect everyone. We need women.

What do you think of the Clinton sex scandals that happend in Washington? Does the public have a right to know what men in executive leadership positions do?

Private life should not be covered by the media; a man is responsible for his job not his private life.

Must men in public life be married? Does a CEO have to be a 'good family man'?

Men in public life need not be perfect family men. It is amazing that even the American public now tolerates this, i.e. the public is not especially upset with Clinton, as long as he is doing his job well. This is wise; to insist on public scrutiny of leaders' private lives would damage both public and private institutions in the future.

Juan Luis Cebrián, Chairman, PRISA, one of the two largest media conglomerates in Spain

PRISA holds the controlling interest in Spain's most prominent newspaper (*El Pais*), a private television station (Antenna 3), and various book publishers, magazines and other holdings. It is closely linked to many Spanish and Latin American media business groups.

What do you think of 'family values'? Is the changing nature of the family changing corporations?

Corporations are extremely conservative entities, so most of the executives are too. During the ten years I have been CEO of PRISA, I have noted that if an executive has 'family problems', it is considered that the wife has a problem, the executive doesn't feel he has to stop and deal with it.

Are there many women here working at top levels?

No, they are in the second level. In the top slots, there are only men. Women don't have management responsibility – though the newspaper *El Pais* (one of our companies, of which I was director for many years)

has a deputy editor-in-chief who is a woman. She has been there for several years.

Why aren't there women in the top slots?

There is a problem with women's attitude in the labour market. They don't fight enough for power. Quite often they are better than men, but they choose not to fight, they choose to focus on family, especially the kids, while men focus on power and work. Some women seem to dislike outright competition.

But women can be called terrible names if they try openly for power, i.e. 'Bad because you're powerful' is how women are made to feel... guilty!

Such attitudes are a philosophical tradition of the society, caused in part by education in school and family. They are unnecessary and we should eliminate them. Why do we divide girls when they are only five years old, into separate schools? In this way it is not possible to get to know various members of the opposite sex, and see them at work.

Do you think you have a responsibility to put a woman in one of the top positions of PRISA? You are one of the most powerful men in Spain, and...

Well, it's up to women. During the next few months, I have to make three or four important assignments. Everybody knows it. But no women

'There is a problem with women's attitude in the labour market.' They don't fight enough for power.

are asking for these posts. Why? I hope in the future they will become more involved.

Now, women only ask for things like one year off with wages to have a child, or time to go away and write a book. They don't ask for important posts. Men ask for them. Believe it or not, this makes it easier to appoint a man!

Also, anytime I propose a woman for a top assignment, people ask for a bigger demonstration of her qualities, more proof that she is good, than if she were a man. A woman needs to be several times as good as a man in order to gain corporate power.

I can relate to that. In my books, I always have to prove my ideas. While others may spout their opinions in 'books of ideas', I must prove every sentence – twice.

Old attitudes prejudicial to women do persist. However, women themselves should change their attitudes to power.

Many men ask me for favours and things through e-mail, through letters, they come and stand at my desk. This makes it easier to use men, because they are knocking at the door. On the other hand, I have to admit it's a little bit difficult, having a woman standing at my desk asking for something.

Why? If there are so few women in top executive positions, are you saying this is women's fault? Women say that, though they are qualified, they are passed over for higher appointments, the truly top jobs. When I ask why, they tell me 'They just don't see your qualifications. I am over-qualified for what I am doing, but I have hit a glass ceiling, like most other women...'

The relationships on a board or in a group are different if the members are all men. If there is even one woman there, the attitude of the men changes. It's difficult to describe. The attitude is like, 'There is a woman, so we have to be careful!'

Careful of what?

Well, it's just a completely different atmosphere. There is a complicity between men, we share attitudes, culture. There are things that only happen between men.

Do men prefer to be with other men, feel more comfortable – men with men? It sounds like men have two identities, one with other men, one with women...

Here's an example from this very morning. I have a four-year-old daughter. Early today I took her to school. (I don't usually.) I saw a few men there, but mostly women, of course. We men were 10–15% (and half of these were retired, grand fathers, etc.). This low figure is not because 'men have to work'; it was early enough for men to go there before work.

The women were talking to the kids, but the men were walking around, not speaking. I asked myself, why? Men do not feel comfortable there. We don't believe this is part of the normal way of life of men; the management of the family belongs to women. Women feel secure in the family, but men only feel secure, experience their real identity, in work.

They only experience their own identity with other men at work? Well, how can women be integrated into the top echelons of corporations, in that case?

Quotas could be useful. If, as a man, I know that I have an obligation to appoint women – maybe 25–30% women – then I'll do it, no problem. Labour equality laws are very important. The force of tradition is so strong that it is impossible to change the situation otherwise.

The experience of Scandinavian countries using quotas, enforcing the hiring of a certain percentage of women, shows that quotas work. In countries that have used them, the situation now is good. It takes one or two decades, that's all. Then, after the whole system has been affected positively, we can forget quotas and return to meritocracy.

Non-public companies, privatized companies, would not be affected by quota laws, except on a voluntary basis. Such corporations might have a moral duty to human rights and to equality, but this will be a matter of choice, not obligation. The government's regulations concerning justice wouldn't be enforceable. Many more corporations in Spain will be privatized now.

That is very sobering. How then would quota legislation help? If a government's legislation would not apply to most corporations, would each company have to design its own moral charter?

Quite a few women are on boards of directors in Spain, but this has nothing to do with being a woman. The board of directors of a private company consists of its owners. For example, we are a private company, not a public one, and so our board consists of the owners of the company. One or two of these are women, but they do not discuss women's rights.

What, then, is the solution? Will men promote women? Or are men sometimes hesitant to appoint women to important posts, because of male-female politics?

If the woman is pretty, there would be a big problem. People would say things. If she is capable and ugly, it's easier.

After the Clinton and other sex scandals, must executives keep a tight rein on their private lives, always present themselves as 'good family men'? Can an executive be single and date various people?

In this country, people cannot believe what has happened to Clinton. For one thing, it is difficult for a man like Clinton to have a usual sex life. Where can he go? He can't call a hotel and book a room, after all, just like anybody else.

Sexual harassment has not become an issue in Spain. I believe in the Latin cultures it is very difficult to decide when courtesy or a Don Juan attitude becomes sexual harassment. Just think of the universities, for example: professors have many students around, it's easy for them to have a relationship that may or may not be sexual. The whole idea of sexual harassment is difficult to define.

I think that sexual harassment is an issue everywhere, but since it has been such a 'part of life', it has been invisible. Now that women are beginning to take a full part in public and business life, they feel it is crucial to deal with this issue. Alhough it was once considered an 'American issue', cases are now emerging in France, Germany, England and elsewhere; many corporations will find themselves faced with lawsuits in countries other than their home base, now that they have become global or international. Obviously, to get ahead at work, in most cases women have to have the good will of male superiors; this can create an explosive situation. Given this, it is striking that so many of the new corporate female/male executive relationships are working well. Sexual harassment lawsuits – although in the minority of instances – will continue during this period of transition to full 'integration', as we try to redesign our ideas of the genders and how they relate productively.

Rudolph Giuliani, Mayor and CEO, New York City

The most important corporation in New York City is New York City itself. New York City is the largest employer in the state of New York, with 200,000 employees. Its chairman: Mayor Rudolph Giuliani.

A few years ago, New York City was bankrupt. It couldn't pay its employees, and had to declare itself out of business. Like any other business, it had to dig itself out of the hole. To do this it sold bonds, and other things. Now it's in the pink.

What do you think of the slogan 'return to family values'?

Everyone defines it differently. The idea of keeping families together can be a good one, depending. Of course a good family makes people more stable at work, but there is no formula for a 'good family'. Families today can be composed of different elements.

In fact, today in New York City, 50% of people are single; when people live together, usually they both work; this is the situation for most people now. Everybody works. Businesses here mostly have day care available to people, and also the City of New York provides day care for poor people, so parents with young children are able to work, not kept from working.

How is New York City dealing with the integration of women into its executive pool, upper management?

There are many women here in important posts. In fact, one-third of the top core staff are women. The deputy mayor is a woman; the sheriff of New York City is a woman (Teresa Mason), the Director of the New York City Federal Affairs Office is a woman (Alice Tetelman), chair of the NYC Commission on Human Rights is Marta B. Varela, and so on. Deborah Weeks is First Deputy Commissioner of the Department of Business Services.

We have 50 commissioners. Of the fifteen inner circle advisers, one-third are women! Every morning, we start the day with a morning meeting of the most important members of the staff, to set the agenda for the day. About half of the members of this 20–25 person meeting are women.

When will there be a female mayor running New York City? How is it that New York City has never had a female CEO?

I ran against a woman in the last election campaign. Next time, there will be more women running, they will be better organized, and with more backing.

What do you think of the idea some corporations have that women working increases the unemployment ranks?

In New York City, about half of the workforce is women, and we have very low unemployment too. Our economy is healthy and unemployment is lower than almost anywhere, although women are in the workforce in big numbers. Clearly, then, any argument saying that the exclusion of women from the workforce would keep employment high and therefore be healthy for the economy is false.

Excluding women would be to cut ourselves off as a society, like cutting off half your potential. Why do that? To put it another way, if you believe in competition, the more people competing will cause the best result. In business, women make an enormous contribution, women are needed, belong there in the workplace. They have a right to be treated in exactly the same way as men. In business, you should notice that he, she or it is doing a good job. The job is neuter. Discrimination against women is illegal. (Gay and lesbian discrimination is also illegal, but more stubborn to wipe out.)

'Excluding women would be to cut ourselves off as a society, like cutting off half your potential. Why do that?'

It is in the interest of corporations to notice women's performance and potential. Why? Fair play inside the management team increases performance – this is what we have learned.

What do you think of the examination of Clinton's private life? Must politicians and businessmen be 'perfect examples' of 'good married men'? Can they fall in and out of love, display emotions? Do the media have the right to look at the private life of a public figure like Clinton? Must a CEO be 'morally perfect'?

Since Roosevelt, all US presidents have been married. I think there were only one or two presidents ever who were not married. But somebody's private life is only relevant when it affects their public life; this should not be an excuse for voyeurism. People or the press can be fascinated with a famous figure's private life, when it has no relevance to his or her job. In the case of Clinton, whatever the allegations, his performance is good.

Are there cases of sexual harassment among the 200,000 full-time employees of New York City?

Sexual harassment – none! This is a very sophisticated city. People here know how to conduct themselves, they don't get involved in this sort of thing.

As a supervisor, I stay out of people's private affairs. When people go through life, they are always going to have personal problems. The question is, how do they handle them?

Part of promoting women today seems to revolve around the question of the mentor–protégé relationship. This has worked well between men. Can a man have a female protégée? Or will people accuse him of being involved with her or of sexual harassment, etc.?

You will always be criticized, you have to let these things roll off your back. You may be accused of having an affair with the woman (by whispering voices around you, or enemies attacking you), but you can't let it get to you, you have to do what is right. If a woman working next to you is best qualified for a promotion, you have to go with it. It would be an insult to her to deny her the job – and a betrayal of yourself.

Naoki Ogino, Chairman and Managing Director, Editorial Board of Directors, Yomiuri Shimbun, Tokyo

Yomiuri, one of two top Japanese newspapers, even owns its own baseball team.

Do you have women on your board of directors?

No, there are no women on the board of directors, nor are there women in most other Japanese corporations, not in top management. This is normal.

In 1922, Yomiuri Shimbun began to take applications from both men and women, but only since 1972 have there been women on our staff. Therefore only young women are in the corporation now, they are too young to be on the board of directors yet.

Would men on your board be comfortable with having women on the board?

Oh yes, I would – at least!

How are changes in the Japanese family affecting people who work for you?

The social system and the family are changing now, but these changes are not finished, of course. I sometimes wonder where they are going... Today 25% of marriages in Japan end in divorce, and those divorces are mostly initiated by women, even though there is a traditional word in Japanese used to label a divorced women in a very unkind and cruel way. There is a stigma against her. A new study by *Asahi*, our competitor, shows that 50% of Japanese women aged 20–29 say they do not want to get married. We have not had a phenomenon like this in Japan before, with many young women saying they would prefer not to marry and to continue to work.

Are women who work in your corporation better off married with children – or can they get ahead successfully if they are single?

Children are no impediment to women advancing at Yomiuri. However, realistically, most women stay at home for a while after having a baby, although neither the government nor the corporation pays her any financial compensation or support during this time. The official rules of the corporation say she can stay home for one year, but in reality, of course, she can only do this if her husband pays for it.

How do women get a job at your corporation?

To get a job here, everyone must pass an exam. Women get higher grades on the exam, usually, than men, so at first, women get better jobs, but by age 45, men are ahead of them, men have the better jobs.

Why?

The best jobs here for women are as journalists, so I am speaking of journalists, not executives or managers. Journalists work very hard and late – until midnight – and men can tolerate this more than women. Some families understand that it's OK if a woman stays late at night working, but others do not.

I'm confused. Why, in the cases where there are not problems of children or jealous husbands worried about how late a wife stays out, are not those women arriving at top positions?

In 1972 Yomiuri opened its doors equally to women. These women are now only in their 50s so they are not old enough to be on the board of directors. Strangely, however, there are still six male journalists for every woman journalist, even today. This is puzzling...

Our company has more women than our chief competitor, *Asahi*, the other leading paper in Japan (they have no baseball team, either). We are more advanced. We like working with women, because women are cheerful and feel positive, whereas men tend

to be negative. Men sometimes have an inferiority complex towards women when they are younger and first start the job, but after five or six years, the men get ahead of the women anyway.

Women's advancement is part of a coming social change, but it is a change that women themselves will have to make. I was born in Tokyo in 1934. I originally got into journalism because I wanted to understand politicians and how politics worked. My family didn't expect me to become an important person like I have become. In the future, women will also have to find their own way, little by little.

> 'Women's advancement is part of a coming social change, but it is a change that women themselves will have to make.'

The traditional peace or power balance between men and women in Japan was, for 150 years, that women were at home, taking men's salary and running the household, taking care of children and husbands. But now relationships between couples are based less on economics and more on emotion, so therefore they are seeking a new adjustment between them. It's a time of disequilibrium. We must change our way of thinking, but this will take another 30 years.

As I went away, I pondered what this could mean, that the change would take 'another 30 years'. I wondered whether this meant that women could not hope to advance into executive positions until sometime many years away. I wondered if most Japanese leaders of institutions would say the same thing…

Dr Yukiyasu Sezai, President, Nihon University, Japan

Nihon University is the largest institution of higher education in Japan, with 100,000 students and fourteen faculties on 90 campuses all over the country, the headquarters being in Tokyo. The president of these campuses is elected every four years by the various faculties' professors.

Do you have women at the executive level of your organization?

No, unfortunately, this is not yet the case. However, we are considering this possibility.

Is it difficult for women in Japan to advance into executive positions?

There has been an enormous gap between women's intelligence and ability, and their finding responsible, high positions inside governments and corporations.

What is the cause of this difficulty?

From my perspective, men in corporations need to change. Corporations need to have training programmes to help men overcome fears of gossip when they promote or support women. Women also need training to not fear shocking men or knocking men out with their new power!

'From my perspective, men in corporations need to change. Corporations need to have training programmes to help men overcome fears of gossip when they promote or support women.'

Some women prefer the old ways and do not like to be advanced in a corporation, because marriage is still their only goal, and a career could be negative for this goal. Marriage in Japan can be dangerous for women's careers, because having children means staying home for a while, yet many companies do not give maternity leave. (This is a matter for individual unions to negotiate; some companies at least provide day care centres for children, though no maternity leave.)

Do men in corporate management generally accept the idea that they could be equal colleagues with women? Are there sexual scandals in Japan such as the recent Clinton-Lewinsky affair in the US?

Maybe in Japan men are not afraid of being seen to have a sexual affair, they could be proud because it makes them appear more macho. We have observed Clinton, and what has happened, but the Japanese attitude would be different; we have our own moral standards, and will proceed at our own pace with redefining the relationship between men and women at work.

Yet Toshiba had to pay US$4 million because of a lawsuit it lost over a sexual harassment case in the US. Now that corporations are often international, integration of women into the workplace and especially into management and executive positions will take on an international human rights flavour, so that a new kind of relationship between men and women will become urgently necessary, won't it? Even if a corporation is Japanese, it will face international pressures in other areas of the world where it is based.

Yes, there is no way to go but forward. Japan changed after World War II and accepted Western influences, such as women getting rights they had never had before. Now there are new influences coming to Japan: not only is internet a new force, but also international relations are more close than ever before – so there's no way to go but forward. It would not be possible to go back, even if we wanted to.

I believe that people in Japan now are looking for a shock, a new open, important change. Many people tell me that it's a good time to make a break with the past. There is a revolution going on, one as important as the Industrial Revolution: the world is becoming internationally connected via internet and modern telecommunications. These communications systems are internationalising and revolutionising our values and economic systems, and those of other cultures around the world, rapidly creating beneficial changes that are needed. Women's advancement will be a major part of these changes.

Mike Wilson, CEO, J. Rothschild Assurance.

J. Rothschild Assurance is a UK-Dublin-based financial services company specializing in investments and pensions, famous all over the world.

What do you think of the slogan 'return to family values'?

It may be a good slogan, but is it realistic? We can't go back to the days when women's main job was pressing men's shirts. Today, family values means different things to different people.

Do men today who run corporations have to be 'good family men'?

Business leaders can find it increasingly difficult today to make their personal lives conform to old stereotypes of 'the perfect family' and long-term 'stability' (= no change).

This is because the world has changed – and also they have changed! Men today are not the same as their grandfathers, they have different ideas of who they are and who they want to be. These have seen James Bond, the Beatles and Bob Dylan – also the Spice Girls. They want to feel they are with the times, but still legitimate citizens in terms of family responsibilities. They don't want to be 'loners' with 'no family' or personal life. But they don't want to be tied down by old definitions of 'the family' either.

Some men feel they only have the choice between being a 'swinging single' or a 'dutiful husband with children' – yet, marriage today can be defined totally differently, as a partnership, with a woman who works at an important job, or even with a person of the same sex. How should CEOs and executives handle their private lives at work?

The macho attitude is, 'your personal life should not affect your business life'. But the truth is, an individual's personal life does affect business. So, if someone is having a difficult time, he should say to his colleagues: 'Look, if I'm not on the ball in the next few days or weeks (months?) it's because I'm going through this and this situation.'

People feel it's weakness to admit anything like this – even to change or be unsure about personal life, or be disturbed. But it's strength to change. No one has a smooth ride throughout their life. Everybody faces these situations sometimes. It's useless to pretend 'everything is fine' all the time.

If anyone pretends everything is OK all the time, they are faking it. Once one of my employees had a nervous breakdown. His wife blamed me. But he was trying to be something he wasn't, this was the problem, not me.

What do you think about Clinton and Monicagate? Must a head of state today be heterosexual, married and monogamous?

People can feel de-legitimatized if their personal life does not resemble a Christmas card layout. They hide and cover this up, becoming distant and nervous at work, for example if they are having an affair, getting a divorce, secretly gay or something else is bothering them.

'People can feel de-legitimatized if their personal life does not resemble a Christmas card layout.'

Personal conflicts arise in everyone's life. Businessmen with private problems should speak to their colleagues – especially those on the board with them. This will create trust. Anyway, if I had those problems that the media could pick up, I'd sure rather put my version on the table first!

Do you believe the public has a right to know about, say, Clinton's private life? Is it a legitimate target of enquiry? Real people can find themselves in awkward situations: what if a well-known CEO suddenly finds himself in love, or wanting to divorce? Does a man today who is publicly visible have to stop his personal life, and only get gratification from his work, or children? Must he present a Hallmark greeting card picture of a reliable man, even if this turns him into a man playing a role in his private life (which he avoids more and more 'because of work', just going through the motions), while life itself passes him by, since he can't 'go overboard', feel too much, get carried away or experiment?

It is right today that private life is a matter of public and business judgement. It is not so simple as to say 'private life should be private'. If you're high profile, it's no good saying you don't like the publicity. You have to stand for what you do, in public and private today. It is not a question of morality but of good dealing with your colleagues. If leaders lie in their private life, you wonder if they won't lie in business.

Here at Rothschild, people's own lifestyle and personal preferences outside of work are their own affair, we only care about their performance on the job. But of course their performance is interconnected with a personal life that works. Everybody has snags and difficult moments, unsureness of direction. Better to let someone know you are trying to figure something out, deal with a knotty problem!

Are women integrated into Rothschild? How are the new issues of women and men working together in management being handled?

Ten per cent of the firm are ladies, I'd love to have more. The rest of the industry has less: generally, women have about an 8% presence in the financial services industry. We have 10%, but we need more. The women are marginally more successful, about 10% higher in productivity.

Why? We can't say exactly. Perhaps they are more determined to prove their point, to succeed. Sometimes they are divorced and want to show they can do it... It's a tough business, there's a high fallout rate. Women won't say they want to compete with men, 'show the world', but maybe they do! And we get the benefit!

There are no women on our board – a pity – but let's be realistic: women do have babies, and take time off.

So shouldn't men get maternity leave, so women can keep on working?

Nonsense! Women are more important for children than fathers, especially at that age.

If you were a woman, then, how would you overcome this impasse? What would you want corporations to do?

If I were a woman??! Well, I don't know... But we here at Rothschild are a meritocracy, although admittedly, old attitudes against women die hard.

Do you agree with some corporations who say having women in the workforce doubles the unemployment rate, and therefore see women staying at home in the family as a way of keeping the unemployment figures down?

Keeping women out of employment would be a contrived way of improving the figures. We need women to work. It's not reasonable to hold women back because of this thinking. We should encourage women in their careers. We shouldn't tell them to go home and do the ironing. More women would be good for everybody.

One CEO told me, 'feminism was an experiment we tried, but we found it didn't work'. Do you agree?

No, that's ridiculous! We need the skills of women today. A corporation should be a meritocracy.

If only 15% of women work for the firm, how do you account for this? Is Rothschild afraid to hire them? Do fewer women apply to you?

Is it so easy as to say that women drop out of their corporate jobs at a certain stage because they have a 'nesting instinct' or 'mothering drive'? Or, at a certain stage do they just find that things at work are so tough on them ('one of the few women making this her career', etc. etc.) that domestic bliss sounds like paradise? In other words, do they believe they will find a better atmosphere at home compared to a hostile work environment that calls them a 'tough cookie' if they stay, etc.?

As a woman, still, you stand out: a simple trip to the water cooler can cause comment; some say you are not fitting in, and others note 'her skirt is too long/short, etc.' How a woman stands or sits in a meeting is almost always remarked on, while a man's behaviour might not be. Many women tell me that at a certain point, they no longer want to deal with 'all this'. They want to drop out.

Sometimes women grow so tired of fighting the stereotypes, this atmosphere makes them so exhausted, that they wind up thinking: 'Oh, staying at home and having children will be a picnic compared to this!' Things in an office can be such a hassle for a woman that she decides to go home and have babies instead. Or just not return after a supposedly short maternity leave.

Yes, there is a woman who is head of a competing firm, Pierson, and she got an extraordinary amount of press attention, especially for being a woman. It must have been difficult.

Today many countries in the Middle East force women to stop working and prohibit their education, keeping them out of the workforce, especially out of positions of power. Do you think that the anti-woman policies of Middle Eastern corporations will affect European corporations, especially those who want to do business with them?

No, the West is more advanced. The policies of non-Western countries to women will not influence Western corporations.

Look at Madeline Albright, she is negotiating for the US in countries where women are not expected to be seen in those positions. This shows Western leadership, i.e. appointing a women to such a position, and not hiding her in a job that does not cause culture shock to those she is meeting. But do you think corporations have the same courage, i.e. don't you think corporations will be afraid to have women at the top who would have to make deals with, for example, powerful Arab men?

The West is more advanced, and will go forward with women's rights, even while places like the Middle East may go backwards for a time.

Most of these leaders are similar in expressing a belief that 'women in the future' will be a regular part of the executive corporate world.

Do they think it is the 'thing to say' to express enthusiasm about women, that doing this makes them seem 'young and trendy, with it' – or will they take steps to implement changes?

Strikingly, most of these men vary in how they see men's motivations and needs, men's own new relationship to the changes.

Information from Hite Research: Icons of the Heart

The question: do some CEOs see 'their' company as a 'big family' with 'all the boys and girls' acting 'just like big kids' – or are the new demographics (50 per cent of people in major world cities living 'single', families changing composition) having an effect, creating a new corporate environment with new kinds of relationships emerging inside 'hierarchies'?

My research on 'the family' – (and the ongoing changes in individual self-identity inside relationships and out) seems to me to apply to how some corporations are run.

What are basic achetypes of 'family' that influence how we see the opposite sex, and ourselves? Are the archetypes undergoing change?

Changing Archetypes of Family, Love and Identity

Democratization of the family

One constantly hears that 'the family' is in trouble, that it doesn't work any more, and we must find ways to help it. That we must 'preserve family values'. But let's look closely at these seemingly obvious statements. The 'family' is changing, but in what way?

Constant headlines in the press announce such items as 'divorce statistics on the rise', or 'alarming new statistics on children suffering abuse' or 'battering and violence against women in the home'. Many conclude that these reports reflect the breakdown not only of family but also of society and civilization: and that, if we could only put 'the family' back together, we would end our problems and 'once again' have a perfectly peaceful and prosperous, harmonious society.

Yet, is this true? Statistics on violence in the home were not gathered during the supposedly blissful 1950s, golden age of the nuclear family when society preferred to push its 'personal problems' under the rug (or send them to the psychiatrist's couch). Today, if people are leaving the traditional family, as the statistics seem to imply – whether through divorce, changing the composition of their family or style of their family life – who are we to say they are making the 'wrong decisions'?

If 'the family' doesn't work, what does this mean? If the family doesn't work, maybe there is something wrong with its structure. Why assume that humans are flawed and the family structure is fine and good?

People today are concerned about the quality of their marriage or personal partnership. Rightly they want to live in a way that makes them happy and makes others around them happy as well. They want acceptance from society, but, at the same time, they want their relationships to reflect qualities they can be proud of, such as honesty, equality and mutual respect.

Today, people are creating a social revolution by applying the ideas of democracy and justice to their private lives. Many people are torn in their personal lives between doing 'what they should do' and what they feel is right – between following the form of 'family' and appearing 'normal'; and gravitating to the relationships that are working for them.

I believe that this conflict inside people today is caused by the ideas of democracy and justice, so praised in public life and government for the last 200 years, now penetrating people's consciousness about their personal lives. Not only do people feel they have the right to think for themselves about voting, decide whom they elect to government, but, also, they have the right to decide the shape of their personal lives.

'The family', that is, human love and support systems for raising children, is not in danger of collapsing, what is happening is that finally democracy is catching up with the old hierarchical father-dominated family: the family is being democratized. We are all, most of us, taking part in the process. Almost no one wants to go back to the days before women had (at least in theory) equal rights in the home, before there were laws against the battering of women (who are no longer property, but individuals with their own inherent rights), before the freedom for women and men to divorce if they can no longer form a loving unit with the other person… all these things are advances over the old 'traditional family'.

And yet, current 'back to family values' reactionary rhetoric strives to end these positive developments. 'Traditional values' hype attempts to legitimize women's old status as 'servers' by romantically labelling it 'family values' while denigrating the gains women have made, improvements in the family which clearly must benefit men and children.

What we must decide is, is the 'family' as traditionally defined in deep trouble – or are we in a productive process of change, a process of democratizing and revolutionizing the family for the better?

What is democratization of the family?
The democratization of the family, as I term it,[2] means two things: that relationships inside the family are becoming more equal – that all members, especially the woman and man, make decisions equally and give each other emotional support; and that now people have choices of kinds of families they form. Families today need not only be of the reproductive type, but can include networks of friends, as well as 'single- mother' families or dual-mother families.

Individuals have the right to challenge the official idea of the family and to find improved ways of living their lives. Why should we think that institutions, including ideological, 'religious' institutions such as the 'traditional family' are good and the individual who disagrees with them is wrong? Individuals throughout the course of history have challenged institutions, and for the better. Martin Luther challenged the church officialdom of his time, Gandhi challenged the British government on behalf of Indian citizens and Martin Luther King challenged the US government on behalf of blacks in the United States.

Individuals have the right to challenge the official idea of the family and to find improved ways of living their lives.

What does the phrase 'traditional family' mean?
When we think of 'family', images of 1950s' advertisements float through our heads: Dad smiling, Mom staying home, washing and ironing, surrounded by their clean and obedient 2.2 children. Or, reflecting an earlier image, we think of the archetype of the Christian 'holy family', which we see especially at Christmas with crèche scenes.

Our perception of 'the family' is filtered through the model of the 'holy family' with its reproductive icons of Jesus, Mary and Joseph. The family as we think of it is one of mythological archetype, based on hierarchy and reproduction, the ideal father a nice 'king in his castle'. Surely, you might comment, in this day and age people no longer think like that, the modern family is not a religious one, most people are not Catholics – most of the

2 *The Hite Report on the Family.*

families in the US and the UK are not of the old nuclear variety. Yet the images linger on in our minds, and we measure ourselves (or find ourselves being measured in newspapers) against the three leading icons of this 'traditional family', held up to be the only 'right' kind of family (every other family being flawed or wrong-headed, tragic).

The icons of the 'holy family' surround us in some of the most glorious art and symbolism of Western history. In the sumptuous images and colours of great painting, in the intricate works of architecture and music, the story of the 'holy family' is told and retold. Artists such as Titian, Raphael and Michaelangelo were commissioned by the church to create masterpieces out of biblical themes, as were composers such as Bach and Handel. The church was the primary sponsor of art for centuries.

No matter how beautiful (especially in its promise of 'true love'), this family model is an essentially repressive one, teaching authoritarian psychological patterns and a belief in the unchanging rightness of male power. In this hierarchical family, love and power are inextricably linked, a pattern that has damaging effects on not only all family members but also on the politics of the wider society. How can there be a successful democracy in public life if there is an authoritarian model in private life? If we all learn, therefore, to think and react hierarchically? The emotional spectrum we come to believe represents 'human nature' reflects this background.

Now that families are becoming different, we are seeing people question things in their upbringing that for centuries have not been questioned. We are beginning to see people ask themselves exactly what 'love' is and try to build families based on love that does not exactly fit into the system, or follow the old models of 'right living'. People feel unsure, even guilty about the new lives they are constructing.

Whether or not most people's lives fit into the 'traditional' hierarchical Holy Family model archetype, most people feel a certain admiration and nostalgia for the symbols. Why? Why do the icons hold our hearts? So used have we become to these symbols, that we continue to believe – no matter what statistics we see in the newspapers about divorce, violence in the home, mental breakdown – that the icons and the system they represent are right, fair and just. After all, we are told, the 'holy family' is a religious symbol, so who can criticize it? We assume without thinking that this model is the only 'natural' form of family and that if there are problems, it must be the individual who is at fault, not the institution.

We cannot even begin to imagine that our beautiful family system, the object of all those magnificent paintings and symbols, might not at heart be good or right. What is 'reality', we wonder – the icons, or our lives? What should 'reality' be? Shouldn't it be a 'harmonious family' like the icon? Aren't we flawed as individuals if it is not? And who is to 'blame'?

How can there be a successful democracy in public life if there is an authoritarian model in private life?

Yet, it seems to me, the statistics we are seeing do not represent a 'decline' in the family or a collapse of civilization. What is happening is a transformation, not a collapse. It may be one of the most important turning points in several centuries, the creation of a new social base that will engender an advanced and improved democratic political structure.

Too many people, all their lives, live out a play-enacted version of themselves, a shadow-self tailored for public consumption, displaying 'appropriate' social behaviour in public life; while underneath, in private, an undergrowth of confused feelings of joy, fear, eroticism and pain exist, all jumbled together.

Too many people, all their lives, live out a play-enacted version of themselves, a shadow-self tailored for public consumption, displaying 'appropriate' social behaviour in public life.

This is beginning to change. Most people today have discovered in their own lives that trying to copy one archetype of how to construct their personal lives does not permit them to relate honestly to the people around them or on the level they would like. So they are seeking in their own lives to find what does work, thus leading to the diversity of choices we see today and the new government statistics on changing lifestyles all over the Western world.

What we are witnessing now – and participating in – is a revolution in the family. The way we live our lives, with whom and how, is being questioned and debated in a groundbreaking and important revolution. The fundamentalist reactionary forces that are calling for the 'preservation of family values', opposing this democratization, are wrong to insist that the revolution is causing harm, and have no statistical base for such claims. This is an excellent revolution that has been needed for a very long time. The problems we are seeing in 'the family' are caused by its antiquated authoritarianism, not by the humanizing and equalizing process of democratization now going on in family and private life.

We should have faith in ourselves, believe in our own experience and history – not be afraid, but continue with confidence to the future.

We should have faith in ourselves, believe in our own experience and history – not be afraid, but continue with confidence to the future.

Your Opinion…

What is your opinion and experience? What do you think? What have been *your* experiences of what's been discussed in this chapter?

Please use this space to write your remarks, or alternatively you may e-mail comments to the *Sex and Business* website at www.sexandbusiness.com/myopinion. Naturally, you may express yourself anonymously.

_____

_____

_____

_____

_____

_____

Men managing women often have to face women's unexpressed or hidden fears and resentment towards them – fears and resentments women almost can't help having, since they have been shown, over and over, that men hold the power, or most of it. This creates, or tends to create, a love/hate or fear/worship relationship, making it difficult for real dialogue to take place.

Although more and more women are finding a solid footing inside larger Fortune 500 companies, the number of women at the top, statistically, is still small, especially in upper management and on boards of directors. Why? The reasons usually cited for this – 'we can't find qualified women', 'we are hiring young women now as trainees and hope they will work up to the top' or 'the problem for women is that they must interrupt their careers for childbearing' – are not the real reasons for this deficit. Prejudice is.

How much do men

know about working

with women?

Is a New Male Psychology Emerging?

More and more men today not only 'understand' and 'want to help' women – often they have seen their own daughters, wives, sisters and others transforming themselves but still hitting barriers of the 'glass ceiling' at their jobs and in their careers – but also find they themselves are much different from their fathers' generation, and want to change even more.

Think of the many books published during the last two decades on 'personal growth' – 'self-help' for women and 'business secrets' for men. Both are helping the person reading them think through issues of self-identity and how they see the world. Now, after so many years, a sea-change is taking place, as people everywhere have changed or begun to change their view of themselves and others.

Men now, according to my research and the statistics around us, seem to say that they are quietly undergoing a revolution on their own terms, in their own inner values and beliefs – beliefs about the importance of work, how work should be structured, how private life should be lived, how time should be spent. Many men are rethinking the ultimate values of life, what it means to be alive and part of this world.

Men's new ideas and changes are beginning to make themselves felt at the workplace.

We will see more and more of these changes coming in the future. They will happen faster if we can chase away the bogeyman of puberty initiation rites for boys – that make men later fear reprisals from other men at work if they promote women, or begin to act in more individual ways (see Growing Up Male, page 120).

How Much Do Men Know about Working with Women?

How well are men doing working with female colleagues? Managing women? How many men feel comfortable hiring and firing women, helping them achieve their maximum result, find new directions, get promotions and take successful new initiatives for the company and their careers? How many feel comfortable taking orders from a woman?

How many men feel that they themselves are burdened by an outdated 'male psychology' and want to redesign their own mental software?

Today, with more women at work in so many different kinds of jobs, men and women are having to adjust, create new kinds of relationships from scratch. As long as most women in the office were secretaries, and a man could 'tell them what to do', the relationship may not have been too different from a relationship at home with a sister, daughter or mother (a 'helping person'). Now, however, men are called on to relate in some new undefined way to 'women as equals'.

Men are called on to relate in some new undefined way to 'women as equals'.

In fact, although men have had female secretaries for most of the 20th century, many never really felt comfortable with that relationship. It was neither a love relationship nor a family relationship, the two ways men were educated to see women.

Although, of course, most men believe that it is right to accept women at work as equals, how many – knowing that women have been educated to feel that power and aggression are bad and 'unfeminine' – feel that part of their job is helping women overcome inhibitions about 'power'? Make sure women around them have some power?

How many men feel that they themselves are burdened by an outdated 'male psychology' and want to redesign their own mental software?

Many men today have female bosses, female colleagues and, especially, many young female employees. The young women are expected to move up into middle management and possibly later into executive slots. Are the men managing them now grooming them to move up (secretaries were never expected to move up, they would never 'grow up' to 'threaten' a man), take more responsibility, make more money – or are most men still tending to favour other men, 'the guys'?

Although most of us today smile and say, with a toss of the head, 'Oh yes, we get on well! We're the New Generation!', in fact, things are slightly more complicated.

How is it going?

Mini Hite Report: Statistics

What men say

'How do you feel working with female colleagues?'
29% sometimes I feel uncomfortable and confused about the right approach
51% I am bending over backwards not to discriminate or use stereotypes
20% too much is made of gender, I just try to be myself

'How do you work with women under you?'
18% I help them move ahead
11% I can't ask them out drinking with the rest of us, so they miss out on being part of the inner group
19% they turn to me for help with their work, and I turn to them for help with my private life. Is this OK?
31% no problems
21% there are no women at work I deal with

What women say

'How do you feel working with male colleagues?'
63% sometimes I feel uncomfortable and confused about the right approach
14% I am bending over backwards not to discriminate or use stereotypes
23% too much is made of gender, I just try to be myself

'If you have a male boss, how does he relate to you?'
27% treats me fairly
51% doesn't understand me, undervalues me, but doesn't realize he's doing it
22% discriminates heavily against me in favour of male colleagues and knows it

People in Transition: What Do They Say?

What are men's experiences today in working with women?

'In my third year with the company, suddenly I was put in charge of a division with mostly female employees. This was a large computer company, and I went from spending my days with mostly male techies, to overseeing a large pool of women assembling parts (the small delicate parts inside the works). This blew my mind! I never learned so much in such a short span of time. I learned to be something like an athletic coach, cheering them on, setting targets and rewarding achievement. But whenever one tried to talk to me on a one-to-one basis ("My mother is sick and I must…"), I was hopeless. I had two or three near mutinies, but I had to succeed, it was the only way up (to advance) in the company, so I stuck it out. I don't know what made the company think it could put me in charge of 200 women (but it doesn't have many women managers, maybe that was the reason) – I had to learn quick to drop my prejudices, and get on with work without my attitudes showing. If any of the techies I had lunch with tried to make jokes about my department and "all my girls", I gave him a lesson in manners.'

'There is one woman under me who is particularly bright. She takes on more and more responsibility, and I can see that she easily outstrips the men around her in abilities. I'm thinking about promoting her to one of the top spots, in fact, but I don't want to arouse a hornets' nest of warring men around me. She is excellent at her job, but her political skills… I don't know. On the other hand, what could she do to calm a bunch of men if she's promoted over them? Maybe I'd do best just to keep her in her place, keep her where she is. She's doing a good job for us, she could do more staying where she is, she's making good money. I wonder how she would react to not being promoted.'

'I had to promote a woman to the board. I was chairman and it just seemed odd that there wasn't even one. Besides, my family was making fun of me and the company every night at dinner, calling it that old fuddy-duddy tank of guys. My daughter is an attorney, she's as sharp as they come. She's been on my case about this for years, and I decided she was right. When I looked around the firm, I couldn't see an appropriate woman right off the bat. This made me notice that the firm was not "woman-friendly", I guess it was not grooming women to move up or be visible – when I looked, they "weren't there". I asked every head of department into my office for a meeting, and explained our problem. I asked all of them (all men) to recommend one woman from their division that they thought had exceptional potential. Then there was a qualifying test for the ten women, and the best one was put directly onto the board. OK, she isn't quite old enough or experienced for the slot, but she's growing into it amazingly fast. In fact, she's already made some good suggestions at our meetings, and I'm not sorry at all that I did it. It's had a good effect on the morale of the other women, probably, and maybe it even makes men work harder (scared to lose their jobs)!'

'Julia used to be my secretary in the daytime, then the evening shift secretary was Livia. Both of them accepted the job because they told me they wanted an entry into the firm, not because they wanted to be "secretaries forever". I promised that after a few years getting their feet wet, if they deserved it, I would look around for good jobs for

Women say men still sometimes create a feeling that women are out of place at work.

them within the firm, jobs with responsibility. In the meantime, Julia and I fell in love. The problem was, I am married, and in my position, I cannot (and don't want to) dump my wife and family. I solved the entire situation finally by finding Julia a top job overseas: she manages an entire division! Were the boys surprised when I told them she was coming! Not happy at all, but then, it's better to have a new director come from outside than from the group already there. She takes a fresh look. We'll see.'

'I'm only 28 but I have a lot of women working under me. The trouble is, I can never decide which ones to promote, which to fire, and which to be patient a little longer with. My mind is confused between liking one of them, seeing the work she produces (doesn't produce!), or just thinking she's an asset because she improves the atmosphere of the place. I mean, keeping up morale is a big part of work, isn't it? If someone is unpleasant to work with (and some of the women really are!), can they help the company? I know they don't help me. I fire them.'

'It's incorrect, so kill me, but I like women at the office with good legs. I find an old, dull, fat bird a real turn-off, and I don't want to work with anyone like that, no matter how smart she is. I know this is way off base, so don't quote my name.'

Women say men still sometimes create a feeling that women are out of place at work:

'Men in my office have different ways of behaving with me, though we are all colleagues on the same level. Some know how to become friends, others seem not to know and stumble along making inappropriate semi-passes (probably they're not even turned on, they just don't know how else to approach me) – while others are fearful of acting in the least friendly (afraid of offending "the wife" or what???), so that they act stiff as rods! Caricatures of real people. I don't think this says so much about the different chemistry between me and certain men as it does about some men's lack of experience, or general attitude towards women. If a man grew up with his sister, he has a much better chance of being relaxed with women. Some men, especially those who never had a sister or cousin or women friends, can only think in terms of showing women how dominant they are. They show their desire to dominate me in different ways: the unfriendly guy is showing his dominance by keeping me shut out, and the ones making semi-passes (remarks and innuendoes) are trying to imply a sexual relationship and in this way dominate me – I guess in the past, a man "having" a woman symbolized him dominating her. The men who do this are not stupid in general, it's just with me at work that they freeze up and act bonkers. Too bad.'

'My husband died suddenly two months ago. I am 53 and have been working all of our married life, we have two children. Now that I am a widow I feel that my younger male colleagues think I should stop working (so they can have my job?). They keep saying things to me like, "We know you must feel terrible, it must be difficult for you to come to work, wouldn't you be happier staying at home?" and so on. They are looking at me and making gestures like I am unusual, maybe not quite "normal", why do I want to come to work anyway?? This attitude is not helping me. First of all, without my job I would not have much income. Secondly, without my job, should I just stay at home all day crying? Thirdly, I have a right to my job, I like working. Fourth, I will need my pension (to get it, I have to continue working, of course)!'

Brain Software Commands

SOFTWARE TO DELETE

Women are inferior. Women are not made for business, but for love and sex.

SOFTWARE TO INSTALL

Women, like men, have many sides to their personalities and identity. Women vary.

SOFTWARE TO DELETE

Men are lessened by women's 'encroachment' into the office; it lessens men's status.

SOFTWARE TO INSTALL

Having women work with men in the office enhances work, adds to the energy and talent available. This benefits me.

Brain Game 4.1

Clichés about women: the software in your head (and how to de-program it)

Imagine you, a male executive, are discussing money and negotiating a contract with a woman executive.

How would you behave differently than if you were conducting the same negotiation with a man?

You can learn a lot from your answer.

Points to think about re women and money:

- What does money mean to women, and is this different from what it means to men?

- Why can discussions of money between men and women be hard to handle, in a way discussions between men about money rarely are?

- Would you be afraid of negotiating a pay rise or pay cut with a woman, more than with a man?

- How comfortable would you be hiring a woman and discussing her salary?

Question: Does any amount of politeness to a woman, any amount of promotions or awards, make up for lack of equal pay?

(A British study showed it will cost £400 million for the British government to begin giving women equal pay (May 1999, *Observer*).

A Catch-22: How Can a Woman Ask for a Promotion?

There is a Catch-22 for women at work: a woman won't get promoted, in all likelihood, unless she tells people she wants a particular job, and if she does tell them, they may call her 'too aggressive', 'unfeminine' and dominating' – 'a bitch on wheels' – to get the job!

If a woman tries to engage in the work strategies necessary to gain promotion, sometimes colleagues become negative and call this 'bitchy behaviour', although they wouldn't say the same thing about a man.

Brain Software Commands

⊖ SOFTWARE TO DELETE

Women, if they speak about money, are rude and grasping, money-hungry. Women would be more graceful if they did not care about money.

⊕ SOFTWARE TO INSTALL

Women have as much right as men to be paid for their work. It is normal for women to discuss money with others.

'You Can't Trust a Woman in Business'

There has been an old attitude – 'you can trust a man, but not a woman', 'a man's word is his bond', etc. while women are 'changeable'. As the famous aria proclaims 'La donna è mobile'!

Yet statistics show that women are more likely than men to repay bank loans and other business debts. (A small study by the International Monetary Fund in 1994–5 brought in surprising results.) 'Housewives' often manage the finances and budget, do the financial planning for the family – yet they are considered, in cliché, incapable of adding up figures, 'they just spend money'.

This cliché is pervasive. Early in the 20th century, women did not have the right to have their own bank accounts; in France, for example, women only achieved this right in 1964. The idea that 'women can't handle money' is harmful, of course, to women's career advancement.

Many women go into business for themselves (two-thirds of all new businesses are begun by women, and a high percentage of them are successful after five years) because they find their path so blocked inside companies. Yet even there, the same dynamics surface. Consider the story of a young woman in Italy:

'I began my business financing advertising fifteen years ago. I have been highly successful. Recently one of my main accounts pulled out, because (he claimed) he had received a less expensive and better offer from someone else. I was surprised, because we had a ten-year contract, and it is only half over. I took one of the major shareholders of my small firm out to dinner, with his wife, and mentioned the situation to him. I had thought, given the fact that he had been making quite a handsome profit for these fifteen years and I had never asked him for anything before, that he would help me think of a strategy to keep the business going, and therefore keep his dividends coming. I thought he had a good opinion of me as a reliable businesswoman. In the middle of the dinner, he told me he would sell his shares, he wanted out. His wife tried to reason with him, but he had made up his mind. Now I feel very strange, like my track record doesn't mean anything. Why? He says he wants to be sure of his money. He has been sure with me for fifteen years. Why can't he trust me?'

Equality: The Big Issue

Behind many management issues lies the issue of gender, its unrealistic stereotypes, and a very real history of discrimination and inequality.

Behind many management issues lies the issue of gender, its unrealistic stereotypes, and a very real history of discrimination and inequality.

Sometimes there is an unspoken resentment about this: women may resent men for having an advantage over them (most men expect to hire and promote men, not women), while men may resent women (but be unable to say so) because now they have to compete with more

people (women too...), work is no longer the private male preserve it was, 'only for the guys'.

Men managing women often have to face women's unexpressed or hidden fears and resentment towards them – fears and resentments women almost can't help having, since they have been shown, over and over, that men hold the power, or most of it. This creates, or tends to create, a love/hate or fear/worship relationship, making it difficult for real dialogue to take place.

Although more and more women are finding a solid footing inside larger Fortune 500 companies, the number of women at the top, statistically, is still small, especially in upper management and on boards of directors. Why? The reasons usually cited for this – 'we can't find qualified women', 'we are hiring young women now as trainees and hope they will work up to the top' or 'the problem for women is that they must interrupt their careers for childbearing' – are not the real reasons for this deficit. Prejudice is.

Quite a few male executives feel uncomfortable with this disequilibrium, and would like to change it, but don't want to face the clichés some of their colleagues may throw at them, i.e. the sexual politics of the situation. A male executive instinctively realizes he does not want to be pointed out as 'the one who wanted her here', to insist on promoting or hiring a woman, as he may be accused of having a sexual affair with her (and this is the reason he hired or promoted her). How a man who wants to hire woman can avoid these problems is explained in Chapters 3 and 5.

Sometimes a man who is uncomfortable with a woman looks for a personality defect in her to justify his feeling of dislike or repulsion. In fact, what he may be experiencing is his own prejudice – although he may not realize this is the case. When in doubt, a man could try the mental gymnastic of imagining he is in the same situation with a black man; how would his feelings change or stay the same?

Male managers and colleagues can find ways out of these impasses, new possibilities for getting the full potential out of all the personalities at work, including those of women – but how?

First, men needn't waste time feeling guilty because they have power over women at work (if a man says he doesn't feel guilty, he may be experiencing hidden guilt) – but they should become more creative, active, helping to change women's status in a variety of ways. In addition, both men and women must consciously strive to overcome ingrained attitudes leading to distance and distrust. Specifically, what can men do?

Both men and women must consciously strive to overcome ingrained attitudes leading to distance and distrust.

Brain Game 4.2

Ethical issues for men in corporations vis-à-vis women
Question: If you are a woman's colleague and it comes to your attention that her salary is (wrongly) less than yours, and you think this could be part of the company's pattern of sexual discrimination, what should you do? If you think she is being underpaid compared to you, even if it is not part of a larger pattern, what should you do?

After all, it is not your fault; you do not make company policy, not to mention preparing the corporate budget annually. Still, what should you do. Should you take any action?

Here are some possible choices, maybe you can think of others:

1. Start an employees' discussion group to see if there are gender problems such as lack of equal pay. (Are women as a group being underpaid by the company? Or, are men overpaid!) Of course, this could be a big risk, you could be fired!

2. Talk openly with your colleague, advising her to ask for a raise (to your level); tip her off how much (but ask her to be discreet and not mention you).

3. Speak to a male superior and say you're concerned the company could be at risk for gender discrimination in pay practices, and suggest her salary be improved. In this case should you tell your colleague of the step you have taken?

4. Do nothing. It's up to women themselves to fight for equal pay.

Ethical issues for women in corporations vis-à-vis men

Is the situation one-sided? Are women 'angels', while men hold 'all the power' and are 'bad' for not sharing it? After all, the name of the game in business is competition. Why shouldn't men take advantage of whatever they can in their bid to succeed? Should women learn the same lesson?

Indeed, some women have. Now that eighties' political correctness is no longer a new fad, many women in the late nineties have caught onto the idea that a little lipstick can help a lot on the unequal playing field called 'business'.

> Now that eighties' political correctness is no longer a new fad, many women in the late nineties have caught onto the idea that a little lipstick can help a lot on the unequal playing field called 'business'.

Are women ethically at fault for using the tactics of feminine wiles? Are they unfair at the office, or just equalizing the playing field with men, who already have an in-built advantage? (See Chapter 6.)

Problems Men Can Have Promoting Women

There seems to be a block: the percentage of women on boards and in higher management is pitifully small. What reasons do men in power give for this, according to my research?

'The women are just not *there*. You want to put them into responsible top positions, but they are just not there. It's not a question of prejudice.' (CEO of UK publishing company, May 1999)

The three reasons CEOs in my sample gave me for not having women at the tops of their corporations are:

❶ 'We're hiring young MBAs now who are women – they have the best academic scores anyway – and eventually they will rise to the top.' (Currently there are no or very few qualified women of that age and on that level.)

❷ 'It disturbs the working atmosphere on the board of directors if we bring a woman in; men, for whatever reason, work best together and prefer to work together.'

❸ 'It's tragic but women's childbearing bodily functions (biology) and family demands interrupt their careers: just when they should be getting along with their careers, in the important period of their thirties, they must take time off, time out, to have children and begin raising them. This is not anyone's fault, but it means that women have lost valuable time in gaining experience inside the company.'

Another executive, editor of one of the world's leading newspapers, had given the issue considerable thought:

'I used to think that hiring young female MBAs was the answer, when I started working 30 years ago. However, I have seen that it is not. Something happens during women's thirties, so that women leave corporations. We lose women during their thirties. My conclusion? It is necessary for companies to make special efforts to keep women in their thirties. Otherwise, they all just go. Companies keep hiring bright young women, but where are they twenty years later? Women who should be rising in the corporation are no longer there. There seems to be a myriad reasons – marriage, pregnancy, childraising, negativity of the workplace to women, non-promotion and valuing of women at work, negative stereotypes about professional and "career women" putting on the defensive psychologically, lack of day care for children, and so on. The bottom line: companies must make special efforts to overcome this hurdle, or they will lose women. Time alone will not solve this problem.'

Realistic, not to mention futuristic, analyses of women's future inside corporations are hard to find. Here is one:

'I am positive about women's emergence into corporate leadership in the future, only for one reason. Why? Because the fundamental balance of sexual power has shifted: women won't shut up any more. I mean this in a positive sense and quite seriously. There are many signs of this, i.e. Monica Lewinsky speaking up about her relationship with President Clinton, Princess Diana talking on television about her private life, and... The Hite Report on Female Sexuality where women spoke about their sexuality and bodies in amazing detail, for the first time! The double standard, fears that women must be quiet and docile, don't keep women quiet any more.'

Some executives say a word in favour of quotas for hiring women:

'There is still huge discrimination against women, to the extent that even women themselves believe they cannot make it, they are not as good. For this reason, quotas can be very positive. A CEO can use it to hide behind when he promotes women: "Believe me, I didn't want to put her in that position, but I had to. They made me do it!" With quotas there, no one can criticize him, as they tend to do.'

Debates in countries such as France and Germany are ongoing as to whether their parliaments should install tough quota systems, a mandatory 50 per cent participation in government jobs at all levels for women.

Debates in countries such as France and Germany are ongoing as to whether their parliaments should install tough quota systems, a mandatory 50 per cent participation in government jobs at all levels for women.

As one CEO of a major international firm put it:

'Women are very bright, as bright as men, but tragically for them, they must stop work to bear and raise children right in the middle of their careers; when they go back to work, they have lost several of the most important years for developing themselves at work. It is sad, but simply the fact. We are hiring many young female MBAs now, and with time they will rise up in the corporation, and end the male dominance inside of the corporation.'

Yet the hiring of young women, expecting them to move up in the corporation doesn't seem to work; all those bright young women fall by the wayside for some reason. To make sure that women are participating fully in corporations, companies must make special efforts to put them there – both in helping women in their thirties work even though they are beginning families or face other demands; and by appointing senior women to high-level posts – looking for them and *finding* them.

Women's Ghettos Inside Corporations

Ghettos? Is this an exaggeration? One woman explains:

'I am a woman running a small business of my own. I have many corporate clients, so I get to see what is happening with women on all sides – including at my own bank. I have three banks for my business (it's good to be diversified!), and would you believe that at each bank, there is the same situation? It can't be just a coincidence. I have had these accounts for over ten years. At first, I usually had a male account executive, during the early 1990s, but by the late 1990s my accounts had all be moved to be handled by a woman in her early thirties – or if my accounts were not moved, then in any case, I found that suddenly a woman was in charge of my account. At all three banks, this woman is the only woman at that level amidst a pool of her equals, male account executives (and bosses above her, all men).

'The system works against her, in every case – and therefore against me. At one, for example, I have never been able to get a line of credit! When I tried on three different occasions over the years to fill in the proper form, speak to the bank about

this, etc. I was met with a closed door. When I asked the woman account executive, she informed me that "Mr ____ makes this decision, at least for the branch – but he must also refer it to the next higher division, for their decision, which is final." I felt like if I were the client of one of the men, there would be more trust, but being the client of a woman, she was always under pressure to be more conservative than the men in her decisions and actions lest they criticize her or find fault, costing her her job. Who suffers? Me. When I try to move my account to a male executive I am perceived as being "dissatisfied with a woman", and expected to give a "good reason" – which could also cost her her job. The cards are stacked against her and me. I can only move my account to another bank, and this takes valuable time away from my business...

'At another bank, when I called to speak to the woman in charge of my account, I was told on various occasions that she was "on vacation", yet she had just returned from a vacation. When I insisted that I must talk to someone, even if she was not there, no one seemed to feel that this was a serious matter; I must wait for her to return, since only a woman can deal with another woman! On another day, I found her in tears. When I asked why, she told me that her all-male colleagues continued to address her as "Miss" although she told them repeatedly to call her Mrs, thus being disrespectful. She felt that they did everything they could in little ways to try to destabilize her and trip her up, claiming that her figures were wrong, that she could not count, etc. As it turned out, when she came back from "vacation", she told me that during the previous month, the men in her division had been promoted, everyone except her... This had made her so depressed that she became ill. I'm sure she was. So was I; my account was in shambles because of her absence and their refusal to help.

'The third bank is similar. There, one young woman is bravely trying to make her way up the ladder. She is very good. But when she is not there, no one will service her clients – thus making her seem unprofessional. Every item must be passed for approval to her boss, a man who controls everything. Finally, one day, I spoke with him and this seemed to improve things. I notice that a new young man has been given a job parallel to my account executive, and he may be moved up ahead of her before long.'

The current stage of integration of women into corporate management now often involves ghettos for women inside corporations. Perhaps this is a natural stage, but I think it can be dangerous, a dead-end. This tendency can be overcome by the simple mental exercises I suggest throughout this book.

Developing stage 2 and 3 colleague relationships with the opposite sex – and avoiding cliché pitfalls that can ruin them – are the direction we need to move in. You can also profitably read about how to develop a working friendship (friendship without fear) in Chapter 8.

Which Women Should Male Executives Promote?

Women at work looking for men to marry

'My ex-secretary is now a PA for a football team. She's 30 and is always talking to me (we still speak of the phone, and sometimes get together for a drink) about how she wants to meet the right man and settle down and have babies. She tells the men she goes out with this, and they shy away, she says – like once she was walking down the street with her boyfriend, and when a stroller passed by with two babies in it, she couldn't resist stopping to look adoringly at them, but when he saw this look on her face, he became terrified and never called her again! My secretary (ex) is a lot of fun. I don't know why the women at work never seemed to like her.'

Charming as this woman must have been, it does not sound like she took her position at work, or as a woman outside the home, very seriously. (Or it could be that she somehow feels that telling her bosses she is 'really only interested in babies' makes her completely non-threatening and non-competitive, so they will accept her even more!) If she does not take her own position at work very seriously, in all likelihood she will not take the other women at work very seriously either: what good would they be to her, if she is primarily interested in finding the 'right man' and 'making babies'? Such an attitude would be irritating to women at work who do take their jobs seriously and hope to advance.

Problems taking women seriously

'I like having young women working here. They bring a lot of energy and enthusiasm, and don't expect too much – like some men do. One girl is cute as a button. Has one of the best track records in her university, her graduate scores were among the top ten. She doesn't brag, however. With her perky ways, I'm sure she'll get ahead in the company – if this is what she eventually wants. (I bet some bright young man will steal her away, though! She'll wind up wanting to have babies and stay home, like my wife…) The new generation of women will take over the world someday.'

What's 'wrong' with this point of view? This executive is praising women's contribution at work, yet there is a lurking suspicion listening to him that he might be uncomfortable with this same woman were she to continue in the company and arrive at a very senior position and be more near his own age. He may be able to accept 'the new young women' as long as they are young and as long as they pose no threat to him, i.e. are much too young and junior for his job – and besides may quit anyway in favour of marriage and children!

Quite a number of CEOs – from Japan to Switzerland – put forward the idea, without any prompting on my part, that the new generation of women would take over companies and the world in the 21st century! That women would somehow save the world, and save companies. This may be simply projecting women's traditional role as 'peacemaker' and 'idealist', 'solver of all problems', onto women's situation at work. Ironically, some of these same CEOs may be hiring and promoting the very women who do not have these particular skills, preferring women who 1) do not threaten them, and 2) 'think like the boys', i.e. fit in with corporate structures as they stand.

How can a man promote a woman at work without arousing controversy?

How can a man promote a woman at work, or have a woman protégée, without being 'suspect', i.e. hearing rumours he is having a sexual relationship with her?

Will a male executive be accused of having a sexual affair if he tries to promote a woman to an important position, or tries to have a female protégée? What should he do about this, how should he handle this? How should a woman, if she is in the position of being promoted or hired by a man, handle this? How can she best make the transition into a mostly male executive environment?

Male executives today are often aware of the small number of women in key positions and know the potential of hiring women with good qualifications. Yet, not usually stated, are the very real risks a male executive may run in trying to 'improve society', 'help

women get ahead' or even just 'do the best thing for the corporation'.

Male executives today are often aware of the small number of women in key positions and know the potential of hiring women with good qualifications. Yet, not usually stated, are the very real risks a male executive may run in trying to 'improve society', 'help women get ahead' or even just 'do the best thing for the corporation'.

Although, of course, it isn't fair that society still can make assumptions and judgements about inter-gender relationships, even (especially?) at work, the fact is that these clichés still surround us. This doesn't mean the world isn't changing or that we can't lead in this important change, we can. It just means watching out.

There are practical steps male executives can take to avoid charges of sexual involvement when promoting a woman, or having a female protégée inside the corporation, such as the one used by Laurenz Fritz when he was chairman of Alcatel (as he explains in Chapter 3).

Similar steps can be taken in the not-so-frequent case of a woman hiring or promoting a man.

Brain Software Commands

SOFTWARE TO DELETE

'It's all in our natures.'

'Mother Nature will have her way.'

SOFTWARE TO INSTALL

'Human beings are complex.'

How Can a Man Best Work with Female Colleagues at the Office?

Do:

- Appraise your working partner(s) for her skills and assets, as well as weak spots.

- Try to imagine the most productive way you could combine your talents.

- Present the possibility of working towards this goal together to her. (Say, 'Let's present a project jointly at the next board meeting, what do you say? The project I have in mind is what we were talking about the other day, i.e. bridges in Australia, or boats in Africa, or whatever. Here's how I see proceeding...')

Do not, when trying to talk to a female colleague:

1. Fall silent and wait for her to begin discussion of a work project.

2. Imagine that she doesn't like you.

3. Imagine that she has a crush on you.

4. Imagine that her private life is a shambles, and she is just dying to talk about it.

5. Imply to her that your private life is a shambles, and you might see her as a new girlfriend.

6. Focus on her faults or weak points (or yours), expecting either of you to fail.

7. Lose interest when she speaks more than two sentences.

The Bad Boy Planet: Out-of-Date Software

Out-of-date software you may be carrying around in your head...

Test your software. Find out where you are on the planet of male clichés...

1. Do you see Darth Vader as

   - rebel
   - corporate establishment power figure
   - neither?

2. Is the Star Trek philosophy

   - macho
   - feminist
   - neuter?

3. Is your favourite film idol a man or a woman? Has it ever been someone of the opposite sex?

To understand your score, keep reading this book: all will be made clear to you.

Things men (used to) say that women don't like (they sense discrimination)

'Just call my girl, she'll help you out', I hear men say, regarding their secretaries.

One of our receptionists was told by an older guy, 'You should meet my son!' She felt patronized, why did she want to meet his son? Did he assume that her life was so miserable – that she was a 'mere receptionist', only 'waiting to meet a man, Prince Charming, to take her away from all this'?

To move her up in social status, escape from this oppression, i.e. her job?

What do I feel if I see a woman in a short skirt at the office? If she's good-looking, I think, good for her. She has the confidence to wear it. I guess she's proud of her own legs, she wants us to see them. Some of my colleagues I've heard remark, 'Look at those legs, what a pair of crumpets!'

Of course, neither women nor men can stop and pay attention to every nuance of every conversation, since after all, work is the main order of the day. One can just tell oneself: 'Don't pay attention, don't think about it, just get on with things.' This is productive much of the time. The only downside is that one can get so used to 'not paying attention', and responding with a knee-jerk 'Fine, OK' attitude, that this can seem to be one's real persona. You can even forget, in the end, how you really feel about certain remarks!

Another out-dated male cliché about how to relate to women:

Junior version: 'I thought I should pull her ponytail for no reason because I saw a kid spit on his mom in a breakfast food commercial, and everyone seemed to like it and admire him.'

Senior version: 'I made a sexual innuendo towards her in front of the other men at the office. She didn't like it, but the men had a sneaking admiration for me for doing it.'

Brain Game 4.3

How to establish a good dialogue – useful if there's a problem

A male executive is talking to a female project manager, but somehow there is not a great feeling that things are moving ahead... what to do?

Sit down. Smile. It can help any situation.

Think of the most profound thing you can think of and say it. (Searching for something to say? Try the weather, nature is profound, after all.) Make sure it is less than two sentences long, give the other person a chance to respond.

Ask what she likes most and least about the project she's on.

Ask more questions and follow up: listen attentively. Don't yawn, look at your watch or answer the telephone (except briefly if necessary) during this attentive listening.

After, summarize what you think you heard her say, to make sure you are both on the same wavelength, then, if she agrees with your summary, continue with your thoughts and reactions.

Software Check-up: The Seven Deadly Sins

There are Seven Deadly Sins to avoid in order to communicate well with women you work with.

These are communication blocking tricks that men often use in private life (give away unenlightened attitudes). Can you spot them at work?

These behaviours create a pattern that one frustrated women describes like this:

'Usually I try to talk to him calmly at first and get no response. Then I am forced to state my points more bluntly, and he tells me I am attacking him. I can't win. He doesn't really listen to what I am saying.'

There are seven classic ways women say men have to silence them.

The seven classic ways women say men have to silence them:

1 **The silent treatment.** Men often try to shut women up with the classic silent treatment. The result is that the woman either shouts and a fight ensues, or she too becomes silent and cold. Either way the problem is never resolved.

2 **Pretending it never happened.** How do women feel when the man 'deals' with something they bring up by simply ignoring the fact that they have said anything at all?

3 **Changing the subject.** Many men try to change the subject in a variety of ways if they don't want to discuss something, yet facing a problem – if it comes to that – will clear the air. The situation need not be resolved during the conversation, but putting the block on the table will allow for further reflection and, eventually, a solution.

4 **Saying the problem is petty.** This is guaranteed to insult the other person! Even if the stated problem does seem petty, it is important to hear it, since it may be hiding a deeper problem that is difficult to enunciate. To point out to a person that an issue is fairly trivial is a way of saying that you do not find it interesting or important, i.e. you do not find what the other person is saying important enough to listen to.

5 **'A woman shouldn't complain because it makes a man feel guilty.'** Another common response might be called 'irrational aggression' or 'bullying the person you've just flattened'. Attacking a woman whose feelings are hurt – just because they are hurt and she has the nerve to say so – is another common tactic. In the man's mind, he is attacking her 'back', she deserves it, because she is making him feel guilty. (But where does this guilt really come from?)

6 **'What you feel is incorrect.'** Speaking of condescension...! Another way some men shut a woman up is by telling her, after she has spoken, that her feelings are 'wrong' or 'incorrect'.

7 **'You're crazy!'** Some men try to silence women by saying their thoughts and opinions are silly, crazy or funny – and then

can't understand why a woman may raise her voice in protest or become upset.

These attitudes of silent indifference, ridicule and put downs, clichés of daily life in private relationships (and at work), have the effect of silencing women before they have spoken, so fearful are they of provoking this kind of negative response. Women now don't want to be accused of being 'just like a woman'... The person initiating these negative responses seems to be saying he doesn't have to bother with the woman's side of the story, her views. The attitude expressed is: 'Take it or leave it.' This forces the other person to either fight back or silently and meekly accept the situation and say nothing.

Many women at work clam up altogether, 'keeping their head down', because they know where attempts at dialogue can lead. Rather than trying to make a point, they simply avoid problems. They fear being called aggressive. This is not good for company morale or progress.

Of course, what women really want is a two-way respectful dialogue, 'emotional equality' – acceptance, respect. Men can benefit, both privately and at work, by checking out whether any of these attitudes are still hanging about in their heads.

What women really want is a two-way respectful dialogue, 'emotional equality' – acceptance, respect. Men can benefit, both privately and at work, by checking out whether any of these attitudes are still hanging about in their heads.

Brain Game 4.4

Do women talk too much?

Topic: Who does most of the talking in mixed groups? Check yourself in the next conversation with someone of the opposite sex: how many minutes do you talk? How many minutes do you listen?

SOFTWARE TO DELETE

Women talk too much.

SOFTWARE TO INSTALL

Women are often intimidated at work and don't speak up enough; it is difficult for them to feel they will get the attention and time necessary to be heard. You may have to encourage them to speak, and take time to listen carefully.

Brain Game 4.5

Gender – behaviour in meetings

Scene: A group meeting is taking place, the weekly conference of all the heads of departments. Two members out of seven are women.

Do the women 'stick together'? This is a difficult situation for them. If they support one another's suggestions and ideas, then they are in danger of being seen as 'the sisterhood', illogically supporting 'another woman against the men' – whether this is true or not. If they don't support the other, they are in danger of being stereotyped as 'those women who can never get along, what bitches and cats!'

Of course, you would never be guilty of thinking such a thing! No, you are far too good, I have no doubt whatsoever. But just in case there is some small fragment of this idea lurking in the back of your mental software, take one minute to think this through.

Questions to test yourself

Men and women can read each others' signals without falling back into old clichés left over from days gone by, from dating stereotypes or in a new way than they did (or do) in private life. Women, for example, can adopt a point of view that observes men together on a playing field, thinking in terms of a team with its members competing yet working together to 'score points', hoping to learn such team skills to win. Men can remind themselves that most men grew up to believe that they would inhabit an all-male or mostly male work environment, as executives, and keep an eye out for possible irrational prejudices towards women at work.

Whether or not we could all make ourselves into robots who logically follow our rational conclusions... we should not expect people to deny themselves their own individual ways of expressing their moods and personalities with each other. It is natural that – even after reading this book! – there will be days on which either a man or a woman just can't deal with it all, and decides 'heck with it', I'm just going to 'be myself'. It's OK.

Ideas and Aids

Shortcuts men can use to improve their relationships with women (overnight) – success guaranteed

Learn to think like a woman when you want to.

Learn to think like a woman when you want to. (This doesn't mean, 'I'll manipulate him to get what I want by giving him sex', as some men fantasize when they dream of being female! It means having to face the expectations people have of you *because* you're a woman.)

Remember that male authority figures can seem frighteningly powerful, intimidating, to many women, as well as men in groups.

Learn to talk and interact without pressing women's 'buttons', understanding what it is like to be brought up as a woman – just as women must understand (see Chapter 5) what it's like to be 'male'. (After all, men have their own masculine complexes that women have to compensate for when speaking with men.)

Don't be afraid: many men feel a hidden loyalty conflict, i.e. am I going to antagonize my wife by having good relationships with career women at the office? Will the 'men's club' at work still accept me if I seem to be friendly with lots of women?

Some men feel more than necessarily nervous, guilty or worried about potential conflicts between their wives and women at work. Why? (See Executive Wives, page 81.)

Do you really believe in equality? Test yourself on pages 65–66.

Do you really believe in equality?

Go on, break the ice! Establish a dialogue, be the first man in your group to dare to have a woman protégée or invite a woman into the men's group (drinking beer?) after work (if she wants to come)! Listen and speak about women's ideas in meetings. Why not?!

Try this cliché on for size:

'Women are out of place at men's meetings.' Ask yourself: 'Can I support a woman in private but not in public, like at a meeting?' Take this test... if a woman presents an idea in a meeting, could you stand up and second it as quickly as if it had been a man presenting the idea?

'What's Love Got to Do with It'???!?

Men sometimes project images of women in private life onto women at work, seeing women basically in terms of private life – as potential sexual or romantic mates. They wonder, when they meet them, whether they are 'happily mated' or single. (And the reverse is true: women wonder about men!)

This is not surprising, since we were all brought up this way. Yet this side-issue keeps men and women from working as well as they might with each other. Here is some good software to erase!

Some of the clichés about love ('real men' don't need it, 'women are desperate for love', and so on) add to the confusion that can crop up between a man and a woman when they work together.

The culture teaches men and women different values about love. It is rather negative to men, i.e. when a man announces to his friends and family, with joy in his eyes, that he has found the love of his life, he is in love and wants to get married, he is often met with doubting, indulgent smiles: 'Don't rush into anything, it's just your hormones, give it time, you'll get her out of your system.' Thus society warns men against women and love every day with little remarks: 'Don't let a pretty face turn your head', 'Don't let a woman wrap you around her little finger', 'Are you sure you can trust her, isn't she going to use you?', 'Don't let her get her hooks into you! You're just a meal ticket for her...' and so on. The hero in Ernest Hemmingway's classic novel, *A Farewell to Arms,* loses his wife because his best friend tries to get him to 'forget her, don't let a woman make a fool of you'.

The culture teaches men and women different values about love.

A woman, making a similar announcement about her engagement, usually receives a totally different response: cheers all round, encouragement for getting married: i.e. 'Did he pop the question?', 'Did you say yes?', 'Will you be happy? Have children?', 'When is the wedding date?', 'Congratulations!'

According to my research, the majority of men I studied (7,000) did not marry the woman they

most passionately loved, and are proud of this, because they feel they did not let their emotions take control, run away with them; they remained 'rational and in charge'. Loving 'too much' they felt they would lose control. Marrying a woman they felt more 'sure of', of course, often led to a less emotionally intimate and rewarding life and relationship.

The lesson for the office: men may have an unconscious hangover from these cultural truisms, i.e. it's not good to hang out with a woman, because other men will laugh at you, show you less respect, you will be seen as 'weak' not 'strong'...

Are Women 'Fixated on Love', more than Work?

Many men still have programmed in their mental software some kind of inevitable connection between women, sex and romance – along with a side-program stating that these will interfere with a woman's performance at work. (These things do not automatically interfere with work inside corporations, myths to the contrary; consider, for example, the myth that women are sick and stay home from work more often than men, due to menstrual difficulties, etc. while statistics show that men are absent 'sick' one-third more days per year than female colleagues.)

Where does the idea that women are 'fixated on romance' come from?

The 19th century was full of depictions of romantic female heroines who died for love. These tragic heroines – Tosca (Puccini's operatic heroine), Madame Bovary (Flaubert), Anna Karenina (Tolstoy)

– all died in the midst of a heroic private struggle to remain true to themselves, be their own person. My theory: historically, women's self-expression first took place in personal life, rather than in a career or profession because personal life was the only canvas on which women at that time were allowed to write. Before the 20th century, when women in large numbers were increasingly able to have careers, the only stage on which women could show their heroism and strength of character was the private stage of love and family.

In the 19th century, love began to be redefined, as women's role as simple family 'helpmates' was undermined by the new democratic ideals – for the better. Yet society often still punished women who 'gave all for love'; thus these novels and opera plots were relevant and authentic: women who behaved 'unconventionally' in love often did die tragic deaths.

During these two centuries, as women were growing and expanding out of the predefined roles of mother, daughter and sister, they experienced in passionate love the adventure denied them in public life (women could not have their own bank accounts, frequently could not inherit property, etc.). This is not to deny the importance, to both men and women, of passionate love, only to point out that novels focusing on women and private life were making a connection that is no longer a nerve centre – at least no more so for women than for men.

But thus was born a cliché: women as victims of love and romance, addicted to love. The contemporary version of this in business may be: women leave corporations in great numbers in their thirties because they fall in love, want to get pregnant, get pregnant, have emotional personal lives – i.e. women must sacrifice, 'die', for love. The same scenario, in other words. One could point out that lurking even further in the background of all these clichés is the spectre of Maria, the mother of Jesus, who was 'pure' because she conceived and gave birth without sex. This is the old double morality we all grew up with: having sex tarnishes women, and so – abracadabra – 'sex' and passionate love mean women are destined to leave their jobs when they are in their thirties!

Do some corporate chiefs think this is, after all, the best policy, since 'daughters' should not be sexual – and those who are must pay for their 'sin' by losing their jobs or careers?

In short, many people still project stereotypes of their relationships in family and personal life onto each other at work, inappropriately, sometimes with tragic consequences. This projection does not make for good business judgements.

Many people still project stereotypes of their relationships in family and personal life onto each other at work, inappropriately, sometimes with tragic consequences.

Where does the idea that women are 'fixated on romance' come from?

'Keeping Women Happy'

Are executive wives jealous of the new career women?

Wives, secretaries and the new professional women: how do they feel about each other?

Do men have a special job keeping them from being angry at each other? Keeping them from feeling one is getting more favours than the other? Or is this old software?

The old divisions between wives and working women are disappearing, as more and more women work outside the home – not only for money but also because they find that having this kind of contact with the world, on their own terms, is refreshing and rewarding.

A wife explains:

'Naturally, when I called his office and always heard the same voice, the melodious voice of a young and pleasant woman, I wanted to know what she was like. When I asked him, he sounded evasive, so I became insecure: the next time I called her, my tone of voice was probably wary. Hers became wary too. Heaven knows what opinion she may have had of me. Linda was her name, but she had to call me Mrs Phillips (my name is Gloria). Now that I am working too (I even have my own secretary, who he has to call to get me!), I understand much more easily that just because Linda worked with him all day every day did not mean there was "something between them". But in those days, wow, was it heavy! So I would be cold to him when he came home at night, looking for reassurance, but he didn't know why. A distance crept in between us – a

distance still there to this day. I mean, my taking a job as a way of having my own life has been a benefit, but I'm sure it was in part created by this strange fear and envy I had of Linda and all the other women "out there".'

Society in the past was structured so that wives were excluded from the world of work, they were supposed to stay home and take care of children. They didn't have their own place of work outside the home to go. This bred a feeling of exclusion from 'the outside world' (seen in the climactic film *The Stepford Wives,* zombie robot wives), thus these women were often prey to jealousy towards other women who did have access to that world. Today, fortunately, many women have a choice of the kind of work they do, whether at home in the family or out in the world, and so the same fertile ground is not there for serious jealousy, although some of this residue remains.

In the old tradition, it was inappropriate for a woman to be out in the world 'gallivanting around' after a 'certain age'; there were 'good women and bad women'. The 'good women' were wives and mothers, and the 'bad girls' were those who were sexually free, not wives or mothers. While the 'nice girls' were allowed to 'look around freely' for a mate during their early twenties, beyond that age women who were not married were looked at strangely – i.e. 'Not married yet? What's a nice girl like you doing without a husband? You should have children!'

Executive Wives and the 'New Career Women'

The old image of the executive wife is of a woman who helps her husband entertain, has his children, maintains good grooming and comportment to help build her husband's image, and is selflessly loving and patient.

Is this image (still) true for most wives of executives?

One wife, typical of many, explains:

'I wish I could enjoy more the security of the position of "wife", but I find this role anything but secure... My husband does a lot of work attending openings, cocktails, etc. with other executives. This often goes on to involving dinner with clients. This functions, in a way, as his social life. I see him in the morning, and at night before bed (then when we're sleeping! We sleep together every night in the same big bed, and I love this, he does too.) Sometimes I attend the functions with him, but most of the time I'm only invited when "all the other spouses" come too.

'Should I be happy for him when he comes home excited by someone he's spent the evening with. I try to be, otherwise I'm like an "old, boring wife" – although I'm only 36 and quite good-looking!

'In the beginning (we've been married many years), his late hours used to upset me more, but now I've come to adjust – after all, it's his career and without it, how could we have paid the bills? Yet it's a high price to pay, sometimes I wish we were in business together. After the children went to school (when they were five and six), I looked around and found a good job for myself. I had to do this to maintain my self-confidence. I just couldn't go on being limited in

my circle of friends to other moms and the local grocer. Maybe I just felt competitive with him, maybe I wanted to "show him" – but I believe it was for myself and because I feel I need contact with the world, there is a lot I can contribute. I like being known as a person in my own right.

'Sometimes I go out to dinner with colleagues too now. I don't always tell him with who, what was said, or how these dinners came about – as he usually doesn't tell me. Has this hurt or improved our sex life and our relationship? It has increased my confidence at least. Before, when he wanted to make love to me, or "accepted my advances", I still didn't feel he really wanted *me;* in the back of my mind was the doubt that maybe he was just doing it because I was handy and he was randy – to be blunt. Yes, he would tell me I was good-looking, and give me small presents from time to time, but was it all out of guilt? I guess he had (and has) a mixture of feelings for me. I think sometimes that his full-time "other life" (he's at work, whatever that means, 12–14 hours a day, while he's with me – not counting sleep – 3–4 hours a day) will eventually make me accept the advances of another man. Yes, men do try!

'A female colleague? This takes a lot of will power, but...'

This wife explained how she tried to psychologically adjust, over the years, to her husband having 'two lives', a life with her, and a separate life with his colleagues at work including female colleagues.

Another wife explains how she feels about the 'new executive women' at work, i.e. the increasing number of women her husband now works with on a daily basis:

'It used to be that I was the only woman in my husband's life. I may still be the one he sleeps with at night, I mean really sleeping, not sex most of the time – but am I the one who has most of his attention? I don't know anymore. I am sure it is right for companies not to discriminate against women, to let them get ahead and be executives too, if that is what they want. But it feels to me like these women couldn't care less about me, it's like some of the company dinners we attended where women ignore me and seem to be trying to get ahead by flashing their bodies around at the men, or wangling long conversations with them. I am invisible to these women, I am unimportant, I don't count.

'Maybe they're right. My function was to bring up the children, and take care of my husband's daily needs. Over the years, he talked less and less to me about his job or the newspapers, political matters and books I was reading, he just (we just) got on with things. This meant me getting him up in the morning, feeding him and the kids, he went off to work, then he would come home sometime in the evening (late or early), talk about practical matters (the electric bill, a computer at school for one of the kids, etc.), then sleep. At first I used to fight with him and insist on "weekends" together. He interpreted this to mean that "he should pay attention to me"! Of course, that was great, but he never seemed to think of these times as times he would get as much as I did, i.e. I paid attention to him, was interested in him sexually, emotionally and intellectually. He made me feel like these "weekends" were a chore to him, so gradually I lost interest in

insisting on them. He never brought up the decreasing amount of quality time (I hate this phrase) we had with each other.

'Now I hear him mention a new woman chief of sales in his office – what the other men said about her, what she's doing, etc. If I ask questions about her (her age, marital status, etc.) I'm accused of being jealous. (I am – but it's natural and he could take this as a compliment.) I guess I'm still in love with him, or else I have no sense of self-worth left and use him as my reference point, because now I find myself watching what I wear in the morning when I serve him breakfast (imagining to myself, do I look as slick as she might look? Will he think I am more desirable as a woman than her? Yick!) I don't feel our marriage is threatened, but I wonder what it is I am getting out of marriage now. Is it enough?'

A woman with her own status and job describes attending a conference with her husband as 'the wife':

'I went to an executive sales conference with my husband. I have a full-time important job elsewhere, but we planned this in advance, so I was able to get time off. It was a weird experience – although I had fun too. I wanted to help my husband by being "the right wife", yet I wasn't sure how to proceed: should I talk to other (90% male) executives about my own work and views? Or would this seem competitive to my husband, i.e. would it be better for his advancement and status to just enhance him by showing that I love and think highly of him, and am a team player? Or should I talk to the men at his company who can promote him, try to subtly motivate them to pick him for moving up? Hell, I don't know if he even wants to move up.

'I was surprised that quite a few of the male executives had wives who work in related fields. These men seemed quite comfortable with "the new woman" and I admired them for having an equal mate. Many of them had had children together earlier, then the woman went "back to work" or began a job; maybe the husband had helped her get started, or maybe they met because they were working in similar fields. Maybe their marriages lasted over the long term because they had something in common besides "the children".

'On the other hand, there were many men there on their own, with wives at home, and a third group of men who had flashy dates with them, men who seemed to want to make a point of "hanging out" with their buddies, be part of "the gang" at work, the women almost old-fashioned ornaments – even though the women (the situation wasn't their fault after all) were dressed in the latest style black mini-dresses, little slip-like things with low backs, hair long and flowing, tanned faces etc. These women looked very insecure and were trying hard to be glamorous and look comfortable, and like they were having fun. I hoped they were.

'I didn't relate much to those women, or the men with them. I was afraid, I guess, that they were so nervous about their status that if I tried to talk to them, they might perceive me as "not one of their group", and "reject me". I tried to play it cool, look as good as I could myself, and talk when anyone addressed me but not initiate

controversial topics (this could make any conversation interesting), let my husband take the lead. Later I wondered, and I asked him, how would you feel if I took you to a convention of mine, with mostly female executives? (Of course this is hypothetical, since no corporation I have known of has mostly female executives!) I asked him, would you behave as "supportively" as I did, or would you resent it? He assured me he would love to be in this role, but I have my doubts...

'Anyway, this was my experience at his version of summer camp. I would love to talk to him more about it, but he is very sensitive and tends to worry that I didn't like it. This isn't true, so I guess it's better just to tell him about the parts I enjoyed. Especially having sex with him in the room!

How are most executive husbands feeling today? Do they feel comfortable with an 'equal' working wife?

How are most executive husbands feeling today? Do they feel comfortable with an 'equal' working wife?

'It takes a strong ego for me to let my wife go out every day and earn a living, knowing that in the process she meets and works with mostly men. All kinds of men – young ones, old and rich ones, middle-range "fascinating guys" like me! Who knows, maybe she could fall for one of them, or anyway one of them could sure fall for her, she looks sharp when she takes off for the office in her perky suits, driving her sporty car. I'd be interested. Are they? She doesn't tell me, well, she make references and hints, but then she's always home at night with me, so nothing too major can be going on. Anyway, I just have to live with it if I want to have a wife who's not staying at home and nagging me because "you don't pay enough attention to me". This is the case of one of my friends. A situation I'd rather avoid. How can you maintain sexual interest in someone like that ?'

'I don't mind my wife working – as long as she does not have a job that's more important than mine. I mean, it's just too much for me, to be constantly comparing myself and my importance and worth with her. I had a girlfriend like this. She was exciting, I could never keep up with her, she seemed crazy about me, she wanted to get married. Finally, I couldn't marry her because I decided I would always feel like the second wheel, less important and less dynamic. Logically, there would have been advantages – she made quite a bit of money that we could have spent to buy a house together, and she had friends who could frankly help me move ahead with my career, her family was well-connected and so on, but everybody was always talking about her, we would be at dinner and she would tell me her latest business coup and how much money it brought in and I had nothing so dramatic to tell about my day. It made me feel small.'

'Now my wife, whom I also love, works at a job that is more ordinary and loves to hear at night about my day, she thinks my job is the important job in the family, and tries to help me think through how to get further with things I am trying to do – even if to some people these things might seem trivial. I feel I have a real partnership with her, but I just felt like an

appendage when my girlfriend's job was more important. Am I a jerk?'

In contrast to these views, however, 1999 trend features in newspapers (*Independent,* May 1999) claim that 'executive wives' are coming back into fashion.

For some, it seemed during the 1980s that 'the new career women' were a kind of futuristic 'bad girl', a strange exotic mixture of power and glamour, to be feared. ('Women will take over if you let them...') 'Back-to-basics' traditionalists praised women who 'left all that' to return to home and family. Statistics, however, told another story: the steady movement of more and more women into the workplace, in every sector and on every level – except at the top.

How Do Secretaries and Women Colleagues see Wives?

How should women at work relate to 'wives'? Should they speak to their male colleagues about them, acknowledge the wife in conversation with the man, so that the man understands that the working woman accepts and appreciates the reality and presence of 'another woman' in her colleague's life? Or is this not really the responsibility of women at work?

'Once in a while his wife would call the office, and I would pick up the telephone (if he was away from his desk, etc.). This always made me feel tense. What should I say? "Hi, I'm Sally, I work with your husband nine hours a day, but don't worry, I'm no threat...?" Or, "Hi, I'm Sally, I'm having a great time working for your husband nine hours a day, I hope he'll promote me, so I have to be as scintillating and clever as possible. I hope you'll understand. I'm sorry if he compares you and me because we're both women, it's not my fault, there's nothing I can do about it".'

Yeah, a tough one.

And what about men at the office who have girlfriends? Is it inappropriate office behaviour to ask about them, or refer to them ('Hey, hey, John, going away for the weekend again!')? Not doing so may leave one in the position of seeming to make a play oneself, just by being friendly. Should one therefore be cold? If a man breaks up with his girlfriend, however, then the woman in the office who tried to be polite and ask from time to time, may now seem to be an agony aunt who can be told about the various stages of trial and error of the break-up, new dates, etc. This can have a peripheral effect of making a woman's work less promotable, because the woman herself seems 'obsessed with trivial matters of love and private life'!!! But not always...

How should a woman, a secretary, relate to a man at work who clearly has an affair going on, unbeknown to his wife – when both the wife and 'other woman' are calling him at work?

How should a woman, a secretary, relate to a man at work who clearly has an affair going on, unbeknown to his wife – when both the wife and 'other woman' are calling him at work?

'I didn't know whether to ignore it when my boss became involved with Sheila. She kept calling, asking to speak to "John" – so, since she was using his first name, it soon became clear to me the situation. She probably did that because

'Female psychology' – is there such a thing?

usually I asked the person how to spell their name, their telephone number, and what the call is in reference to. Maybe she wanted to quickly make it clear to me that this was personal. Maybe he told her to say this, to call him at work and ask for him like his. But I have met his wife and speak to her every day on the telephone. I feel like I am involved in lying about something when I don't want to be involved. I don't know what to do. I guess nothing, but I don't feel good about it. Should I speak to him? He would think I was meddling, and anyway, it's his life. Maybe he and his wife have problems I don't know about. Maybe he wants to leave his marriage or something, and this is one way he has of thinking about that possibility, trying it out, sort of. Or maybe just spreading his wings at age 52, who knows? But I feel weird every time she calls.'

---

1 See *The Hite Report on Female Sexuality;* this book demonstrated that most women do orgasm easily during exterior or clitoral stimulation, and do not have a problem having orgasm (especially on their own).

2 See *Women and Love,* the third Hite Report, a study of 3,500 women discussing 'What is love?'

Would she feel less weird if she were not also a woman, and did not know well the probable feelings of both women, i.e. the 'new woman' and the 'old woman'?

Is this men's problem, or women's problem? A non-answerable question; the solution is a new psychological landscape (wipe the old and put a new one on the screen).

Female Psychology – Has It Changed?

'Female psychology' – is there such a thing? This is, of course, the way women's software has been shaped by society – and most women have been in the process of changing theirs for at least the last 25 years. 'The female' has been the subject of endless books, diatribes and lectures for centuries, many filled with vast quantities of prejudice and negativity, sometimes using the designation 'religious' to cover this prejudice. For example, before the 1970s, people generally said women 'had a problem having orgasm' because of 'mental blocks' and 'because they are so emotional' etc.[1] Today, many of the clichés that remain about women (especially strong are clichés about women, 'love' and romance) are just as off the wall.[2]

However, women share a number of *culturally* created complexes that men do not have – although men have others, just as unfortunate and just as unnecessary – for example, a tendency towards lack of self-esteem and insecurity, that each woman finds her own way of fighting against. Some women, finding that their weak point is bumpy and fragile love relationships, use eruptions and fighting as part of their psychological armour, a way of staving off the stereotypes, a way of avoiding feeling weak and insecure (their parents' voices inside their own heads?), keeping their own identity intact.

If a man can manage, he should try to help women around him compensate (just as women understand men's inner need to placate 'masculine stereotypes') for this background, i.e. women are less, women are weak, women can't make it, etc. etc., created by the social fabric.

Some men, however, reacting to their own social background telling them it is 'weak' when people cry, shout, 'become hysterical' or need help, take the opposite approach and ignore any signs of difficulties, just 'setting the example' of a stiff upper lip. Sometimes this can be the right approach, but usually a few words exchanged are better.

Men Thinking Like Women: New Tendencies Fight Old Clichés

Can a man think like a woman?

Can a man think like a woman?

'Yeah, man, I'll take a curling iron to my mind, sure, that'll be the day. I'd rather roast in hell.

Think like a girl? Me??! NEVER!'

This idea is not too popular... in some quarters.

Men working with women can profit by trying to become expert at 'thinking like a woman', understanding female ways of communicating (insofar as they may be different), and the software demons women have to fight in their own minds ('If you're too successful, no one will like you, etc.).

Ironically, ever since childhood, most men have been taught to avoid thinking 'like a woman' (since women are illogical by nature, weak-brained!) – in fact, this was considered the worst thing a man could do. Boys are endlessly told 'be cool!', 'don't be a sissy', don't be a cry baby like a girl' and other cruel things. How ironic that now it will benefit men to do just the reverse. It will help their careers if they can learn to communicate in the 'female way'; in fact, for both men and women, it is now an advantage to be able to think either 'male' or 'female' ('I have rights' vs 'How can I be helpful?'), speak both 'languages' – or combine them for optimum results.

Brain Game 4.6 – For Men

If a woman shows any signs of 'traditional female emotions', how should a man react?:

- become aggressive and cool to keep the situation in check

- point out the behaviour and its irrationality

- change the subject

- other.

Brain Software Commands – For Men

— SOFTWARE TO DELETE

'The new female class of career women on the move are ballsy and unfeminine.'

+ SOFTWARE TO INSTALL

'The new group of women at work are just as vulnerable – and 'tough' as men always were (and were not).'

— SOFTWARE TO DELETE

'Career women are not as moral as wives and mothers, but wives and mothers are boring compared to career women.'

+ SOFTWARE TO INSTALL

'Working status has nothing to do with sexual or moral status. There are good people in every category.'

Check to see if the software you have installed is working.

Think about one of your female colleagues, and compare your thoughts about her with your thoughts about a friend's wife, your wife, your mother, etc. How do they differ? Are you being rational?

What Should a Man's Management Style Be?

Should men change their style of management when working with women? Try to adapt to a different way of communicating?

There is much discussion of women's different style of management. Sometimes it is said that women manage work more like managing a family or a household, meaning, possibly, in a familiar style. Men, presumably, have a style of management that is more rigid, more military, more hierarchical. This may or may not be true, in individual cases.

As one middle management executive puts it:

'I find that when I'm speaking to "the new woman" at work I'm much more careful about what I say than when I'm speaking to one of the men. I'm sure the men will know what I mean, but with the women, I'm not sure. I come across like a timid nice guy, then they're surprised when I fire one of them for not doing her job.'

Is he communicating well with women? Or is he speaking tentatively, giving a message that 'communication is difficult, there is a gulf between us'?

While of course it is a lot to ask, and scores of books have been written about 'how to be a good manager', in fact, managers today have to adapt to 'new rules' and make sure good interaction is taking place with the female employees as well as the males. If women don't feel free to speak up and express opinions, rough sailing is on the horizon as issues and views go unaired. Most managers easily have the capacity to communicate and also listen well when they want to; the hidden problem here (to be addressed in depth later) may be in the faulty software in their minds, flashing warning signs when communication with women is going too well: 'Danger! Can I trust a woman with this information?'

Information has been one of the male powers, and women (until the 20th century, uneducated in the West, and still in vast parts of the world, illiterate) were denied it. Traces of this feeling, that women 'don't need to bother their pretty little heads' about such matters, 'leave that to the men' remain. While there is an appeal to women's egos in the 'you're too pretty to bow your head down at a desk all day' approach, underlying such a statement can be an attitude that also denies the woman any right to have enough information to truly get ahead. When communication is blocked, ask yourself as a manager if you are withholding information that could be useful.

Women have been educated, generally, to be the 'helpmates' in relationships with men and children; this was their role in the family. Men, in contrast, were educated to take charge of things, take action, initiate decisions. It may be awkward for a male manager to think of himself as a 'helpmate', and yet this is one of the two basic roads open to managers. One basic means of managing people is to help them, the other is to rule them. In the former, managers take decisions after forming a consensus among workers; in the latter, managers take decisions and then tell the others, subliminally daring them to complain or be fired. Men have been more praised in films and television programmes for having the dominator style, especially with women. They have been ridiculed for being 'soft', a 'softie', if they seemed to get along too well with women!

One powerful CEO told me that he thought his business partner was a softie, but he was not:

'It was always that way, even 25 years ago. I always had to pick up the pieces after he made a problem. He's weak, too soft. He's too much in love with his wife, he relies on her too much, all he wants is to be around her. He doesn't have the stomach for office wars, I have. That's why the ship has got where it is, I have quadrupled the worth of this company and taken it to the top. How do I see my style of management? I am sort of like the chauffeur, the driver of the company. I steer the car. Nobody has to tell me how to steer it, I know.'

This same CEO, when asked about the promotion of women or the position of women inside his large company, delighted in mentioning the various women who had tried to advance in the company under him and their fates. None had made it onto the board or top executive level, it seems. Why? 'Because women feel conflicted about their childbearing status and take decisions harmful to their careers.'

Needless to say, this management style will not create an atmosphere that will get the best results out of all the people there.

How Do Women React to Male Power?

Women's reactions to working for men: daddies and other men in authority

Men should become aware of women's sensitive feelings about male power. Remembering that we come from a society that has given most women special lessons in this area, lessons that can influence women's reactions to male managers and men in power. (Of course, men too can have their own problems with male authority figures, see page 127.

Men should become aware of women's sensitive feelings about male power.

Sometimes a male-dominant workplace intimidates women. Especially when a man is in a position of power over a woman at work, emotional buttons can be pushed, creating feelings of danger, security or uncertainty. Such situations may cause some women to behave subserviently, others rebelliously. (Neither posture is the best for working...)

One of the other problems men can face in forming good working relationships with women comes from a problem women often grow up with: the problem of too much obedience to their father – and, by example, thus to men in power. This can inhibit a woman from behaving naturally, or speaking up when she has something to say.

Any special problems women have working with male superiors are easy to understand – after all, men, too, can have a tough time psychologically dealing with 'the boss'. Sometimes women feel intimidated by men, because 1) men have power, they can give and take away a job or promotion; 2) most girls learned in their families that the father (or brother) is top dog, and special attitudes should be observed towards him, special respect; 3) many women have experiences dating men that make them wary of how men will behave

towards them at work. (As one woman puts it: 'Will he reject me if I'm too friendly, like a useless girlfriend? I know the rules: a woman should not call a man for a date, or seem to be chasing after him, need him; he should want her and chase after her!')

A male superior may help a woman by understanding the historical entity known as 'woman' and also the way women have changed and are changing. (Women can understand men in the same way, understanding what 'masculinity' was supposed to be, defined by the culture, and how men feel about it all today.)

Listen to these women's experiences applying for a job or promotion from a man:

'I had a job interview with the head of the department. I planned what to wear the evening before, carefully, making sure that I looked neat but not overly dressed in any way. I washed my hair too – my hair is long and straight, brown, so it can look somewhat sensual without being overtly provocative – though this changes if I put on tight jeans or a short evening dress. As I went out the door the next morning, my roommate said she thought I looked like the perfect executive.

'I got to his office, and his secretary asked me to wait a few minutes, he was busy on the telephone. I wondered what she thought of me, and if she would talk about me after I left, if he would ask her opinion of "what she thought of another woman". The whole situation was intimidating, it put me on guard. But I tried to remain relaxed and feeling positive. Finally I was shown in, and things went OK. But I wondered if, after I left, they would talk about me. Would he ask her opinion of me, of what I was wearing, what she thought of me "as a woman"? I wondered what kind of relationship they had – friendly, intimate or hostile – and did she want to be "the only woman" there, working with him?'

A male superior may help a woman by understanding the historical entity known as 'woman' and also the way women have changed and are changing.

'I'm waiting for a promotion decision. I'm the only woman on the list. I know it's wrong to think, but sometimes I worry that his secretary will say bad things about me to him, behind my back, because she is jealous that I have a career and she doesn't, I could have a better salary too! Of course, it's natural he wants someone in my job who has the support of others he must also work with, but it's difficult to know how a woman feels about you, and whether she will say I'm OK or not. It makes me nervous. I feel I can't speak to her directly about this, she would say, "What do you mean?" looking cold and imperious. Why do I imagine this?

'Am I being realistic or ridiculous? She could have power over me. Maybe I'm paranoid because I want the job so much? But men seem not to trust their own judgement when hiring women, they turn to other women around them to make the decision! So every woman

who is "non-threatening" is hired and promoted, those who are not dangerous in any way, either to the man's job, or to the woman's beauty rating... not the person best-qualified for the company, like I am!'

Today, however, women in business try to 'see' gender less, and treat women and men with exactly the same friendliness and courtesy, professionalism.

Daddies and Daughters

The archetype of the CEO as 'father'
Don't fall into this old cliché!

Should a woman try to be Special Buddies with her corporate chief executive/the 'father'?

Should a woman try to be Special Buddies with her corporate chief executive/ the 'father'?

'If you can get the father's/CEO's favour, then you can gain status and get a better job' – this is one inevitable way (in the current situation) women may think of trying to unblock their careers, lift the glass ceiling.

Stored in the back of all our software are lurking nasty thoughts of sexual influence as power: how to worm one's way into power, be 'in style' and so on. But there is another part of us that is growing stronger in the new climate of expecting the workplace to be a meritocracy, a side of business that wants to create a more equal, better atmosphere that is more exciting and less predictable – less boring – the famous meritocracy that capitalism promises work will be.

Yet when female employees are confronted with nameless discrimination coming from male executives, they face some rather stark and bleak choices, at times. In women's less powerful moments, it seems that the attention and personal status the chief's favour will give us is appealing. Men do this too, when they try to be 'buddies' with the chief.

The temptation for a woman to flirt or take on a 'good sweet daughter' role with a man more powerful than her inside the company can be almost irresistible, especially with a man she feels is uncomfortable with equality, i.e. 'she's aggressive, she wants my place'. Or if not flirt, at least use feminine 'softness' and graceful ways to implicitly 'ask for' gentler treatment. Since this may be her only means of protection, it is almost impossible to blame her. Yet, while such behaviours may protect her in the short term, they will usually not get her promoted, so what choices is she left with? To become a feared 'ball-breaker'? To band with other women in the firm to put forth her 'demands'? To go above that man's head to someone higher? But what if that someone is a man with the same mental software? Etc. etc. etc.

One solution to this Catch-22 could be a new category of employee – gender managers – to whom employees can turn for counselling, advice and new ideas. Like a doctor or an attorney (or referee), the job description of the GM promises that he or she will not repeat what has been said in confidence to others.

To be a flirt or a 'good daughter' at work?
The dilemma for women, dealing with men in power, is a little like this: no matter what strategy you try, you can come up on the short-end. For example, if you dress very visibly, you are seen for your body; if you dress invisibly, you are taken for granted. How do you get taken seriously at work?

The dilemma for women, dealing with men in power, is a little like this: no matter what strategy you try, you can come up on the short-end.

One woman explains: 'I can't stop flirting. I'm hopeless. I'm addicted to flirting!' Another has an opposite problem: 'I come on like a sister, and they take me for granted, like "She's a good egg, she'll do our work for us, and cover for us when we stay out all day!"'

Many women hate themselves for taking on one or other of these roles: 'I feel confused! I'm always dissing myself for being too flirty, making strategies vis-à-vis using my female ways with men. But face it, I'm a brainwashed victim of my Kultur...'

Or is she? After all, women still are not statistically 'equal'. As long as they are not (in numbers and equal pay), won't they still need lots of special strategies? Or should they form organizations with other women, would this be more effective?

In the relationship with 'the father' (or a male authority figure), some girls or daughters also experience an 'erotic' or 'special' feeling – a fact that in my research seems to suggest a connection with an acceptance of sexually harassing behaviour later from male 'superiors', even sometimes a feeling of 'guilty' complicity with it and pleasure in it, a feeling that it marks one as 'special' and 'chosen'. Understandable, given women's situation, but not the way things should be, not a choice a women should be faced with.

The answer to this dilemma lies in the new relationships between men and women, not in the woman or the man as individuals.

What is the traditional identity of a 'good daughter'? 'Being a good daughter' used to mean breaking the basic rules of the system. The duty of a 'good daughter' was to be 'pretty' and 'go along', never upset anyone too much. Yet the duty of an adult is to think for herself, create a real way of life for herself, and by implication, for others.

Sometimes, to make a better system, you have to break your pact with the old one. Although this may seem to hurt others at the time, and even yourself, in the end it will be better for everyone.

Sometimes, to make a better system, you have to break your pact with the old one.

Most women already know that, in order to 'grow up' into the new system coming about,

they have to stop being overly 'nice', as they were taught ('it's ladylike and graceful'), and think in new ways. Most women began working on this part of their mental software a few years ago. Enormous progress has been made, but there are still hidden corners, unidentified behaviour, that comes from the software we think we have already rid ourselves of. Here is one example. In news reports and my interviews with CEOs, it is said over and over again: 'Women work harder, they do not demand the special perks that men do, such as big offices, free cars etc., they do not expect such big promotions... this make them better employees today.' Doesn't this sound like the 'good daughter', trying earnestly to prove her worth? It's never bad to be excellent at your work, of course, but maybe this is not the only good strategy for women's situation today: the 'good daughter' role education should not block women from advancing and taking more power at work.

Office clothing
Does this mean a 'mature woman' is 'tough' – using her 'male' side? What is happening to women at work? Many women feel it is now hip, smart, to be a little masculine – 'tough', unemotional, don't show any signs you're female, dress down in black male-type clothing, 'give the right signals' (you're one of them?). Lately, however, women have begun to notice that 'dressing like men' did not make men at work think women were 'no longer like women' and therefore deserving of being promoted 'just like men'. Thus today there is something of a backlash in clothing styles. 'Girlie fashions' are in. This does not mean that women don't like work, or offices, or that they want to 'go back' to their

identity as 'just girls'; it means that women don't see so much point in attempting to copy the uniform style of the Western male business suit – or the 'tough male management style'.

The status of men is so great in society that even their clothing is copied by women and 'minorities' (hoping to fit in?). Yet traditional female styles of clothing represent a lingering vestige of 'female identity': women had at least the right to decorate their bodies in the way they wanted (men did not). While some may argue that 'men's clothing' is more utilitarian, is this really true? Men constantly complain that their suits are hot and uncomfortable, they want to take their ties off as soon as possible; are they wearing a form of chador? Others argue that female clothing is a way of decorating the female body to attract men, i.e. a sign of oppression and exploitation. There is not space here to reason through the various pathways of this idea that of course has merit; however, briefly, is uniform prison-style attire such as 'suits' a sign of liberation? As to women's clothing being too body revealing, women can be proud of their bodies and wearing such clothes can be for themselves and not to be 'on display'. Traditional 'female behaviours', such as being seductive (yes, men too), enjoying flowers, lipstick and perfume, decorating the house, even liking the colour pink, should be available to both women and men.

Brain Software Commands – For Women

How can women change their attitudes to men in power?

Follow these simple steps and exercises to change your software, your relationship to powerful 'father figures' (and 'the system').

SOFTWARE TO DELETE

'He's after me, or I bet I could get him! Is he vulnerable to women if they act sweet? Daughterly? Sexy? Young and fresh?'

SOFTWARE TO INSTALL

'Personal sexual politics are in 99 per cent of cases a dead-end. I should be reasonable and do a good job, then if he does not appreciate or understand, I can look around in the company for someone else to work for here.'

And... 'I'll try to offer him reliable collegiality and see if he responds positively.' (See also Chapter 5.)

'There should be an internet pool of names of "oversexed male executives" who promise work favours and don't deliver.'

A suggestion received from one anonymous female executive: 'There should be an internet pool of names of "oversexed male executives" who promise work favours and don't deliver – men with reputations women should watch out for. Names could be suggested anonymously, then if a name comes up twice, it would automatically be put on the list... Does this sound outrageous?'

Information from Hite Research: Growing Up Female
Does how girls grow up in families – the family as it has generally been defined – have any relationship to how women in corporations often relate to their bosses or men in authority?

Let's look at what my research in the 1990s shows women describing about their fathers and feelings for their fathers. Are there any parallels with corporate life?

Daughters and Daddies

Male authority figures: girls and their fathers
'I idolized Daddy but never understood him.'

Friendship: the future model for father–daughter relationships.

Friendship: the future model for father–daughter relationships.

Girls very often describe their father and their feelings for him in extreme ways: either he was the most wonderful father ever, or he was a monster – rarely anything in between. Why?

What needs to be developed is a new friendship between fathers and daughters – relationships in which fathers reach out a hand to their daughters, provide a real relationship that neither excludes the mother, nor ridicules or trivializes her. This will give the daughter, too, the pride and confidence for her future life at work and personally.

Today there is an atmosphere hanging over many fathers and daughters – 'Warning! Heterosexual impulses possible!' This socially constructed message makes spontaneous relationships almost impossible, as a 'red light' is always blinking subliminally and so distracting fathers, making them slightly nervous, questioning their own feelings. 'Better to abstain from trying to be friends, lest too close a relationship look sexual.' This alienation in father–daughter relationships causes nervousness and distance to grow, sometimes including anger and disappointment. The majority of fathers who replied to my questionnaire did not feel sexual attraction for their daughters, but remain terrified of the possibility.

Frequently, also, an element of sexism interferes with these potential friendships: when fathers treat their daughters as 'mere females', 'not important', trivializing their interests and work, daughters are pressured to try communicating via other means, i.e. subtle flirtation, etc.

Potential friendships between fathers and daughters can also be hampered by family politics, i.e. the position of the mother at the bottom of the family hierarchy, and the girl's consequent fear of betraying the mother by befriending the father. Many girls feel they're involved in a constant balancing act. They want to 'play fair' and not offend either side.

Love and longing: girls' feelings for their father

Many girls feel a strange mixture of emotions: closeness and distance, fear and longing, joy and fury – all mixed together:

'As a child I learned from my mother that the best way to handle my father was to ignore him. I learned from my father that the proper attitude towards my mother was ridicule. She was treated as if she were stupid, even though she was a college graduate. She eventually divorced him, and he never forgave her for leaving him. It hurt his pride.

'I was close to my father until he remarried when I was about eleven. His wife was jealous and possessive and wouldn't let me be alone with him. She especially disliked his being affectionate with me. Before that, we'd been affectionate and had talked alone a lot. I was afraid of her and I lost respect for him.

'As I developed physically, I seemed to remind him of my mother. He made remarks about my body, so that I felt ashamed and covered it up. He forced his affection on me while I tried to get away and my stepmother fumed at me. Thirty years later I learned from my mother that he had treated her the same way and had even spoken to her the same way. I don't know what it means, but it was an awful way for a girl to grow up. I was afraid of him, mainly because he hurt me with the mean things he said. He wouldn't let me argue or think for myself. He didn't want me to date or marry. When I was 35, he told me I wasn't old enough to talk back to him!

'My father and his second wife fought for ten years before they settled down. After my brother and I left, their family consisted of themselves and their two children. They all got along fine. She's been a wonderful wife to him and I've learned a lot about marriage from her.

She's now one of my best friends, believe it or not.

'My father and I spent our lifetime together fighting. Although I was his favourite child, my relationship with him was always one of conflict. I wanted to please him but could never do anything well enough to merit a word of praise from him. Oh, how I wanted that! Eventually, I just quit trying and felt more hate than love.'

'My father was very authoritarian, whereas my mother was gentle, loving and warm. He never praised us to our faces, but he did to others. Maybe pride and love are the same thing.

'Despite everything, I was aware that the love was there, especially for me. I sensed that I was my father's favourite. He was always scrupulously fair with us all, but this special love for me was confirmed when he died this year; my mother told me of things from my childhood (letters, drawings, compositions) that he had kept hidden away and she had only now found.

'Throughout my adult life, I had avoided him as much as possible, until I heard that he had contracted a fatal illness. Then, all that suppressed love for him came flooding back, and I managed to tell him that I loved him before he died. He never said the words to me (not once in my whole life!), but I knew he wanted to from the expression in his eyes and from the way he held me so tightly one day when I went to visit him. I feel sad that he was never able to express love through words and touch. How much easier that would have been for his children, and his wife, and himself.'

A hallmark of most girls' statements about their father is their frequently self-contradictory nature; almost three-quarters of girls' replies contain contradictory, even disjointed statements: 'We went places together. I never feared him. He is a lot like me. I have a hard time accepting him and I love him a lot.' Listen to these descriptions:

'My father was the meany of the neighbourhood. We were scared of him. In our house, we never argued: he screamed, we listened. But when we went on family vacations, it was entirely different. Those are very fond memories for me, he seemed relaxed and friendly.'

'My father was not affectionate, but he was playful, carrying me on his shoulders and tickling me. He was a strict disciplinarian and I feared him when he was angry. He would let me come with him when he went to work on the farm, and teach me about nature and old customs. He seemed to know everything. I respected him very much, and did what he said. Today I am frustrated with him because he is so stubborn about what he thinks is correct. But he did raise a large family of two girls and three boys, and gave us all a strong set of values to live by.'

What is the reason for these confusing jumbles of emotions? One is that the archetypes (including fear of 'sexual motives') make it difficult for family members to realistically see one another, since the archetypes keep getting in the way; the facts of the relationship are only 'seen' and experienced through the mythological gauze of the 'shoulds' and 'shouldn'ts' of the archetypes. Thus individuals have difficulty forming valid relationships, based on their individual feelings and experiences. This is as true of the mother–daughter relationships as it is of father–daughter relationships.

Affection (and later betrayal?) from the father: patterns of withdrawal of affection

One girl describes how her relationship with her father went through several stages, stages described by many other girls:

'I felt closer to my father. He wasn't extremely affectionate, but I could hug him (not my mom). And he would rock me to sleep in his lap. He was my protector from my older sister. I loved him. We did quite a few things together, like skiing, skating and fishing. He would take me to the beach, even though he didn't know how to swim.

'It was me he woke in the morning for school, got me ready and made breakfast. I never feared him, I only feared his disappointment.

'But when I was a teenager, our relationship became more strained. Major disagreements arose when I started camping in mixed groups. He never forbade my going, but he would ask me if I "thought that was the best thing to do". I got used to not quite telling the whole story.

'He didn't want me to go away to college either. I felt as if I was going to university against his wishes. He wanted me to do secretarial work. He also didn't like it when my mother went to work outside the house. Later when I lived with a guy for a year when I was 22, Dad didn't speak to me for at least a month, and never came to visit us or called.

'Then, later, when my father became very ill and was going to have an operation, we became close again. I had just broken up with my long-time boyfriend (the same one). I was afraid that my father was going to die and not know how much I loved him, and so I started sharing more with him. Showing him the more private side of me. It is amazing how little my father and I knew about each other's feelings at that time. When I first told him I loved him (it was just before his operation), he cried. Now I hug or kiss him whenever I feel like giving him love, and he's giving it back to me.'

Many girls report that while their fathers are affectionate when they are children, there is a complete change, sometimes an abrupt change, later. Some girls remember a wonderful degree of affection in their early years:

'He called me his "Little Princess", and I loved him. We were frequently together as a family at weekends. When my mother died, he came to fill the role of both parents.'

'I adored my father. My father was so affectionate – he would hold my hand when we went out, he put his arm around me lots of times, and scratched my back every night.'

'How was he close to me? By reading me bedtime stories, singing for me, taking me out to the park, the cinema, buying things for me, teaching me to fish, play chess, football and wrestling, letting me laugh, and bathing me. I was his "Cinderella".'

Betrayal

Many girls who recall early affection from their father also bitterly describe how they felt betrayed by him later:

'After the divorce, my father let us down. He never called – as if we had never been born.'

'My father let me down when I told him my brother had sexually abused me. He didn't take it seriously. He never punished my brother at all.'

'He calls me unjustified names, just because I wear lipstick and short skirts.'

'My mother divorced my father when I was five. He remarried soon after and didn't keep in touch.'

Do fathers have a right to be 'free' of the children? An unwritten rule in society seems to say: if a man divorces, it is socially acceptable for him to rarely or even never see his 'former' children; whereas, if a mother were to do this, she would be considered disreputable. The archetypal role of the mother dictates that a mother must stay with her child, be loving and nurturing, no matter what – while the archetype of the 'father' is much more remote and independent.

The change in fathers' behaviour towards daughters: from affection to silent withdrawal, or nagging criticism

By the time a girl is 12 or so, her relationship with her father has often become quite strained, distant and alienated, sometimes entailing violent or angry outbursts. Girls feel confused and ask themselves: 'What happened? What did I do?' They try to improve their behaviour, often, waiting for the father to 'see' that they are truly loveable ('like before').

This 'waiting for a lost love to return' can become a lifelong emotional pattern in future relationships with men. Living with longing and hope for approval from a distant father, a woman may later pick 'distant' men, hoping to make them 'see' her, love her. She may believe, as she did about her father, that no matter how cold or heartless, the man loves her underneath it all. This is especially true since most mothers reassure their daughters, no matter what: 'Yes, he loves you really.'

Many fathers develop attitudes of alienation and cynicism, becoming known for their cutting remarks and potential violence. Why? This pattern has everything to do with the training for masculinity which boys undergo; it is not 'biologically inevitable'.

Many fathers develop attitudes of alienation and cynicism, becoming known for their cutting remarks and potential violence. Why? This pattern has everything to do with the training for masculinity which boys undergo; it is not 'biologically inevitable'.

As girls describe their fathers' emotional and physical withdrawal:

'I always regret that I stopped kissing my father goodnight, but I've been too shy to start again. We used to play games before bed, like him throwing us into the air and giving us piggy-back rides when we went walking. But when we were too old for that, nothing else took its place. With my mother, we kept on talking, and doing things around the house together. But with my father nothing. The last time we were close (touching) was hugging goodbye at the airport.'

'When I was young, he was affectionate with me (not with my brothers). He would hold me, and speak softly. He wouldn't spank me as hard as he would my brothers. Then we started to argue, when I was 12. Now I avoid controversial opinions in front of him. I think he's confused and trying to find peace with God. He is not the father I remember.'

'I spent lots of time with my father as a child, usually doing outdoorsy things. But from the age of 13 on, we didn't spend much time together – I don't think he could begin to understand an adolescent girl. We didn't get along again until several years after my parents were divorced and I'd been living at college.'

'I loved him as a child, hated him as an adolescent (he became very critical), and now I have mixed feelings of love, respect and bitterness. We communicate best by mail. After three days in person I want to strangle him because he has to have his way all of the time.'

Others 'leave' their father, whom they loved when they were younger, because of the 'betrayal' or bad relationship that develops.

Of course, fathers can have life-cycle problems to deal with that have nothing directly to do with the children. The anger many teenage girls see in their fathers correlates with feelings many men in *The Hite Report on Male Sexuality* describe having in their forties and fifties. Many feel that although they do almost everything they should as a man, taking care of the family, being there, earning a living, somehow they aren't appreciated or satisfied. Many feel empty.

The archetype of the father
'I feared his displeasure but respected him greatly.'

The majority of girls (and boys) say something very much like this in answer to questions about their feelings for their father. The word 'respect' is used ten times more frequently in replies about fathers than in replies about mothers.

Children's statements about their fathers are less effusive than those about their mothers. There is a different, more remote tone: the answers describe a person who is much less well-known, indeed, answers often specifically state this: 'He was a quiet person, hard to know', or 'We rarely saw him, he didn't talk much.'

How well do these children understand their father? Are they responding to an archetype or a real father?

One girl's statement is typical: 'Although I don't remember talking to him about important things, still I love him and respect him today.'

Why does she love and respect him? She doesn't say. Does she know?

Does she repeat it as a kind of talisman to ward off the father–god's anger and punishment?

Can girls criticize their father or is this 'disrespectful'?

Girls' principal complaint about their father is that he is overly critical of them:

'I didn't like him. He was always so critical of me. He said he was trying to help. It was always "for my own good".'

'My father used to put me down, but in subtle, intellectually disguised ways. Emotionally, he was destructive.'

Many children, both boys and girls, fear openly criticizing their father, because they have learned to fear the father's punishment. This fear of male authority figures can last throughout life. The strange jumble of feelings in many girls' statements about their fathers represents, in part, fear and confusion.

Children's statements about their fathers are less effusive than those about their mothers.

A special secret closeness with fathers

'My mother doesn't generally know my deepest, darkest secrets, whereas my father does.'

A large number of girls felt that there has been a 'special relationship', that they had been their father's favourite. This special relationship was almost never acknowledged in words between father and daughter:

'I was crazy about my father. I think I was his favourite of three girls, although I caused him all kinds of pain by reading, running away and getting kicked out of school! He wasn't impatient like my mother. He was wonderful to me. Even after I got kicked out of school, he helped me to get into another very good school. I think my mother resented me. I don't blame her. What a hard time she had.'

'I was closer to my father than to my mother. He was much more demonstrative, affectionate and emotional. I always felt sorry for my mother. My father ruled the family with a strong hand, and this included her. He insisted on total obedience. My mother indirectly taught us to fear him by her example of waiting on him hand and foot.'

'I loved my grandfather. He always wrote me little notes and left me surprises, and I know he loved me. My grandmother would scream and shout at me and hit me too... I guess she had good reasons, and I know I probably could have felt the same in her position, but there was just something great about my grandfather, he made me happy, terribly happy. We had a secret bond, a true understanding.'

Gender inequality in the parents' relationship: its effect on children

'Most of the emotional energy of the house was focused on my father.'

Why do families fight? The biggest problem in 'the family', ironically, is gender. Lack of equality between parents creates unstable conditions for many children.

Why do families fight? The biggest problem in 'the family', ironically, is gender. Lack of equality between parents creates unstable conditions for many children.

We see constant mentions in the press of 'divorce statistics on the rise', read hysterical warnings about 'families collapsing' and so on. The underlying cause of this 'collapse' which is really a process of democratization and diversification of families that will benefit us all – is the traditional, unequal 'emotional contract' between men and women.

When asked to describe their families, most girls focus on the gender power difference between their father and mother, the tensions this creates and how they felt strongly that they were called on emotionally to 'take sides', not necessarily by the parents themselves, but by the situation. Sixty-five per cent say they felt torn, forced to take sides or juggle the two sides much of the time they were children.

The dilemma of feeling emotionally torn between her two parents is painted vividly by one young woman:

'I can remember lying in bed between my parents when I was about six. I would give one leg to each of them – my mother and my father. I wanted to support each of them, not let either one of them think I loved them less. This was very hard, because there was a terrible crack in the middle of the mattress between them where I would lie!'

Feeling this tension, which is built into the patriarchal structure, makes children uneasy, as they try to understand and wrestle with the dilemma of gender inequality, usually for several years, while they are growing up. Which side is morally correct? What do the parents really feel for each other?

Divided loyalties: love as guilt

'We would all scramble when Dad's car pulled up at night and scurry to finish setting the table, so that dinner would be on the table when he walked in. Whatever we were talking about, we would stop. I don't remember him ever being late for dinner. My father was very demanding of my mother, and we all feared him. He was very distant. I loved him, but I didn't like him.'

Do women in corporate offices feel a divided sense of loyalty to male executives and their female colleagues?

Growing up being scared of the father, or seeing one's mother tiptoe around him, creates a habit of acceding to males, especially males in power. This can create enormous problems for women later, in both public and private life.

Do women in corporate offices feel a divided sense of loyalty to male executives and their female colleagues?

Who is the 'new woman' – 'those new career women', 'the young woman of today'? Can we say who the new woman is, independent of the reverse of the archetypes, i.e. not like the old 'mother–wife–Maria role' – or the reverse cliché of a sassy 'bad girl' or a 'ballsy career woman'?

Perhaps not. This is not because 'the new woman' doesn't exist; she does. But it is very difficult for us to put into words what we mean, because of the overwhelming weight of the stereotypes (and vocabulary with such values built into every word).

For this reason, I propose one new archetype. This archetype has nothing to do with the ancient 'Madonna–whore' dichotomy; the character proposed is neither a new version of Maria nor a sexy rock star or up-to-date sex symbol.

In Search of Alice

I have been thinking more and more about Alice – Alice in Wonderland, of course. In fact, I nominate Alice for iconic status, along with Oedipus and other symbols of questioning youths, in our psychological pantheon.

It seems to me that Alice, with her intelligent irreverence for a (from her point of view) topsy-turvy world, is an apt archetype for the identity of girls at puberty. And if we imagine Alice grown up, her character would also be a good model for adult 'girls'.

It is odd, when you think of it, that there is no daughter in the Christian holy family. The Holy Family is composed of Mary, Joseph and Jesus. This, the model on which we in the West were supposed to build our lives, has left girls in an awkward position. Who were they supposed to be? Lurking in the background was the character of Eve, the unmarried girl–woman, who, by being sexual, supposedly caused the downfall of 'mankind' (humanity).

Lurking in the background was the character of Eve, the unmarried girl–woman, who, by being sexual, supposedly caused the downfall of 'mankind' (humanity).

Were all the little Alices of this world supposed to identify with her? Is this why single women are constantly being asked: 'Are you married yet, dear? And do you have any children?' Only when Alice becomes a mother, 'Maria', can she stop being questioned about her identity.

Freud's naming of young men as 'Oedipus', facing heroic struggles, follows along the Holy Family model, in that the son is seen as a great protagonist, dealing with serious issues, worthy of notice. Yet Freud's naming of girls, i.e. 'Elektra' was not successful. In fact, most of his theories about women have turned out, with time, to be untrue; he understood very little about women. For example, one of his now disproved theses was that at puberty, girls should change the stimulation they need for orgasm from the clitoris to the vagina.

Similarly, he seems to have believed that girls have puberty in the same way that boys do. Although he never really looked into the matter, this assumption was taken up by psychological theory. I, too, had somehow assumed it to be true. However, my own research indicates something entirely different: while girls may have what we call reproductive puberty, they do not usually have puberty in the sense that boys do, i.e. a sexual awakening. Most girls can orgasm completely long before they are able to reproduce, through self-stimulation. Many parents tell me they have noticed their small daughters masturbating, and had to tell them: 'Please don't do that, or only do it in your own room.' The implications for psychological revision are startling. This suggests a theory of childhood that is totally different from Freud's.

In other ways, too, as Alice could tell you, girls are seen through a distorting lens by much of psychological theory. Girls are given few or no models of girlhood or young womanhood, the only proper role for females it would seem, is to 'grow up' and become 'full women' by getting married and becoming mothers, performing motherly functions; heroic activities are slated, still today, for boys' futures. There are many examples of boy heroes, young, unmarried men as important protagonists: neither Jesus Christ nor James Dean had to get married to 'prove himself'. Yet when young women are active or challenge authority, they are often labelled 'angry', 'neurotic' or 'maladjusted'; conversely, if they are loyal and 'serving' they can be labelled 'masochistic', even 'self-destructive'.

Girls are seen through a distorting lens by much of psychological theory.

I propose a more positive new icon: Alice. With her intelligence and clear-eyed questions and observations about the status quo and its rules and regulations, she speaks for many girls and women.

It is unfortunate that traditional psychology presents the family as a biological given, rather than a political or social institution, with pros and cons, an institution one can choose or not. It has allowed the 'family' to assume the proportions of a sacred, mythological never-changing reality ('biology'), putting the burden on the individual to 'adjust' to the institution, rather than allowing individuals to build flexible families of all kinds that suit them. The overly rigid family system causes problems for both boys and girls, but perhaps particularly for girls.

It is unfortunate that traditional psychology presents the family as a biological given, rather than a political or social institution, with pros and cons, an institution one can choose or not.

Sexuality is an integral part of the personal identity which girls must try, in this semi-invisible, not-so-friendly-to-them context, to formulate. This is made harder by its being denied, or silenced, not 'seen' – or if noted, frequently declared 'bad', i.e. the oft-repeated reminder 'good girls keep their legs together'. Why can't girls and women be proud of their vulvas and of their ability to orgasm and be sexual?

The symbol of society's denial and negativity toward female sexuality is the silence and gloom surrounding menstruation. Still today, there is generally not even a thought on the onset of a girl's menstruation, of giving her a celebration or a special dinner, to welcome her into a new phase of her life, celebrate the changes going on in her body. In very few families is the father even informed. A celebration would do much to alter the negative atmosphere which has hung over female sexuality identity for centuries, an atmosphere that has labelled menstruation 'the curse', female sexual feelings 'wicked' and sexual appearance in women as 'cheap' and 'whorish'. There should be a new movement of support and respect for girls to take pride in their bodies and their sexuality.

These basic issues, how girls are brought up, are essential for men to understand, in order to reprogram their mental software about who women are – even who they themselves are – and how to work in a new way with women, their teammates.

Your Opinion…

What is your opinion and experience? What do you think? What have been *your* experiences of what's been discussed in this chapter?

Please use this space to write your remarks, or alternatively you may e-mail comments to the *Sex and Business* website at www.sexandbusiness.com/myopinion. Naturally, you may express yourself anonymously.

_____

_____

_____

_____

_____

_____

Many men today, as much as women, want to change the atmosphere and have better relationships, but it is difficult for men to behave differently at work than 'traditional male-bonding behaviour'. Why? Because not 'playing the game with the guys' could cost them their job. As boys learn at puberty, the approval of other men ('the older boys at school') is very hard to come by, and once you've got it, you'd better not lose it (especially not by behaving with disloyalty, i.e. hanging out with women) or you'll be ousted from the group. Bye-bye job.

How much

money

does he have?

'How Much Money Does He Have?': Are Old Clichés Still Active?

Are the clichés about men still heard? Such as, 'work makes the man' or 'a good man is a successful man at business', etc. These remarks tend to measure a man's worth not in terms of his character or personality, but in terms of his financial assets.

Two key issues still define male status today: identity at work and identity in sex. Most men themselves, according to my research, also see their own self-worth in terms of these two areas.

Men's identity at work – especially in business – is, however, changing. As business becomes ever more globally competitive, its members are developing a nervous, age-conscious, I'm-going-to-prove-I'm-still-young quality. Yet, at the same time that they deal with such 'superficial' pressures (created by the fashion and cosmetic business' new advertising campaigns to men, showing very young men dressed à la 'office'),[1] many men are trying hard to think independently and clearly about issues of the day, especially social issues relating to male identity and women's new role in society. Many have sons and daughters, whom they see struggling together in school: they want to have a world in which both can take a good place.

Many men are quietly undertaking the work on their psyches that women have been making on theirs for the last 25 years: men want to keep their minds open to new ideas, re-balance themselves, rethink basic issues, such as what

they think their place in the world should be – as men, as white men, as Western men, fathers, sons and lovers. It's a time of questioning and self-discovery.

According to *The Hite Report on the Family,* on the deepest level, Western archetypes of 'who a man can be' come from the archetypes of the Holy Family, the basic role models and reproductive icons of the society. The two mythic roles model offered to men are Joseph, the father, and Jesus, the rebel-son. In most offices, the 'father' is the CEO or office manager, the 'rebel-sons' are the younger (usually!) salesmen, middle managers and others.

With the current shifts, many of today's businessmen are unsure 'who a man really is', or should be. Men's traditional identity as 'righteous hard workers' has been assaulted from all sides – by women, minorities, environmentalists, their own families (who want them to change), etc. Men are working harder than ever, yet feel less appreciated and valued than ever before.

Who are men? This chapter contains some keys to understanding men and the male psyche today.

How Do Women Describe Working With Male Colleagues?

'I'm a woman who sells life insurance and investment plans. Most of my colleagues, the other sales representatives, are men (well, all of them!). I get along very well with them. There are one or two who make a stupid comment now and then, but they're considered slightly

---

1 Doubtless, the new ads for men's shaving cosmetics, perfumes and underwear, showing very young men, are having an impact; the cult of 'the young' is also felt through the influence and popularity of rock music stars.

jerky in other ways by their other colleagues, too. Most of the guys seem to take me in their stride – I can't notice that they treat me any different than they do each other. Of course, I don't have to get promotions from them. I either bring in the sales or I don't. The figures are there in black and white.'

'My colleagues drive me nuts. Most of them are men, at least the ones who make the most noise and have the highest profile – they seem to have power and know where they are going. The women are more silent, you're never sure if they plan to stay in the company or they are just passing time. The guys are clearly out there pushing and shoving to get ahead, make their mark. The only problem is that they push and shove me too, and not always in a very nice way. I can't shove them back the same way or they suddenly judge me for being "not very feminine". It's no good my telling them they're not being fair. They don't care.'

'The guys where I work seem to be good blokes, nice, never a touch of sexist prejudice, always treat me right, but not special, etc. etc. I sincerely like some of them. But why do I get the feeling that just underneath the surface, things are not quite what they seem? They seem nice, but I can't put my finger on it, it's just that – well, maybe it's that everyone on the next level above me is male. So there's an expectation that the guys are doing well, but maybe I'm the runt of the group. I don't know, I can't explain it, but I feel somehow odd. Even though they're behaving perfectly.'

'The men at the last place I worked, a supermarket, ganged up against me. They played tricks and called me "stinky" and other awful things. They put a piece of dead meat (mince) in my locker and waited for it to smell, then offered me a Tampax. Not very nice. I got the message and left. My mother couldn't believe they did that.'

'My experience as a woman with lots of male colleagues is that I am generally taken for granted. I am left out when it's time for football and beer, also at the office when they talk about things... I am just expected to do my work and keep silent.'

'My male colleagues push the Power Button every ten minutes, I mean they point out how important they are in some subtle way. My modesty doesn't help at all, no points for it, I feel like I'm out and they're in...'

'Lots of men I work with want to see all the women here as "little sisters" they can help. Heaven forbid if one of us gets a raise or a promotion! Then she's not the "little sister" any more but the "little bitch"...'

How do women describe working with men in groups? (What is the men-in-suits – or boys-in-T-shirts – brigade?)

Most relationships between male and female colleagues can work out, if they are basically one-to-one.

A problem often occurs when there is a group of men present – when a woman is working with not one man, but several, i.e. she is dealing with a group of men. Men in groups can act quite differently from men on their own, especially when they are dealing with a woman. In this situation, the woman – and may it be one woman or a handful of women – is usually facing a larger number of men: women are still a minority in management jobs in business, so she and the women present are minority members in most groups at work. (Question: Is it inevitable 'human nature' for men to gravitate in groups towards other men, and women to group together?)

Men in groups can act quite differently from men on their own, especially when they are dealing with a woman.

Why does men's behaviour change when other men are present? Often in mixed groups, a man feels torn between relating to his female colleague(s) and relating to the men in the group. This same pressure can work on women: relating to a male colleague may be going OK, but if a group of women is witnessing it, this can make it more tense.

It is easier for two people to get a relationship going, including an easy interchange, than it is for an entire office to 'get it right'. As the business day involves meetings with various people, the atmosphere in an office, plus the colleagues working alongside the project the two people are developing, affect their interaction.

The heart of today's change, the ground where the 'battle' for a new interaction is really taking place, is between colleagues on essentially the same level. Much is said about senior men promoting junior women, but the testing ground

for the 'new equality' is between 'equal colleagues'. The test comes when a man is called on to 'bond with' his female colleague in the presence of a group of men.

Many men today, as much as women, want to change the atmosphere and have better relationships, but it is difficult for men to behave differently at work than 'traditional male-bonding behaviour'. Why? Because not 'playing the game with the guys' could cost them their job. As boys learn at puberty, the approval of other men ('the older boys at school') is very hard to come by, and once you've got it, you'd better not lose it (especially not by behaving with disloyalty, i.e. hanging out with women) or you'll be ousted from the group. Bye-bye job.

How do women feel in these situations?
Women describe what's going on in their offices:

'At my office there is something I call the boys' brigade. As women, we are less visible and tend to get passed over for promotions, while the brigade goes marching on. Is it because we don't hang out drinking or watching football? Should we form our own brigades? I feel like some kind of bystander watching.'

'Men in groups at the office have a kind of pack mentality that is intimidating to me.'

'I went to a business conference. There were male speakers ("experts"), and an audience of women and men. I noticed at intermission that the women there were divided into two very distinct groups, clearly split. Some of them were dressed in very seductive, tight dresses with jewellery; they were laughing and being vivacious, while men were hanging all over them. Other women were dressed in almost dowdy greys and blacks, standing timidly in corners, looking on. The contrast between the two groups of women was stark. I thought, I can't be in either of these groups. What should I do?'

'I'm a good-looking woman, I get a lot of attention at company conventions and so on. What bothers me is that I don't feel this attention is getting me anywhere, in fact, I have the distinct impression that it is causing me to be marginalized, sidelined. Is this right, or am I just experiencing what every woman experiences, no matter how she looks? I don't know, I just know that I see a group of men above me at work, all the people on the next level are men, and I know they won't be breaking that rule anytime soon (they're all quite young anyway), especially not to bring me up onto their level. They want to play the dating game with me and let me stay where I am – while they rise. They talk amongst themselves, they have a casual camaraderie on airplanes on the way to meetings and conventions, they work well as a group together. They are extremely friendly and polite with me, but they still give me the feeling that they are a group, and I am, well, I am somebody who doesn't matter a whole lot. It's that they are "nice guys", so they are nice to me. But they don't have to be.'

Why are men stand-offish with women? A double standard, as men experience it

Women often observe that men seem to be non-communicative with them, stand-offish, stiff rather than open or at ease – yet with other men, they can be relaxed, comfortable and communicate well, laughing and chatting. What causes the difference? Why are men tense with women?

Why are men tense with women?

Most often, people blame men's stiffness with women on women: 'Well you never know when they'll explode', 'Women are difficult, you know how touchy they are', etc.

These clichés do not explain anything. In fact, it could be argued that it is men's stiffness that is causing women to react with the frustration referred to.

According to Hite Research, the problem starts when the traditional family makes too much of gender difference, separating the genders hierarchically, and continues through a traumatic phase in most boys' lives – a phase that has still not been named or identified[2] even today, except by Hite Research,[3] still not taken with the seriousness it should be. (See pages 120–22.) This phase happens around puberty when boys at school, often older boys, begin taunting, hazing and bullying younger boys, saying things like 'Sissy! Mama's boy! He's a wimp, can't take it!'

2 The influence of boys' initiation rites on adult relationships with women: The puberty initiation rites noted in my research, although not discussed by Freud or others (did they think them not worth noting?), emerged clearly as men described their boyhood experiences: most were hazed or taunted, bullied by older boys (or saw this happening to other boys around them) – especially around ages 10–14. These events have a major impact on men's psychological formation at puberty, although the changes they display are usually blamed on 'hormones'. This is equivalent to installing software programming in boys. It is not harmless or a matter of a mysterious 'biology', hormonally inevitable.
   Fortunately, since it is only software, men can change it, delete the old and re-tool for contemporary business and life.

3 See *The Hite Report on the Family*, Bloomsbury, London, 1994.

These puberty rites and initiations teach boys, via bullying, to fear/respect men in groups; they learn that they must fit in somehow with these groups. Part of what is demanded of them is to 'leave mama behind', 'leave the girls behind' and 'join the men' – keep a distance from women, especially in public, and/or demonstrate that they control the woman, can tell her what to do, are dominating her (not the reverse!). Unfortunately, equality is seen as the reverse... If you do not 'keep your woman in her place', other men may ridicule or exclude you as 'not one of them', affecting your job success.

At work, many men – having internalized these lessons about 'staying away from women' to ensure acceptance 'as part of the men's group' – feel nervous with the new presence of career women. (As secretaries, women were more acceptable, since they were seen as 'lesser' and therefore able to be dominated, so in a 'normal' role.)

How Do Men Describe Working with Women?

Many men, even while expressing reservations, seem also genuinely to like working with women – women bosses, secretaries and colleagues, as well as female clients:

'It always makes me feel good when I start my day with a brief chat or "hello" to her. She's usually already at work when I get there. She sees to like to come in early, when it's quiet, to get things sorted out for the day. I admire her command of detail, she's usually on top of the many and varied parts of her work. I feel I can rely on her.'

'The policy writer in the next office to mine is a woman. I can see her (head and shoulders) through the glass partition between our offices, so I know she's working as hard as I am. No time even for a tea or coffee break, the phone is going all the time and there are a thousand letters to write. The office on the other side has a man. I notice that I'm more likely to feel "sympathetic vibes" towards her direction than his – although it's him I talk to from time to time passing his door. Is this because I think it's more appropriate to talk to another man? Anyway, I feel good knowing she's there, somehow.'

Quite a few men sound formal and carefully neutral when describing their female colleagues – especially at the executive level:

'I like having a female colleague. She is the only woman (besides the secretaries, of course) in our crew of about 85. I feel good that she's here; she makes the partnership more complete, there is more a sense of wholeness about it. She is pleasant, hard-working and ambitious. However, I just can't find a way to have a real conversation with her, she's too busy to talk, she just comes in, sits in her seat and gets going. So I have no way to make a connection.'

'The highest level woman in our department is well-known for being one of the biggest performers we have. She makes a fortune for the company. We all went on a trip once, and she brought her mother as her "partner" (most of us brought our spouses). She and her mother went off sightseeing alone most of the time, we almost never saw her. I don't feel terribly comfortable with her, and she probably, doesn't with me or any of us either. We're all careful to be polite, etc.'

Despite liking them, some men don't take women seriously at work – or are careful to describe them not only in terms of work, but also how they picture them as sex partners:

'One of the women in my office is fiery, her temperament is sassy. There's never a day when she doesn't take on somebody or something around her. I get a big kick out of whatever she's saying. I don't know if she's really right for this corporation, but it's nice having her here for a while.'

Men's Reactions to Today's 'Invasion of Women'

At the same time as saying they like working with women (when asked to describe their female colleagues), men present more mixed feelings when asked the question in a different way. When asked how they would feel if there were an equal number of women as men in their office, on the same level – if half of their bosses were women – men feel much less positive.

In fact this evokes a completely different response: 67 per cent of men say that they would be uncomfortable, can't imagine this situation, really.

Are men upset, suffering silently, feeling psychologically disoriented and dislocated dealing with the arrival of career women on the scene – especially since they are not supposed to admit it if they are?

Many men do feel beleaguered, but feel they don't have a right to complain:

'How do we feel? My friend told me right out: "I would have a problem with my wife earning more than me, or having a female boss." Lots of us agree with him.'

Men in my research say that the thing they most resent about being male instead of female (if anything) is the possibility girls have to cry and complain; girls can say what's bothering them – but if a boy or man does this, all the world tells him he's a wimp. Women, men say, get sympathy.

Men's problems adjusting are often overlooked in the understandable focus on the problems women have just getting into the office, above secretarial level. Yet men also deserve sympathy, especially when so many are trying to behave perfectly with their new female colleagues.

The adjustment is a mutual problem, the new work environment and new relationships will be a mutual creation.

The adjustment is a mutual problem, the new work environment and new relationships will be a mutual creation. It's important to hear and understand both sides of the situation.

The following remarks are written anonymously, 'to protect the guilty':

'Ever since Angela arrived in the office – she's supposed to be an executive manager (manageress??) – I feel like I have to be careful, like she will scrutinize my behaviour and give me demerits if I'm not pc. Anything I do could be labelled "laddish" or "insensitive", any joke I make could be "out of place", etc. etc. Work was more fun before she got here.'

'I admire Rita. She's hitting 40, her body's made for tight suits, she's divorced and her career is going full steam. Too bad she's almost old enough to be my mum!'

You Can't Go Home Again: Change is Good

While the changes at work can make women feel they are stepping up – their status improving – men can feel just the opposite. Women are glad to belong to the world of work and corporations, but men feel that now, with women everywhere, they are being demoted. What happened to the privileges men were promised?

While the changes at work can make women feel they are stepping up – their status improving – men can feel just the opposite.

Business used to be, in the 'good old days', a 'world without women... a logical world without emotion'. Or did it? As one executive told me: 'The business world is a module, a special space where, when you enter it, all questions of private life disappear...' (Never mind that emotions are everywhere in corporate culture – envy, greed, desire, hate, affection, love, rage, violence – just not the emotions usually associated with love relationships with women.)

Since business has been basically a male prerogative, to many men on a gut level, women seem like interlopers, deserving whatever treatment they get, from sexual harassment to ridicule to having to prove themselves twice as

much before advancement: 'If they want to be in the workplace like men, they have to take the knocks that come with it. No more protecting them, they have to learn what it's like. If they can't take the heat, they should stay *home*.'

But most men would really not like to go back to 'the good old days'. Most men say that they quite like having women at work, they like the new atmosphere, even though they may complain! The change in their status is irritating, but having women around on an equal level adds a new spirit to business that wasn't there before. The competition is stimulating and challenging.

Most men would really not like to go back to 'the good old days'.

Does this new atmosphere, mixing male and female values, spell business success? Or do men work better with other men than in mixed groups? This is a new social experiment, and it is probably too early to tell; however, in places where inter-gender work relationships have been operating for some time, for example the government of New York City (employing over 100,000 people, and having at one point had a quota system to improve the numbers of female participation) it has increased productivity.

Brain Software Commands – For Men

SOFTWARE TO DELETE

'I grew up to believe work and business would be an all-male environment, and that women do not belong there.'

SOFTWARE TO INSTALL

'Working together with women is normal today, and offers new energy and vitality. I like it.'

What Does Work Mean to Men?

The anatomy of male pride

The changes at work represent a crossroads for men. Why? Because men's definition of who they are is tied up with identity at work and identity in sex. These are the two basic areas of self-esteem for men.

The changes at work represent a crossroads for men. Why? Because men's definition of who they are is tied up with identity at work and identity in sex. These are the two basic areas of self-esteem for men.

Traditionally, masculinity was demonstrated – a man 'proved his worth' – either in the workplace, or in battle. Thus any changes to the workplace are threatening to men's basic identity. This is much more difficult for men than for women, especially since (as noted) the change in status for women is perceived as up, but for men, it's down.

Boys are brought up to believe that they will grow up to have a different life than women, and that they will have more power and privileges. Just look at any kid's morning cereal advertisement or video game!

This does not prepare men to work well with women on an equal footing. Girls are brought up, too, to believe that men will have more money and a mysterious power or way of life that they themselves will not experience. Thus women, too, are not brought up in a way that is helpful to smooth working relationships with men later in life.

Men have been educated to identify with other men, dress like them, cut their hair like them. Men desire the esteem of other men, and fear not being accepted by men, 'the group', 'the ones that matter' and confer social acceptance, status. Women are helpful as part of 'personal life', adjuncts to that status – in the classic outline of who a man was supposed to be. Of course, today quite a few men have surpassed this old dichotomy, and, fortunately, the number is growing.

Some say, women have a womb, they create life; men only have work so 'don't take it away from them, it's all men have got!' Some 'serious' male anthropologists and psychologists (including feminist writers) put this idea about a few years ago to 'explain' male hostility to women (rape, etc.), implying that if men are not let alone to feel special at work, they will develop a terrible inferiority complex. This is not true, or only true in cases of terrible identity problems in the first place; according to my research, men's self-esteem is something each man develops by having a sense of his worth,

not worth based on what others don't have, but on what he himself does have; further, in Hite Research, men often expressed dissatisfaction and disillusion with their work, especially after age 50, asking 'What's the point of it all?' Many men want to see shifts in 'the system'.

There is still a tendency on the part of many men (and women) to think things like: 'Men are made to go out into the jungle of business and do combat. A real man is one who is on top at work, making lots of money, a hard-driving businessman.' The other side of this coin is: 'Love and sex are the basic ways a man should relate to a woman, they give him strength and support for his work; women should not be out in the competitive jungle.' The two-world system.

Sometimes men and women can't accept their prejudice as prejudice, believing they simply have a 'different value system', i.e. 'I'm old-fashioned, I guess... I believe nature made women to stay at home and take care of children.' Or: 'Too much questioning of traditional beliefs is what has got society into such a mess today.' (Is it in a mess? More than usually?)

Keys to Understanding the Male Psyche

Men who are nervous around women...
The basic keys to understanding men – 'who men are' – that emerge out of my research, relate to the pressures on boys during the formative and impressionable years of puberty. During harsh puberty rites (boys' initiation by other men and boys through taunts, bullying and dares into the 'world of men'), boys learn to fear/respect men in groups, fit in with them, and to keep a distance from women especially in

Many men want to see shifts in 'the system'.

public, lest other men punish, ridicule or exclude them.[4]

Two traumas at puberty create male patterns with women, often for life, according to my research: men learn at puberty to fear other men as they are taunted by older boys to 'be one of us or you'll be sorry!' (part of being 'one of us' means not hanging out with women or having them as equals in public). A simultaneous trauma boys undergo is experiencing the insistence by the male group (usually at school) that, to prove membership the boy 'tell the mother off', 'show the mother who's boss' (i.e. him) – betray the mother. In my research, most boys go through about a year of inner turmoil over this 'need' but finally try to conform. Conforming, however, leaves a lifelong nervousness around women, seen most clearly when a man develops feelings of love or close friendship for a woman.

Having to 'betray the mother' publicly, at the same time that he is developing strong sexual feelings (most boys first masturbate to orgasm with ejaculation at puberty), is further confusing to later relationships with women. Boys often masturbate to orgasm in their rooms while their mother is in the next room preparing dinner, or a boy can ejaculate into his bed sheets, knowing that it will be his mother who finds the 'dirty sheet' to wash later; the juxtaposition of these two dramatic or emotionally tense situations combines to create a trauma about sex and disloyalty, so that many boys learn (in this mental software) to combine love and disrespect (or fear) of women. Loving a woman later may make them nervous and uncomfortable, but may also attract them.

In short, men's psycho-sexual identity installed at that time (but later able to be changed, reprogrammed), includes simultaneous love and hate, desire and repulsion towards women: sexual desire is combined with a need to humiliate 'the female'. (See page 125.)

This strange combination, or toxic mixture, can go a long way towards explaining how some men can be involved in sexually harassing less powerful employees. (See Chapter 7.)

The two basic components that most men, as a result of this boyhood training, have to deal with every day in their own minds (their personal software programming), are: 1) fear of other men in groups and 2) pressure to appear to dominate women, at least in public – countered by the new pressures not to appear to be dominating women!

4 According to Hite Research, this taunting/hazing teaches boys that love is connected with 'silly girls' feelings', and that 'sex' is properly had with 'women who are not like your mother', i.e. 'bad girls'. Do some men at work also then automatically try to divide women in their minds into 'the good ones' and the 'bad ones'? This is inappropriate; it is not good business judgement to use old clichés of 'nice girls' to decide how to get business done, who to hire or how to relate to women at work.

What is it like to grow up male?

In my research I studied over 7,000 men and boys, asking them questions about their lives. Sifting through the data and analysing them revealed new perspectives on boys' development and psycho-sexual identity, as well as men's later relationships with women.

What is it like to grow up male?

One of the most striking facts to emerge was that a majority of men claim that they did not marry the woman they most passionately loved, saying they are proud of this, proud to have kept control of themselves, 'done the right thing'. (Why was it 'the right thing'?)

In fact, most men say that being in love makes them nervous, uneasy, therefore they try to overcome any feeling of being 'too close' to a woman – including women at work. As one put it, 'It's like a kind of contamination...'

Question: Why are men often nervous and stand-offish talking to or working with women? Deeper problems from a man's background can be haunting him.

The Secret Trauma of Boys: Breaking Up with the Mother
Boys learn they should no longer stay too close to women, such as their mother, but hang out with other boys.

How boys learn to see women as 'other'[5]
As small children, many boys feel especially close to their mothers, often preferring to spend more time with them than with their fathers. But then, around puberty, they learn that they must reject their mothers, according to my research. They are pressured by the prevailing culture (especially at school) to change their behaviour, with taunts like 'Don't hang onto your mother's apron strings', 'Don't be a wimp', 'Get out of the kitchen and hang out with the boys', and so on. Most of all they are expected to demonstrate their new identity by showing that 'She can't tell me what to do' and distance themselves from their mothers, even ridiculing them publicly, in front of male friends, fathers and brothers.

They learn that, in order to enter the 'male' world – to be respected by other males, get a job and find a place in the world – they must put aside everything that is called 'feminine' ('gushy', 'childish' behaviour) and 'grow up' to 'be a man'. They must repudiate and betray the person for whom they have felt the most love.

The 'breaking up' with the mother puts boys under severe mental and emotional stress. In many, it creates a lifelong pattern of believing that love cannot last, and cannot be counted on. Most boys feel guilty for adopting these new behaviours; they simultaneously feel they are being disloyal to a person they love, and who loves them, and that they have little choice but to do so. Others, in a familiar reversal of psychological logic, come to feel that their mothers have deserted them. And thus they learn that 'women are not to be trusted'. Others take with them a lifelong belief that strong, passionate feelings cause death and destruction and are to be avoided. That work and relationships with other men are more reliable and valuable.

To sum up, at the same time that boys experience a sudden flowering of sexual feelings, they are hit by a traumatic change in their psychological and emotional landscape: they go through a period of emotional turmoil which culminates in the

5 See Simone de Beauvoir, *The Second Sex*, 1953.

'desertion' of the mother. This crisis can affect their relationships with every other woman: in later years they may feel irritated by what they perceive as women's unspoken 'demands' – which are their own buried memories of their mother's hurt and pain. This can make it hard for them to perceive women clearly – rationally or ethically.

At the same time that boys experience a sudden flowering of sexual feelings, they are hit by a traumatic change in their psychological and emotional landscape: they go through a period of emotional turmoil which culminates in the 'desertion' of the mother.

In this light, we could say that the myth of Oedipus and his psychological conflict about his feelings for his mother quite accurately reflects men's lives now in the family system as we know it. The Oedipus legend may have an historical, not psychological, interpretation: i.e. Aeschlus' play about Oedipus represents boys' and men's confusion over whether to be loyal to a matrilineal or patrilineal social system; at that time in history, patriarchy was recently arrived, and traces of the earlier matrilineal system were still everywhere.

'Don't Be Like a Girl!'

Boys' traumatic initiation rites into 'men's world'
How do boys know they should not be 'too close' to girls, or hang out with their mothers and sisters, not prefer women to groups of men and boys?

It is not inevitable 'male nature' to be ambivalent or even hostile during relationships with women. Obviously not all men are. These attitudes are part of an ideology which society endlessly reiterates to boys, especially at puberty. Pressure on boys to express disdain and contempt for their mothers, at the same time that there is pressure to begin to be 'sexual' towards women (but not be 'female'!) – these messages together cause a traffic jam in boys' minds, and can short-circuit their brains (trauma), fusing the two together forever. The block becomes so completely built into structures in the mind that we can't 'see' it anymore.

It is not inevitable 'male nature' to be ambivalent or even hostile during relationships with women.

According to the testimony of boys in my research, it is the taunting of their peers and fathers which teaches them to change their behaviour, stop 'hanging out with your mother', 'go on out with the boys'. This change (the learned feeling that it is somehow dangerous to spend too much time with a woman, or be too friendly) affects the culture we inhabit on many levels, including the political, because it eventually makes men seek to dominate women in politics, the arts, work and private life.

The trauma or initiation boys undergo is reflected in later life. Film and advertising images of the self-sufficient, independent male, disdainful of women and 'things female', influence many men's behaviour at work. Since the late 1950s, when men began to rebel against the family and look to the single male as their role model, men have complained that women 'tie them down' (rather than expressing pleasure that women bring them something). Adventure for men was seen as 'out there', away from the marital home. The cult of the single male was glorified in films after the Second World War; the male hero became an unmarried rebel, à la James Dean, Marlon Brando, Tom Cruise and Arnold Schwarzenegger. The man most admired by other men, it seemed, was the one who was 'free'. The groovy-male-as-single image continued in rock music culture, with The Beatles and Bob Dylan, and in today's rap singer CDs and MTV videos. While there is some slight tendency to 'return to tradition' and 'romance', statistics and advertising continue to turn up images of youngish single men; television commercials aimed at businessmen (Singapore Airlines, Diner's Club, AT&T 'Call USA Direct') all picture a young man in a suit alone somewhere.

Men at work, in short, feel it is not 'groovy' to be too close or friendly with women. It is certainly not status-friendly to work for a woman. There is more status attached to working for a man.

Information from Hite Research:
Sex and Violence

Question: How do men combine the need/desire to be sexual with women, with the need to keep women at a distance, as just described?

Eroticism and betrayal of the mother: Implications for sexual harassment – a new theory

Oedipus in Love
Male psycho-sexual identity is one of the most important bases of the psychology of the culture. In my research into what makes boys and girls behave differently, how they learn as they grow up to see themselves as 'male' or 'female', I ask girls and boys to define what love means to them in the family.

Painful initiation rites: 'He's a mama's boy!'
As children, most boys feel especially close to their mothers, often preferring to spend time with them than their fathers. However, according to my research, around puberty they are pressured by the culture to 'make a choice', i.e. told they must reject her: 'Get out of the kitchen and hang out with the boys, don't tag along with your sister', and so on. Boys are expected to demonstrate their new 'tough identity' by ridiculing and distancing themselves from their mothers, especially in front of male friends, fathers and brothers.

The implications of this have gone unseen, unanalyzed. The pain of the taunting is laughed off: 'Oh, boys will be boys! Their hormones make them rambunctious at that age.' When, however, many haunting and sad stories told by men emerged over and over in my research, their importance began to become clear to me. These are cultural initiation rites, as 'primitive' (or more so) as those of any tribe in 'darkest Africa': these initiation rites change the course of men's lives, and society. Since, however, they are culturally created, we can decide whether to continue them.

Cultural initiation rites, as 'primitive' (or more so) as those of any tribe in 'darkest Africa'... change the course of men's lives, and society.

As a boy named George said:

'When the guys come over and my mother tries to tell me what television show I can watch, it's humiliating. "Turn off that TV!" she calls from the other room, when she hears us listening to heavy metal rock videos. I am so embarrassed, I say "Shut up!" and turn it up even louder. The guys are really impressed – "I guess your mother can't tell you what to do!", the biggest one says to me smiling. I am accepted, then, but it used to upset me. I felt like a traitor, a terrible son, and feared my mother would hate me.'

Boys are taunted mercilessly by other boys at school with phrases like 'mama's boy' (if they won't go along with the other boys), 'Stop being a sissy, un-cool' or 'Act like a man and stop being a turkey, ape-shit'. They learn that they have to make a choice: in order to enter the 'male' world – to be respected by other males, find a place in the world, get a job – they have to put aside what is called 'feminine', 'gushy', 'childish' behaviour and 'grow up', 'act male' – which means, be the opposite of 'feminine'. They often prove this by, in effect, rejecting their mother (or sister) in favour of a group of boys or men, siding with them, 'talking back to her', and so on.

Boys are, in effect, expected by the culture to change their allegiance – and identity – at puberty. While as children, many boys felt especially close to their mother, now they must decisively reject her! This 'breaking up with' the mother as a child puts boys under severe mental and emotional stress. Most feel guilty: they simultaneously feel they are being disloyal to a person they love and who loves them (their mother) – but that they have little choice. ('She shouldn't have told me to turn off the music. I didn't want to hurt her feelings by disobeying her, and saying something mean to her, but what choice did I have? She brought it on herself.') Others, in a familiar reversal of psychological logic, come to feel that she deserted them, 'You can't trust women', etc.

In other words, boys' psychology is affected at an early age by a traumatic psychological and emotional change in landscape which is not taken seriously by psychologists or society – which is not noted by many Freudian or post-Freudian psychologists, who tend to believe it is the result of 'hormones' and therefore 'natural', i.e. boys' closeness to their mothers 'naturally ends because male hormones' at puberty make boys become distant, disassociated from their mothers, stop feeling close to them. But, in fact, according to boys' testimony in my research, it is rather the taunts of their peers at school (and fathers), who ridicule them for associating with 'females' and being 'soft like a girl', which make their behaviour change.

This is a tragic loss of a complete emotional spectrum, an attenuation of their lives for boys, something which affects the culture on many levels, including the political, eventually making men seek to dominate women in the arts, politics and private life. This demand to 'show masculine superiority' is painful for everyone concerned.

The 'desertion' of the mother leaves significant emotional scars on most boys/men: feeling very guilty about having 'betrayed' their mothers, this guilt can shadow their relationships with other women for the rest of their lives. They may feel irritated by what they perceive as women's unspoken demands, i.e. their own buried memory of their mother's hurt and pain. In other words a woman's love brings up buried feelings of guilt and fear, which may easily become displaced onto the 'evil' woman who is 'provoking' or 'seducing' them.

Many women are left to wonder and puzzle over men's erratic behaviour during love affairs or marriages, as they observe men waxing first passionate, loving and desirous, then cold and blocking, even hostile and aggressive, or violent.

In my study of men, the Hite Report on Male Sexuality, I learned that most men do not feel

6 Mernissi, Fatima, *Beyond the Veil*, Saqi Books, London, 1985.

comfortable being in love, and in fact, most men do not marry the woman they most passionately love. Fatima Mernissi, in *Beyond the Veil*,[6] notes a similar phenomenon in men in Islamic culture, saying they feel a great love for a woman would interfere with their love and duty to Allah.

Not only did I find that most men say they did not marry the woman they most passionately loved, but also most men were proud of it. Most are proud they kept 'control of their feelings'. The reasons for this go back to the love scenario they learned when they were small, with the first important woman in their life: it can't last, it's wrong to stay too close to her, you have to learn to be 'your own man', leave home.

Interestingly, in homes where there are not two parents, when boys grow up with only their mother, they are less likely to experience the most intense types of this emotional trauma of separation, and thus more likely to develop stable and important, equal emotional relationships with women later in life.

Bottom line: This 'education' (software programming) causes boys and men to behave irrationally with women, sensing danger where there is none – and displacing a hostile-aggressive fear of 'men' and 'the male system' onto women. At work this means 'instinctively' trying to exclude or avoid women. Fortunately, many men now are trying to change this software.

Sex and Violence: Sexual Harassment and the Development of Boys' Sexual Identity

Why do some men connect eroticism with giving pain to women?

The confusion of emotions for women that boys learn at puberty is also applied in many men's sexual feelings. Sexually, most boys' early sex lives are subliminally, yet potentially associated with feelings for the mother. She is the woman with whom they are most intimate: they have been kissed by her, seen her body, felt her arms around them, know her habits in the bath. She is the one who knows their secrets, had fed and clothed them and physically touched and held them. Yet at puberty, all this changes.

Boys' 'puberty', that is, 'sexual awakening', occurs between the age of ten and twelve when changes in boys' bodies make full orgasm possible for the first time. Most boys begin a very

heavy masturbation sex life – mostly in secret, although half of boys share masturbation and perhaps other sexual acts with other boys (Kinsey, 1948; Hite, 1981 and 1994).[7] 'I remember it as a time of secrets', one boy relates 'a whole and complete second world was opening up around me'. Another remembers lying in bed masturbating while listening to his mother in the kitchen making dinner.

What has not been noted in previous psychological theory is that, at the *same* time that sexual feelings are becoming so strong for boys, boys also go through the moral and emotional crisis in their relationship with their mother, just described.

Disassociating themselves from their mothers, at the same age they are also experiencing the beginning of strong sexual feelings, causes a peculiar love-hate type of sexuality and

7 Kinsey, Alfred, *Sexual Behavior in the Human Male*, W.B. Saunders, Boston, 1948.
  Hite, Shere, *The Hite Report on Male Sexuality*, Knopf, New York, 1981.
  Hite, Shere, *The Hite Report on the Family*, Bloomsbury, London, 1994.

eroticism to develop in boys in relation to women: a sexuality connected with emotions of guilt and anger.

Because their sexuality is awakening at just the time they are learning to reject and ridicule the mother and 'women's ways' – and because, at the same time, many mothers keep coming back and giving more 'love and understanding' the more hostile and difficult a boy becomes (in an attempt to continue the closeness) – the pattern is reinforced. Many men come to believe 'women love pain', 'women are masochists', 'she'll keep loving me no matter what I do' and apply this to other women later in life.

In the boys' new thinking, the mother's continuing to be nurturing is seen as the mother humiliating herself, which affects how they will learn to define 'love' coming from a woman as adults. William is typical in saying:

'It made me begin to wonder, how far can I go before she will stop being so nice to me? I told my friend the other day when he was over, and we broke some glasses in the kitchen: "Let's don't pick them up and see what she does." We made a bet: I said she would pick them up, and he said, no, she'll make you do it. I won.'

Unfortunately this all becomes an erotic-love package which some men take with them throughout their lives (or try to).

After this, is it any surprise that it can seem normal and erotic for men to want to humiliate women at the same time that they want to kiss them? Is this love? Yes and no. Men are in a bind; most do not see patriarchy as a chain, a fence around them, but instead, believe in their glorious rights and privileges.

Question: If others are chained, can they be free?

Although society calls some of the attitudes in men examined here 'human nature', my theory – if correct – is good news, because it means that these attitudes are not 'nature' or dictated by hormones. It means these attitudes are part of an ideology which the society puts in place in boys, especially at puberty, through pressure to express contempt for their mothers and 'things feminine', at the same time that they begin to be 'sexual' toward women. These two messages fuse, and the resultant behaviour becomes so commonplace that we call it 'human nature'.

Many men are restive with the contradictions they sense exist on these topics, and could like to see change, a different landscape. Starting at the end of the 1950s, men began to declare they wanted out of 'the system' (they identified it at that time as 'marriage'; today they are more sophisticated about what it is that makes them feel not free). There is a new quiet crisis in masculinity, in the male soul and psyche – of which the recent widespread call for a return to 'traditionalism' is only a symptom. Such a crisis will not be solved by the preservation of traditional family values, since 'to protect the family as we know it' does not mean, as it sounds, to keep the world safe for loving values. Rather it means, among other things, maintaining the traditional family hierarchy which insists boys switch their allegiance at puberty

Is it any surprise that it can seem normal and erotic for men to want to humiliate women at the same time that they want to kiss them?

from their mother to their father. (Why is it necessary to have a family or social structure in which there is a need to choose??) The 'traditional family' means and always meant: women in the home and subservient, men 'in power', but impoverished emotionally. To follow the 'traditional path' will only lead to further weakening of the social fabric, because of men's unhappiness (feeling cut off), women's frustrations (trying to make love work) and children's discomfort (feeling trapped) with a problematic gender intolerance.

I believe that many individuals are now breaking through these old clichés, the old social 'shoulds' and stereotypes about the family, trying to forge better love alliances with people they care for, build new families of many new types and designs. They are the wave of the future.

Corporations' top executives would be wrong to think the 'new workplace' is only a 'woman's thing', or a concession to women and 'new families'. Balance is an all-employee issue, not a women's or parents' issue.

The New Man at Work?

Although firms incessantly talk about the need for employees to balance work with personal life, even in the supposed 'caring, sharing 90s' policies to encourage such balance go little beyond lip-service. Real Men are expected to Be There. (Work Comes First!) In a 1999 UK survey, most executives agreed that the extra working hours expected leave them with insufficient time and energy for family, friends and outside interests.[8]

It can be hard for the 'new man' to survive in corporate culture as currently structured, i.e. 'the long hours executive work culture', with its assumption that 'more is better', men who are seen to be working 'really hard' long hours are more admired, etc.

Corporations' top executives would be wrong to think the 'new workplace' is only a 'woman's thing', or a concession to women and 'new families'. Balance is an all-employee issue, not a women's or parents' issue. Single and married men have the same needs and problems that were once considered 'only female'. Simply introducing policies such as job sharing or part-time work cannot provide the total answer in a culture where commitment equals long hours, and maintaining a tough macho attitude at

It's time to get over the Marlboro Man complex and look at results, not hours of 'hard work' or gender of employees, foster new management styles.

8 The survey, Enabling Balance: The Importance of Organizational Culture, by Roffey Park Management Institute, reports that almost 70% of managers suffer from increased levels of stress due to rising workloads, 90% agree that extra working hours are expected of a manager today, 86% of the 450 respondents say they work 50 or more hours per week. Most say that long hours leave them with insufficient time and energy for family and friends. (Caroline Glynn, Roffey Park Management; Tel 0193 851 644; National Work Life Forum 492 8787.)

work is de rigeur. It's time to get over the Marlboro Man complex and look at results, not hours of 'hard work' or gender of employees, foster new management styles.

A company with stressed, dissatisfied managers eventually results in a negative corporate image that fails to draw in and keep customers or fresh, young, talented employees. Most young professionals today put quality of life ahead of immediate high salary or career progression. When they feel work is negatively affecting their life, they may leave their employer, who then has the burden of finding a replacement.

However, new businesses are springing up everywhere with a new kind of office interaction, and these tend to have a very high success rate.

Men's Problems with Male Authority Figures

Quite a few men are torn between wanting to be 'a new man' and wanting to work with the 'male establishment authority figures' – the daddies and patriarchs of fable – they believe exist.

Many also have a problem deciding how they want to relate to such authority figures, i.e. fathers. During the 1960s, it was fashionable to declare that 'you can't trust anyone over 35'. 'Young men' believed that old men were all corrupt, had made some kind of trade-off with 'the system', so that they were not longer honest or relevant.

Question: How does a 'young man' make the transition to being an 'older man' in authority without making too many compromises to still be true to himself, stand for something – and like himself?

This can be done, but it is not easy. In today's context, the question of women's status especially challenges men's integrity and sense of fair play. Men at work have very ambivalent feelings about how to treat women, relate to the new situation; obviously, 'letting women be equal at work' is an idea with justice on its side (as their sisters will tell them) – so should they go ahead and work easily with women, blend in, make new choices – or should they try to please the older male authority figures who may prefer signals of an old male-bonding variety?

The challenge is for a man to understand well enough both sides of his identity, his new thinking and his older training, so that he can elegantly move the entire situation to another stage: make the new world of work valid for everyone concerned – the women there, his boss and also himself. I would recommend that any man wishing to do this read more thoroughly some of the excerpts from Hite Research presented in this book, or the entire series of five research reports.

On the subject of men's relationships with their fathers, bosses and other authority figures...

Boys and Their Fathers: Distance and Longing

Although there is a revolution in the family taking place, the relationship between father and son is one of the last places to change.

Although there is a revolution in the family taking place, the relationship between father and son is one of the last places to change.

Boys learn their understanding of authority and seniority (and sometimes relationships with men) from this early relationship, no matter how distant it may have been. (If it was distant, they learn that relationships between men are distant…) For the great majority, the relationship between father and son is not close – although there are exceptions.

Boys in Hite Research (*The Hite Report on Male Sexuality*) stated over and over, in the most poignant and moving statements, that they had not known their fathers very well, that their fathers rarely talked to them about their feelings or relationships. In fact, most boys said that they had never had a real conversation with their fathers about a personal topic. Most expressed a longing to have had some deeper experience of communication and acceptance.

For some, the only contact they had (which they came to enjoy) was through silent companionship such as watching football and soccer games, often on television, together. Watching men in games is especially pleasurable to boys because, in this way, they can achieve a sense of belonging with their fathers and other men that most of them can have in no other way. The 'games' are a metaphor for learning the mysterious rules of male comportment in the society. Through these games, boys and men learn and observe the permitted patterns of 'masculinity' portrayed there, just as women look at fashion magazines for clues as to acceptable comportment.

Like the Michaelangelo fresco of Adam reaching for God's hand in The Creation, in which their fingers never quite touch, men often feel that tantalizing sense of 'almost… almost'. They can almost touch their fathers and yet there is a distance that is unbridgeable. They are left with a feeling that he is unattainable, other, outside and that this is how it must be.

This incomplete relationship affects many men forever. They attempt to reach 'the father', try to make him recognize and see them, the son. This is the same fight that women can have with men in love relationships, essentially trying to get men to 'open up', be more communicative, relate fully to them, 'see' them. A cycle persists of the younger man, or a woman, not being able to 'get through' to the grown-up, perfectly closed man, consequently feeling less and less loved, coming up against his silence and distance, neither feeling able to understand the other.

Boys (like women) often become fascinated by the power of this emotionally silent and mysterious monolith, the older man.

Some men later find themselves turning into versions of their fathers:

'I didn't know my father, really, I didn't know what went on in his head. He went to work, he came home, he got angry at odd moments and everybody seemed to have to help rearrange things so his anger would go away and he, the god, would be pacified. I used to ask my mother what was I supposed to be like – him?

'I always identified with the son in *Death of Salesman.* I didn't want to be that salesman either. So I tried to go along outwardly with the behaviours they all expected of men, damn it, say as little as possible to avoid conflict (or discovery that I was not all I was supposed to be, cracked up to be, I wasn't a 'typical man'). Funny thing, one day my one-year-old son said to his mother (when they thought I wasn't around): "Why doesn't Daddy say anything?" I had managed to look just like my dad looked to me.

'I felt a sharp pain inside me, almost a stabbing blow, as if someone had put a knife in me. I went and sat down on the sofa and hid my face in my arm, I was crying. It also hurt me when my wife, after my son said that, just murmured something like "Oh, your father's just like that. He's in his own world, he can't help it", as if she were alienated too. There was just no place to turn. It was then I knew I had to change, I had to make a different life for myself and everyone around me.'

Although joining the 'world of the fathers' is a frightening experience for many boys and men (and women) – as boys often feel alone and insecure, suddenly in a new, colder and more competitive world, a world they say over and over that their fathers did not explain to them – conquering it can become the biggest adventure they undertake in life. Later, however, according to my research, sometimes on becoming such a 'fearsome male monolith/ power person', many men feel very unsatisfied and disillusioned.

Many younger men now read this writing on the wall and want to find a new way forward. They no longer want the extreme 'revolution' of the 1960s, but they also don't want the 'return to traditional manhood' of the 1980s; they want a new third way, something they are now inventing at work. This is where men's revolution is taking place.

Projections from Private Life?

Do men tend to see women at work via experiences they have had, or clichés about women in private life?

'Good girls' and 'bad girls'

Some men today unconsciously continue shadowy ideas of the double standard of morality for judging women – at work. In a way, this often leads them to think that 'career women' are today's new version of 'bad girls': they are not behaving in the way a 'good woman, wife and mother' should, they are too free and powerful. This attitude is seen in mass media images of 'the new career women' as well, e.g. Demi Moore in *Disclosure* as the wicked career woman, Glenn Close in *Fatal Attraction* as the neurotic career woman, or on covers of *Der Spiegel* (Germany's leading news magazine) or other world magazines, showing the 'new career woman' as a sexual dominatrix with high heels, stockings, tight-skirted business suit, red lipstick and fingernails, etc.

Many younger men now read this writing on the wall and want to find a new way forward. They no longer want the extreme 'revolution' of the 1960s, but they also don't want the 'return to traditional manhood' of the 1980s; they want a new third way, something they are now inventing at work. This is where men's revolution is taking place.

Projections from private life onto the office

Do some men think that 'private life' has moved to work, now that there are an increasing number of women on the scene?

Do some men think that 'private life' has moved to work, now that there are an increasing number of women on the scene?

Men may be using their experiences and relationships with women in private life as a reference point for understanding female colleagues, and how to treat them. While this may be a natural impulse (given lack of experience at work), it isn't a logical way to deal with people at work.

It can be tempting for men at times, in the office, to fall back on cliché images of women – as wife, girlfriend, daughter or mother – to interpret 'female behaviour' in one of these ways. Of course, if a man stops and thinks, he knows that he cannot understand a woman at work by trying to slot her into a convenient reference point (cliché), any more than women can understand men that way.

Yet many men – and women, for that matter – unconsciously project onto work relationships scenarios of private life. For example, one might think: 'Oh, this flirty relationship with my colleague M. is fun, but wait until s/he finds out that I live with someone, then it will all be over. Our project will be finished by then, anyway, I hope. We work well together, but we can't keep it up. I can't stand the strain! Unless I am

prepared to be committed, this relationship has to be short term... because (such thinking assumes) the only relationship possible is an exclusive one, it has to eventually become deeper or it cannot be.'

This sounds logical, on the surface, but why don't such thoughts enter a man's head when he is working on a project with another man? What is in the back of his mind when working with a woman? That it is forbidden to be involved with a female colleague if he 'already' has a personal relationship with a woman? That it is unseemly to work 'too closely' with a woman, because it means you are betraying another woman? Other men he works with?

This could explain why some male bosses might have trouble continuing a many year relationship with a high-level female colleague, i.e. thinking that such an alliance or relationship is really, at bottom, a betrayal of their relationship with their wife (or girlfriend), and so it must be enjoyed for the short term, but eventually end – and not end with the woman's promotion, but with her leaving!

Think of the advantages of building a long-term solid relationship of another kind in that same situation.

If men use the truisms of private life to understand (or misunderstand) the opposite sex

Think of the advantages of building a long-term solid relationship of another kind in that same situation.

at work, they may find they are falling on their faces; this is not reality now (was it ever?).

What about women? Women too can fall back on the truisms of private life to understand (or misunderstand) men at work. Are men more or less the same at work as they are in private life? Can/should women employ the same strategies with men at work, as with men in private?

Men's Attitudes to Love and Sex with Women: Why They Matter at Work

Men are often used to working with other men via one set of rules, while they expect and understand another etiquette with women in private. Since men's lives have been divided into 'public' (work) and 'private', most men have learned two sets of behaviours. Some men try to retain their work mentality in private life, insisting they and women involved with them be 'rational', while other men feel that their most basic, fundamental self ('real self') is their self as it is in private, and try to show as much as possible of that side of themselves at the office, their 'real selves', the more 'human' and emotional side.

The traditional segue-way between women and men has been in love, sex and private life, therefore the attitudes a man learned towards women in private life (while growing up) are the attitudes he may irrationally apply to a woman at work – even though he doesn't know her, doesn't plan to 'get to know her', and couldn't be less interested.

If a man is nervous about his own private life (not sure it's perfect, etc.), then this can also cause his reaction to women at work to be less than rational, less than neutral.

Therefore it can be helpful in business to know as much as possible about the deeper psychology behind men's view of love and sexual relations with women in private.

Information from Hite Research:
Do Men Like Being in Love with Women?

Another striking fact to emerge from my research is that a majority of men claim that they did not marry the woman they most passionately loved, saying that they are proud of this, proud to have kept control of themselves, 'done the right thing'. (Why was it 'the right thing'?)

In fact, most men say that being in love makes them nervous, uneasy, therefore they try to overcome any feeling of being 'too close' to a woman. Does this include women at work? As one put it: 'It's like a kind of contamination...'

What Does Love Mean to Men?

Many men say they want to avoid falling in love. Or if (heaven forbid!) they find themselves in love with a woman, endeavour to 'calm things down' or extricate themselves entirely from the relationship. At times, they may even strike out and hurt a woman if they feel 'too close', perceiving her as a 'threat'.

It is often considered a mark of 'true masculinity' or 'super-stud-dom' to be single – almost all male movie heroes in films are single.

It is often considered a mark of 'true masculinity' or 'super-stud-dom' to be single.

For some men, the foreign quality a woman can seem to have – her sexuality and identity a sort of lunar landscape – is mirrored in his own lack of comprehension of his own psychic landscape when in love – causing a terror of unnameable proportions which is projected onto the woman (or even a man) who is 'causing it'.

A young construction worker (who also graduated from university in political science, but found no job there) is frank in describing his terror in the face of love – as well as the fun he is having with his girlfriend:

'I am living off and on with my lover. I work building and restoring houses and apartments, for the moment. Every day is a real struggle, both with work and with our relationship together, but I love her and we have the best sex life I've ever had – the greatest.

'For me, being in love is not exactly the fairy-tale sugar-coated happily ever after story of the movies, novels and "great" moments in history. At times it has been painful, and a lot of times I have felt unsure of what was going on and my role in it.

'When I first met her, I had decided never to go out with or get involved with anybody again, as it was always a nightmare, including one very difficult relationship which ended in disaster. But I felt this unbelievable sexual, physical and personality attraction to her as soon as I met her. She was so irresistible and sexy I couldn't control myself. I have never desired someone's body as much.'

'When I fell in love with my lover, I felt as if I had discovered my emotions. But immediately I was

also in turmoil. Although she made me feel alive and exhilarated, this great "love" also made me fear obligations. I was afraid. When she told me she needed me, I got scared, because I thought that now I would have to be a "husband" like my father and tied to her.

'When I was in my teens I thought love always implied settling down, getting married, having children, with me getting a job and supporting the lot of them, like my father and grandfather before me. It meant sacrificing one's true feelings to put on the appearance of being happy all the time. I also believed that marriage was inevitable, as everyone just gets married finally, and forgets about what they really want to do. I disliked the idea of traditional marriage on many levels, but felt like a weirdo for not liking it. I thought there was something wrong with me for not liking the "normal" way of life for couples.

'The result was, the relationship got very rocky because I felt so torn between my lover and my ideas of obligation, duty – I felt that I was getting into something that demanded a great deal of sacrifice from me. At times it seemed burdensome, so I would rebel by saying or doing something to hurt her, since I thought she was the cause of my tension. Really it was my idea of her expectations that was burdensome – not her expectations.

'I assumed that I was trapped, because she said she loved me. I also assumed she couldn't hurt me even if I hurt her. I refused to believe she was in control and could leave me if I made her unhappy. I didn't want to believe that she could break up with me. I didn't want to accept her as an equal (emotionally), and I didn't want to be vulnerable. (But I wanted her to be vulnerable.)

'The way I was raised (most men's mothers treat them like kings, so men feel like any other woman should too) it's not worth fighting very much with a woman to make the relationship better since another woman will be glad to please me – at least that's the way I used to think. But every time I decided to give up my lover, I couldn't eat, my stomach felt like it had been stomped on, and I had tension headaches.

'Today I am sure that fighting with my lover helped me to develop as a person. Even though the fights were terrible, it's really a precious thing to know someone so closely.'

A majority of men in my research for *The Hite Report on Male Sexuality* said that they had not married the woman they most loved, and not only that, that they were proud of their decision, felt they had made the right choice. Why? Because they had 'stayed in control of their feelings', and not let 'sexual emotion' take over their lives… never mind that they felt lonely sometimes…

Yet, a majority of these same men were having extra-marital sex during their 'safe love' marriages – and not so long after marriage. Most in middle age felt that somehow life was passing them by, that 'the marriage' had 'tied them down', and given them not enough in return.

Fortunately, this is a part of the male psyche that men are now in process of rethinking – as seen not only in my research, but also in the public debate that accompanied the trial of President Clinton re his sexual relationship with White House intern Monica Lewinsky.

Many men today are questioning their own beliefs, asking themselves: what is the meaning of love, what do I want from it, what is the rightful place of love and a woman in a man's life?

Many men today are questioning their own beliefs, asking themselves: what is the meaning of love, what do I want from it, what is the rightful place of love and a woman in a man's life?

What is Emotional Equality?

Culturally exaggerated 'differences' between women and men throw monkey-wrenches into relationships. They make it seem like men and women are from different planets, and can never communicate or be really happy. This isn't true, but what is the problem?

'I resent him, sometimes, and I don't know why', one woman muses. 'I have a vague sense of doubt and unease, and wonder if our relationship can get better. I feel on the defensive, but when I try to explain things to him, my reasons sound petty.'

Another explains:

'Men in my life hurt me with their power behaviours – like turning their back on me, walking off, shutting the door when I am trying to say something. They think they don't have to listen or be bothered, it's "my problem", my "hysteria". No matter how much I plead, they just show contempt. Like when I ask J. to screw in a light bulb, help out a little around the house without being asked, he just tells me in a nasty voice: "I don't take orders from you." I can't seem to change this pattern, no matter how I try.'

What these women are describing is an entrenched, largely unrecognized system of emotional discrimination. These psychological patterns are often called 'human nature', but they are not. While clichés say there will never be an end to this 'battle of the sexes', that it is built into 'human nature', this 'battle' is neither inevitable, nor 'human nature'.

Words commonly used to label how women feel and behave in various situations are pejorative to women. Consider for example phrases such as 'she's insecure', 'she's aggressive', or a 'nag' or a 'tease'. Where do such phrases come from? There are no such similar phrases generally in common use for men. Underlying inequalities in social and legal status have come to be reflected in psychological jargon, depicting women as 'less psychologically healthy' than men. These labels are a result of prejudice and not reality.

Still today, women often lack positive words to describe what they are feeling and what is happening, especially in personal relationships. This can be frustrating when a woman is trying to make a man 'see' or 'hear' what is going on, or how things could change.

'Superior' psychological status for men is built into our vocabularies and attitudes in private life. This status is made the main focus of each interaction in a relationship, since men are assigned a power identity (called 'normal male behaviour'), and women are/were assigned the 'helper' and 'love-giver' status.

'Superior' psychological status for men is built into our vocabularies and attitudes in private life.

One young man describes a light dawning on him about this:

'At times being in love with her seemed burdensome, so I would say or do something to hurt her... we had a lot of fights. Really it was my idea of her expectations that was burdensome, not her expectations. She didn't expect much, she didn't expect me to pay, she always shared. But it wasn't only money... Today I am sure that fighting with my lover helped me develop as a person. Even though the fights were terrible, I'm glad we stuck together. It's a precious thing to know someone so closely.'

The old 'emotional contract' contains psychological stereotypes which put women at a disadvantage and men in an isolated 'ogre' position, encouraging distrust and psychological warfare. They lead to futile, circular 'discussions' about 'the relationship' making neither person happy.

Now in many relationships and female-male interactions at work, as well, there is a change taking place: a new kind of relating is beginning to emerge. There is an attempt to find a new way of relating, a new relationship with emotional equality.

How Do Women Feel Managing Men?

How do women feel about new interactions with men?

Only 4 per cent of women work in jobs where they oversee a significant number of men, so the response of most women is 'Give us some men to manage, then we'll tell you!'

It sounds like every woman's dream – power reversal: 'Wow! Power over 50 men! A dream come true!', but women working these jobs often tell another story.

'Wow! Power over 50 men! A dream come true!'

Here is just one story from Female Managers Anonymous:

'I had a job, just out of college, managing 200 men. They were a sales force. There were a few incidents, but in general, they treated me very well. Eventually they even became very protective of me, they got bristly if anyone said anything unpleasant to me, etc. There were two groups, some days I would go out working with one, some days with the other; they became very possessive. In the end I left. After six months, I just left. I couldn't take it any more. I felt locked into a role that wasn't who I was, unable to breathe, like they were all observing me all the time...'

Most women say that, typically, a woman is working for a man, or sometimes for another woman. 'Even today', women rarely manage men. Then, when they do, they can describe a discomfort that makes them decide not to continue – a notable exception being Margaret Thatcher, who remained in office as Prime Minister in the UK 'managing men' for many years. Nevertheless, women are starting to hold these jobs, despite the psychological awkwardness and unnecessary stress (due to old gender stereotypes), and will do this more and more in coming years.

A new female psychology is emerging, one that has little time for old stereotypes and one that takes a 'no-nonsense' approach to the tasks in hand.

A new female psychology is emerging, one that has little time for old stereotypes and one that takes a 'no-nonsense' approach to the tasks in hand.

A New Female Psychology at Work

To manage men, what do women need to know?

One woman's advice: 'First of all, you need to know what men really think of you.' Typical clichés men have about women (we all know them if we are brutally honest):

● women get in the way at work

● women never stop talking, especially whinging

● women love to sit around varnishing their nails

● women get moody at certain times of the month (and turn into terrible monsters)

● women go shopping every lunch hour and spend fortunes.

Once you know and face the stereotypes, when they come up, you can laugh them off, knowing they are only hot air, not a realistic assessment of you or your job performance.

This is easier said than done, since it is new for women to be in responsible positions at work. Although women have been getting very high scores on school tests for years, this has not generally translated into most getting top-level jobs later.

The few women who do break through – especially through middle management into upper management – are dealing with some very tough psycho-sexual issues, juggling not only 'home and family' but also 'old thinking' and 'new thinking' inside their own heads. The confusion is increased by a social misunderstanding about what 'new thinking' is: it is not, as is often implied, a free-for-all – you don't have to play by the rules any more'; what is really new that is emerging is an ethical combination of what is right, traditional ethics, with individual judgements – not a simplistic 'let's throw out all the rules and get natural'.

What Should a Woman's Management Style Be?

Clichés about 'the new professional woman' abound – heaven forbid if she is 'the boss'!

Women 'in charge' or with careers are often depicted by media as power-mad monsters. Think of the cartoons of Margaret Thatcher, or feminist leaders, as screaming ogres and tyrants who nobody would want to be around. Or more recently à la *Disclosure* (the film with Michael Douglas) bring to mind film images of them as sexy, seductive predators who are slick, but 'sick'.

This is not the reality! The problem is that women are faced with these stereotyped attitudes in such a way that they are almost forced to bend over backwards to disprove them (the ogre–monster clichés), i.e. to be utterly and abnormally 'nice', 'calm', 'reasonable' and easygoing. The stereotypes are so shrill that often they block men and women's real working relationships. Never mind that things seem to be going fine, the stereotypes 'must be lurking just underneath the surface', look deeper and you'll surely find some hidden, dark desires...

My advice? Delete such software and open a new page.

Listen to your own real experiences, not to ancient hearsay. Women can be wonderful colleagues, bosses and subordinates – or terrible, just as men can. What makes women different as bosses? Mostly, just the socially created atmosphere surrounding the idea of a woman boss.

Can women today dare to show their strength, act powerful at work, or is this dangerous (because people will misinterpret their behaviour, 'see' it only through negative clichés) – as the following woman describes?

'I have the best job at one of the major television stations in the country. How did I get and keep this high-level job? By being as "unthreatening" as possible, and everyone's sob sister. I have never kept any secrets about myself, everyone here knows the problems I have in my marriage, why I took the decision to marry, and so on. So they feel they can tell me what's going on in their private lives, as well. I keep secrets very well, too. I am the only woman on their level here, so the only woman they can really talk to. Certainly they can't talk to each other! Oh no, that would make them seem too vulnerable. But they can talk to me… So I function sort of as the social hostess for the office, the only one they turn to when there's an office party to be organized and so on. Of course I do my work damn well too, so I can never be faulted, but I keep this low-key, I

don't brag or try to win awards like some of them do. I stay behind the scenes and don't promote myself too much; this way I keep on moving up without anybody seeming to notice.

'How did I get so smart? My mother taught me never to compete openly with men.[9] She meant, of course, if you want to get a man to marry you! But it applies just as much to men at work: don't compete, seem to be just a good serviceperson, and they think you're harmless, you're almost "one of them", you can't hurt anybody, "might as well promote her, she doesn't disturb anything". Such a simple principle. Why don't more women use it? Why scream and shout for your jobs, if it's so easy, just being low-key?'

Of course, if this were true, women now would be heads of half the major corporations of the world, and promotions would have happened more generally than they have. Many women do follow this policy of not saying anything controversial at work ('Me a feminist? Whatever gave you that idea? Feminists are too aggressive, I could never be one of them I just do my work, I don't like screaming.')

Since such women are reaping the rewards of the work of feminists who fought for women's right to work and be accepted in corporate jobs, they should review their attitude. Perhaps they need not 'scream', but shouldn't they speak up or in other ways pay back something into the mutual pool of efforts to create a more

9 Yet… if a woman does not act powerful and show her authority at work, she may never be 'seen' for promotion to the CEO level. It's a Catch-22 for women. Look too young and casual, and you'll be unthreatening, but also 'unseen' for your potential and achievements; act too 'mature' and 'serious', and you'll be a threat. Clearly, male and female attitudes on this must change.

equal work playing field? Keeping a low profile doesn't always lead to safety or being rewarded for loyalty, as Jews, gypsies and homosexuals discovered during the Second World War, when they tried to fit in, keep a low profile, in Germany and elsewhere, thus hoping not to be noticed or given a hard time; they were hunted all the same.

The first woman CEO of Hewlett-Packard, appointed July 1999, said she did not want to be seen mainly 'as a woman' but as head of her company. This is understandable and correct; however, since she is the first woman to become head of one of the top 100 Fortune global companies, like it or not, she symbolizes more than 'the right choice for the job'. She is correct to point out that people should judge her for her job performance, not her sex; but she is wrong not to say that she hopes that there will be other women appointed to similar positions in the near future. Trying to blend in and be accepted 'as a normal member of the executive team' isn't always the best strategy (think of Margaret Thatcher). In fact, the reverse way of behaving can provide more job protection in the end, i.e. helping other women and once in a while pointing out that things are changing, that more equality will create a better working environment. In visibility is semi-safety.

Did the television executive just cited resent being the office 'agony aunt'? Yes and no; men didn't have to perform this sort of female emotional role ('sob sister') for each other, men could shine and receive awards and be promoted – but she was proud of herself for having found a way through the thicket, a way to 'beat the system', being the only woman in top management in her company.

Women's styles of power

There is some truth to the idea that many women do have a different managerial style than men's; many people talk about women's coalition-building managing skills, a valuable asset women bring to corporations. What style of management should a woman have? Tough-as-nails was all the rage when the first executive women broke ground, but now that is considered as a little passé. It is OK for a woman, like a man, to opt for whatever style suits her – if he or she is basically tough and brusque, OK, but if the tough-cookie style is only exterior style, today a woman or man can opt for a more moderate style and still be taken seriously in an executive position.

How to Be an Authority Figure

Even today, there are clichés about powerful women, but few real models of women over 40 who hold positions of authority. What should a woman 'look like' as she grows older and more powerful? How should she handle or display her authority? What symbols will others understand, which does a woman herself want? These are the questions for the new models of femininity we are now trying to construct, and which women will construct in the next few years.

Listen to one woman's dilemma – a dilemma shared by many women in authority:

'How do I feel? I feel defensive – sometimes. Other times I feel extremely powerful and brilliant. I am quite senior at my firm. However, I feel like – perhaps I am wrong, I don't know – it is necessary to continue looking "young and vigorous", i.e. like I'm, in my thirties. I'm not, but

I more or less look it. This helps keep me seeming to be "in the swim", but has the disadvantage that younger women in the firm think I am their equivalent! In fact I am senior – by dint of my hard work and number of years with the firm, the amount of responsibility I carry and manage for the company. How can I portray myself with enough power and prestige, while not turning off the men? It's the men who control my pension, etc. Most, well *all,* the board members are men.'

Is power bad? Will you be hated and feared if you are the boss? Will you be only a symbol, no longer yourself? Many people do not want power inside corporations; leaders are lightning rods for love, hate, anger and various forms of emotion...

Is power bad? Will you be hated and feared if you are the boss? Will you be only a symbol, no longer yourself?

One young executive explains her doubts:

'I just can't imagine being "the boss". I feel like people would hate me. I wouldn't have anywhere to go, I would be boxed in and have to stay there and keep doing the same thing until retirement! It looks like a dead-end, to be the boss. I have more freedom where I am. I am not totally married to the system,'

Is this a changing reality – or are people (especially women) simply afraid to dream and take power?

'The boss' represents an authority figure, and sometimes one cannot imagine oneself in that role. If you grew up with a father the whole family hated and feared, this is more likely to be the case, but your view of power later may depend on how the father expressed his power to you.

One person could want to become boss to control others, use power in a crude way – while another could want to use it as a means of designing a new world, painting on the world a beautiful design and a legacy, like Conrad Hilton, or Elizabeth Arden. He or she could change the understanding of the nature of power, of what power and authority are.

Women may doubt themselves (yes, still) managing men and running organizations.

Do women still think of themselves somehow as not the ones with the right to run the world? The ones who must 'get jobs' from men or the system, or who have to find a place, somehow in massively powerful, untouchable entrenched system?

Most women don't think of themselves as the ones who 'see better than anyone else how to run the corporation' but think only: 'Maybe those men are confused, making a mess of it, but what can I do?'

Most women feel that they would not be accepted, that things they do would not have a chance of real success or make an enormous difference. This was what was amazing about Prime Minister Thatcher, that she seemed to believe in her right 'to tell men what to do'. She had a vision and followed it.

Listen to the very legitimate feelings one woman expresses:

'I don't want to blame women here for their slowness in getting ahead – women's progress, in any case, is not slow! – but neither do I want to simply bemoan and commiserate with women in a tough spot. I know women can make it out of this spot – it is only women who can make it to the next step. Women have a right to feel they have every right to run business, just as they already feel they have a right to control their own private lives. This will get them ahead running businesses.'

Many men, too, doubt that the system is theirs. Most do not envision taking over the reins of one of the larger cultural or business institutions, but think this is someone else's right. The reason is that we all grew up 'out of power', with people 'bigger than us' running things. Were we told that we would grow up to take power over them? No, usually we were given the message that we would grow up, we might do great things, but we would never be greater than our parents! Transferring this message to our encounter with the world, we learned that there would always be the 'parents' 'running things' somewhere 'up there', and we should simply try our best to find something to do within the system that we liked and that could make us successful within it and financially solvent.

What if we were brought up to think that the system is in constant process of transformation, and that it needs us to really make it happen? This is or could be the radical promise of 'corporate capitalism' and of democracy: each person is empowered. One of the basic reasons, noted in *The Hite Report on the Family*, for our slow willingness to really take control of 'the system' (that famous 1960s' phrase) is our fear of 'the parents', lingering in our psyche's past childhood. The 'growing up' process is rarely (allowed to be) completed, it seems.

Brain Software Commands – For Women

Many women are developing new mental software to go with the office.

Many find the atmosphere of the workplace a tonic and an aid to making some of the changes in themselves and their lives they want to experience. The work world can be more rewarding than the world of private life: at work, women often say they face less discrimination (!) than in private – even though the difference in pay scales is clear in most firms – because at least at work there is objective proof of the work they are producing, that can be judged by others.

> Most women today have been spending quite a bit of time on rearranging and changing their mental software; the woman you knew last year is probably not at all the one you will get to know this year.

Most women today have been spending quite a bit of time on rearranging and changing their mental software; the woman you knew last year is probably not at all the one you will get to know this year.

⊖ SOFTWARE TO DELETE

❶ If I'm successful, men may hate me.

❷ If I'm successful, women may hate me, call me conceited, power-mad and unsisterly.

❸ If I'm 'too successful', people may call me a 'screaming, demanding bitch' (and no one will love me, I won't feel loveable).

❹ If I'm young, men in charge may like me or be nice to me, but they won't promote me. ('Oh, you'll go off and have babies', 'You're so young and pretty, a nice man will get you!') This can be flattering on one level, but negative and insulting on another.

❺ If I'm older and look like I know what I am doing, this makes some men nervous around me.

They wonder: 'Could she try to unseat me, get my job? Shouldn't she be at home? There must be some reason her work is not really good enough, anyway. Who does she think she is? She's enjoyed a lot of time with the company, now it's time to move on, etc.' Yet most men won't have this attitude with male colleagues, who are indeed trying to get their jobs or be promoted above them. Why? Because this is considered normal! A man even admires another man for trying to get ahead of him.

❻ If I'm not attractive, I won't be able to get and keep a good job. (Or, If I'm too attractive, I won't be able to get and keep a good job.)

Women often have a build-up of frustration and irritation with men – both in personal and work life – since so many men have used old clichés to block women. This build-up can cause a woman to explode at the 99th person (male) who exhibits them, but you can use your inner anger (justified) to 1) move your own thinking radically forward about the situation at your company; 2) show the man doing or saying whatever how elegantly the situation can be better, for both of you. Use your power of intelligence to make the situation work for you.

Brain Software Commands – For Women

SOFTWARE TO DELETE

Someone else 'older and wiser' is running major corporations. I can't even begin to imagine it.

SOFTWARE TO INSTALL

What qualities and experience do I have to bring to the executive level of a large corporation? What would I like to contribute?

Female Authority and Power

Most women are not used to having authority over men, except perhaps over a brother when younger, or over their own children (after a fashion!).

Most women are not used to having authority over men, except perhaps over a brother when younger, or over their own children (after a fashion!).

Sometimes women feel no one respects their authority: 'I'm at the same level as a guy who works with me, Tony. But the secretaries all cue up to him, open doors and refer clients to him. To me, they act like I'm one of them.'

Many women in authority have mixed feelings about their relationship to other women working in the firm with less authority.

A woman boss says:

'How do I relate to the receptionists? I feel very uncomfortable with them, because I feel like, when I arrive in the morning with an important client already waiting, that they're lower in stature than I am, and that this isn't "nice" of me, and also that I can't acknowledge this difference in status like a man could, I don't want to be considered "arrogant" or look like a "dominating woman", so I always smile and say hello. But sometimes they can be arrogant or dismissive with me ("because I'm just a mere woman"?) or "forget" to do things I say, things they don't forget to do for the male executives. I try to smile and act nonchalant in these situations...'

Another woman boss complains about the secretaries in her firm, saying they prefer the men and don't do as good a job for her:

'I used to work as a secretary, and I know quite well what the job is. When you answer the telephone, you state the name of the company or the person whose telephone you are answering then wait to hear what the person calling wants. If whoever she or he wants to speak to is not there or is in a meeting, you offer with enthusiasm to take the person's name and number. Between answering telephone calls, you write letters and do filing, or whatever else. This is the job of a secretary. Without a good secretary, nobody can function.

'But now, some secretaries have a habit of acting like they don't have to do things, if they are the slightest bit complicated or seem unusual to them – especially when they are very young. With some of them, you get the impression that they were hired because they were "cute and non-threatening" to male bosses who had to do the hiring, but that they grew up in households where they only had to exchange their "cuteness" for services rendered by the rest of the household: work and responsibility alien concepts to them. So, if one of these "decoration secretaries" answers the telephone, she doesn't say, "No, so-and-so is not here, can I help you? Can I take a message?" She just says, "No, so-and-so is not here", and if you try to leave your name and telephone number she repeats every time "What?" (getting the number wrong each time) and (about your

name) "Uh, how do you spell it?" Then after several tries, "Hold on a minute...".'

In order to display more authority, women try sometimes to dress 'correctly' or to be overly official. The tendency for women is to fall into one of two categories, i.e. to become in their new role either too official and hard, or too 'nice' and friendly.

It's no wonder that women might be a tad self-conscious in executive positions, with the eyes of the world (their sisters, other women, and men, of course) on them, just waiting to be critical and find an excuse to say they can't do it, can't handle it. Newspaper cartoons picture women in authority positions as 'school teachers' or 'mothers' – because they have no idea of any other picture. Yet women were only school teachers during the last 100 years, women had to invent that career too.

Today, women are breaking out of the old ideas of women as either 'just as good as men' as managers, or 'isn't women's style of management more holistic?', leaving behind such clichés, experimenting with new, individual styles.

Does a woman have the right to 'take power'? Yes.

Does a woman have the right to 'take power'? Yes.

How Women Can Feel Comfortable and Good in Positions of Authority (and So Can Those Around Them...)

'To be powerful, a woman doesn't have to do anything but act like a powerful woman', I have heard it said. Yes, and I would add also think like a powerful woman, that is, not like a 'daughter'

When you think of it, there are no or few positive icons or symbols of women with power over others, although the ancient Greeks had Athena and other symbols of positive power in women. The traditional symbols of modern Western society are all male: Moses, Jesus, The Beatles, Napoleon.

Many women are currently trying to make this shift in their mentality, but they find they are walking a fine line between pleasing themselves and pleasing the powerful corporate fiefdoms around them, usually made up of men, i.e. all-male corporate boards of directors, etc.

Yet it's great when capable women have power, because this gives everyone a feeling of confidence and energy for working towards mutual goals. Places like New York City, whose government employs 100,000 people, show quite clearly how this works. Having benefited a few years ago from a quota system, now the city has had years of experience with women in high places.

It's great when capable women have power, because this gives everyone a feeling of confidence and energy for working towards mutual goals.

Brain Software Commands – For Women

Follow these simple steps and exercises to change your software about power and 'the corporation'.

− SOFTWARE TO DELETE

'I could never make it to the top of the corporation. Anyway, if I did, I couldn't have a proper home life too, so what do I really want?'

+ SOFTWARE TO INSTALL

'If I want to get a lot of power or be on top in this organization, I can. But this will mean putting my mind to it in new ways, i.e. it is not enough to 'be the best' at what I do. This is a naïve and 'safe' way of hoping to get ahead; it says 'I'm good' therefore You, the powerful ones, must graciously bring me into your group. The world is tougher than that. No one will hand me power on a silver platter; I must lead, believe in myself and then others will follow.'

'The reins of this organization are just begging for my touch. I have more to offer this organization than anyone else. Let me set about finding the places of entry, the rungs of the ladder to climb up.'

SOFTWARE TO DELETE

'The best way to get ahead here is simply show how good my work is, to perform to the best of my ability – and this performance will be noted and rewarded.'

SOFTWARE TO INSTALL

'My performance is extremely important, and I will work to do the best job I can. But expecting this to be rewarded may or may not be realistic; therefore, especially as I am a woman, I must put forth my case and also begin to simply take on the role I envision for myself, without "permission".'

SOFTWARE TO DELETE

'What is the best way to put forth my case for wanting to be CEO?'

SOFTWARE TO INSTALL

'What position do I need to be in to have the possibility of taking over power of this organization? Do I need the support of others? Which groups? Groups of men? Groups of women?'

'I have a lot to offer. I will keep putting forward my abilities, and aims – both for my own career and for the company. On the other hand, I won't just 'be the best' but also point out in memos that I am trying to be the best so I can get a promotion, as fast as possible!'

You are a woman at the executive level of a corporation. Most of those you work with and manage are men. Should you deal with this situation, your heightened visibility (are you 'the corporations's experiment in having women in top management'?), by:

- being as low-key as possible, trying to blend in and do nothing controversial, showing that a woman can be a team player too

- being twice as well-prepared as your colleagues, performing better than anyone else, while remaining friendly and 'non-threatening'

- being aloof and removed so that no one will misunderstand you and think they should relate to you 'like a woman'?

Choose one option.

Brain Game 5.2

How can a woman overcome the tendency of some men to resent her and motivate them to want to follow her?

Program yourself like this:

'I am vibrant, amazingly bright, know best where to go with the company. Others here will be happy going there with me, and even happier when they see where we've arrived, all our success!'

Brain Game 5.3

What to do when your higher status makes a man angry

The first issue is to recognize the anger for what it is. This may be difficult, because even to him, the issue spoken of is something different, he may not believe he is angry about 'That'. Hopefully, the situation will never progress so far that it gets out of hand, because you have handled the situation well until now, sensing vulnerability. But there are always some times and some places that are just not manageable!

Follow these steps to make good colleague status again:

Try the Four Ss System (see Chapter 2).

Discussion: Advantages and disadvantages of 'male' and female' approaches to work.

● What are the advantages of traditional male psychology at work?

If traditional male psychology has been to keep one's cards close to the chest, this could be good for not stepping on anyone's toes at the office, but creates problems with interchanging ideas and communicating.

If traditional male psychology has been to keep one's cards close to the chest, this could be good for not stepping on anyone's toes at the office, but creates problems with interchanging ideas and communicating.

● What are the advantages of traditional female psychology at work?

If traditional female psychology has meant being warm and listening to others, this can be good for communication at the office – at least the woman hears others, but perhaps she is not heard or listened to herself, thus forcing her to learn new strategies for stating her points and getting heard.

Brain Software Commands – For Women

SOFTWARE TO DELETE

'Men at work are formidable, stuffy conformists who have lost their individuality – and don't like me because I have mine.'

SOFTWARE TO INSTALL

'Men's behaviour at work is subtle. I want to learn to decipher their language, not necessarily to always speak it, but to converse better.'

When a Man has a Woman Boss

Seminar: Training men not to freak out if a woman is promoted over them.

A special problem for some men may be having a female boss. How can men learn not to freak out if a woman is promoted over them? Sometimes a man, without realizing it, will try to regain dominance over a woman or a situation by putting a woman down, either to colleagues or to the woman directly in front of other men at work – even by a sexual innuendo – to bond with the men in the corporation and exclude the woman as 'punishment'.

This not-new version of 'us vs them' is something that most people, when it is pointed out to them, will try to move beyond. This is especially true when more creative paths are indicated, when other, new ways to view the dynamics of the situation are made clear.

Fear of women in power

How do men feel? Many men still have images springing to mind of school teachers or mothers 'telling them what to do'. And as they learned at puberty, 'a woman telling you what to do should always be told to be quiet!' (See page 123.)

Today this attitude is counterproductive and out of date, so how can a man quickly get rid of such a knee-jerk reaction?

Brain Game 5.4

You are a man and a woman is promoted above you. You react by:

● not complaining, but watching to see how often she does something wrong, to help her by criticizing her errors

● trying to become friends with her

● talking to one of your best friends outside the corporation about your feeling that maybe you were more qualified, but 'today women have to be promoted' – until you can see another strategy for getting ahead at work.

What are the various effects of each of these choices?

Paul once found himself losing out on a promotion, while a woman was given the job. He felt very bad, and also had the job of explaining what had happened to his mother, in whom he had confided his hopes of getting the new job. He found himself saying into the telephone, even though he did not feel right about it: 'They told me they really wanted to promote me, but they couldn't; there's a kind of quota in the company now, unofficially, and they had to promote a certain number of women this year. I'll get the next job, they said.'

It can be embarrassing for a man not to be moved ahead, in a way it is not embarrassing to women, since women have not been expected to 'get ahead' as men have. This puts men in an awkward spot; although quite a few men today say that they would like less work and less responsibility, most don't like to 'lose'; and few really seem to relish the joys of staying home cooking...

Brain Software Commands –
For Men

- SOFTWARE TO DELETE

'I grew up to believe work and business would
be an all-male environment and that women do
not belong there.'

+ SOFTWARE TO INSTALL

'Working together with women is normal and
offers new energy and vitality. I like it.'

- SOFTWARE TO DELETE

'She may be a bitch. I'd better be careful.'

+ SOFTWARE TO INSTALL

'How can we make a good team? How can
working well with her further my career?'

Your Opinion…

What is your opinion and experience? What do you think? What have been *your* experiences of what's been discussed in this chapter?

Please use this space to write your remarks, or alternatively you may e-mail comments to the *Sex and Business* website at www.sexandbusiness.com/myopinion. Naturally, you may express yourself anonymously.

_____

_____

_____

_____

_____

_____

Women have changed their relationships with men enormously during the last 25 years, but only begun to change their relationships with each other. It's as if, for the past two decades, women were hypnotized into thinking that only by fixing their gaze steadily on men, 'making it work with men', could things improve. This was partially true since in realpolitik, men held and still do hold most of the power at work; thus a woman could 'waste her time' relating to another woman. Women were not power centres.

How are women doing,

working

with other women?

How are Women Doing, Working with Other Women?

Today, more and more women find themselves relating to other women at work – in both 'old-style' corporate environments and thriving self-owned businesses – with men as suppliers, consumers and bankers.

This is a new situation, many women working with other women as their bosses, secretaries or as professional colleagues. How do these relationships function?

Although women have psychologically complex work relationships, little attempt has been made to get an overview of the psychology of women's relations at work, especially not in 'the new workplace'.

> Although women have psychologically complex work relationships, little attempt has been made to get an overview of the psychology of women's relations at work, especially not in 'the new workplace'.

Negative clichés abound – 'Women are envious, two-faced snakes – especially career women! They're more ruthless than men, they'll stab another woman in the back at the drop of a hat.' Or: 'Women are moody, touchy and insecure – difficult to work with.' Obviously, such clichés are – to say the least – simplistic. Men fight among themselves just as much as women and people don't say

of them 'they can't work together'. What is really going on?

Relationships between women at work, increasingly important, are still in the process of being sorted out. Old clichés begin to sound ridiculous: 'Put two women together and all hell will break loose', but still hold a grain of truth. Why? Many women have an inferiority complex about being female, as opposed to male, i.e. they believe men are more important at work.

Women, like men, have picked up virus-like stereotypes that preach women's inferiority, 'craziness' or 'desperateness'. (Why should women be different in their view of women than anybody else?!) Women may have good reason to be angry with other women sometimes, because women, too, can hold prejudices against women, and act on them.

Most upsetting is that another woman can use a double standard – hair-raisingly, often without realizing she's doing it – to bully a women into obeying the system's rules and accepting 'her place' as second class in her job. Ridiculously, such views are often not 'seen' as hostile and condescending, but as 'how things are'. (Why take it personally, it's just garden-variety scorn of women...??!)

However, it's no wonder women have a double standard for judging men and women, since these attitudes are engraved at birth – 'It's a Boy!', announced with jubilation, as opposed to 'It's a girl – well, then, she can help her mother with the housework.' But it's doubly disappointing and infuriating when women use this prejudice against other women.

New to today's developing situation, there is a quality of special awareness, mental luminosity, that many women share. A spirit that is growing.

Business Manners Necessary for Women Working Together to be Successful

What are the business manners necessary for women who work together to be successful?

A woman need not be perfect, or 'think perfectly', in order to have better interactions with other women at work. On what basis can she have a successful interaction? Should she treat all women as generic 'women' and 'be nice to women'? Scrutinize the behaviour of each and every woman on the scene to decide which ones are 'good ones' and 'bad ones', those you can trust and those you can't? Should she just avoid dealing with other women, keep her distance psychologically?

Women have changed their relationships with men enormously during the last 25 years, but only begun to change their relationships with each other. It's as if, for the past two decades, women were hypnotized into thinking that only by fixing their gaze steadily on men, 'making it work with men', could things improve. This was partially true since in realpolitik, men held and still do hold most of the power at work; thus a woman could 'waste her time' relating to another woman. Women were not power centres.

Yet this is no longer true. Today, a woman with a career often finds that she must make her relationships with other women succeed

New to today's developing situation, there is a quality of special awareness, mental luminosity, that many women share. A spirit that is growing.

professionally, build power bases with female colleagues. This is a special challenge for women for two reasons: 1) two female colleagues working together often have fingers pointed at them, 'Yeah the girls stick together', etc. (not said about men); and 2) most women do not accept simply imitating male hierarchies in business, but want to make a new style of interaction.

To succeed in existing corporations, women seem to need to make their relationships with each other work in 'male-style' teams, hierarchies. Yet most women are not used to hierarchies with each other (except in mother–daughter relationships), not sure they like or want to participate in them.

Although many women are not happy with the idea of hierarchy as the only way the world can be efficiently organized, the corporate world is based on hierarchical power structures, along the lines of chains of command, as in military units, or soccer/sports teams.

How should women relate to other women in hierarchies? Do some women have the right to power over other women, or should all women be equals?

In order to retain the esprit of solidarity and friendliness many women want, women must now invent work relationships that are

In order to retain the esprit of solidarity and friendliness many women want, women must now invent work relationships that are hierarchical in a new way.

hierarchical in a new way.[1] This restructuring is difficult because of the prevailing atmosphere containing de-validating stereotypes, as noted: 'Oh, women always argue, they're not seriously capable of working together to lead a country or anything else – especially not a business! They should leave serious decision-making to men!'

Nevertheless, women can, together, form real power bases. This is a psychological challenge for women raised to believe that only men are secure power bases. (This lack of confidence may start, according to my research, when a girl loses confidence in her mother's willpower, observing her mother accepting a second-class position in family, finding this depressing and dispiriting – and as a result, beginning to identify with her father and men only, a pattern that continues in work relationships; see *The Hite Report on the Family*.)

Women face an amazing array of challenges. Perhaps the most difficult is combating the

Women face an amazing array of challenges.

obscure psychological prejudices that come at them from various directions, including from inside their own minds. These demons are too often unrecognized as the prejudices they are, or only hazily understood, and pass unchallenged,[2] their sting felt but not consciously registered.

If women are said to be 'edgy' at work, this is not because of their 'natures' (or 'time of the month'...) but because the psychological landscape they are confronted with is a minefield. A woman must be careful to side-step men's fears of 'women taking control', and at the same time, learn how to relate to other women as 'superiors', 'inferiors' and 'equals', depending on the situation – make friends, but still try for promotions and advancement beyond 'the other woman'. This can feel dangerous and uncomfortable.

Also, to add to the confusion, women find there are quite a few 'old-style' women at offices (including young, trendy women) who are not 'conscious' of issues between women; they may frequently hold unexamined stereotypes in their minds, still regarding men as 'better'.

This is confusing if a woman is trying to build collegiality, or a new style of hierarchical respect and courtesy with other women in the office. For example, a woman aware of power issues between women may be surprised when she tries to build bridges with another woman that she is greeted with suspicion and rebuffed. Approaching her colleague in a 'very

---

1 There are now alternatives in business styles, of course. Especially new styles of consensual management are emerging. These non-hierarchical organizations are creating more equal playing fields.

2 Also, most women understandably feel that work is not really 'the time' to have a confrontation about prejudices, their careers will progress best, they believe, if they overlook negative slurs.

friendly' way, she can unwittingly make the other woman feel nervous and doubtful, as if she is expected to be 'friendly' and 'co-operative' simply because she's a woman; she fears getting involved in a marginalized 'women's group' or 'ghetto'...

Other women feel irritated with female colleagues' efforts to initiate relationships, believing:'What's the sense of being with a woman when you can go where the power is, be with a man?' Since such a woman usually knows it is not 'politically correct' to say or admit this, she may smile warmly at other women, feigning interest. How can a woman tell apart the women who do want to develop serious work relationships and alliances, and those who only want to appear 'with it'?

Let's look at the most problematic area, hierarchical relationships among women.

Secretaries' Stories about their Female Bosses

Many women, (especially younger women) say: 'Why aren't women where I work nicer to me, why do they so often stab me in the back?' Or 'My boss is a bat from hell, a bitch on wheels. She is hard to deal with, I think she's jealous or something because I'm younger – what should I do?'

This complaint must be real because it is voiced so often, but it may also reflect gender-based expectations of women, the expectation that women be always 'sweet, helpful and friendly' etc. – things not expected of men. Women are generally expected to be more loving than men, perfect 'little mothers' (more perfect than real mothers are!) to take care of them.

Some secretaries love their bosses, but some hate them. As one secretary describes her female boss:

'My boss loses her temper lots of times – in fact, almost every day there is some terrible crisis that happens – either the computer breaks down or the telephone messages are crucially messed up, or someone changes their mind or refuses to pay once they have received it, or delays, delays, delays – I guess she has a right to get unnerved, but I always seem to get the brunt of it, she claims I am the "cause" of it.

'Like yesterday, she started screaming when she came back from a lunch with one of the clients and saw I had had to stop working, because a computer, mystifyingly, had stopped. I was afraid to go on, so I just waited for her. When she saw I was not finished, she started shouting at me – in front of two other people – and told me I could never do anything by myself, I was never right, and I had to stay late and she would not pay me extra until everything was fixed. I felt humiliated with the two people watching, their mouths open, waiting to see what would happen. I had to agree in front of them or lose my job. I felt humiliated and very small and stupid. But I understand my boss, I think she is trying really hard. Other times, she explains to me and I can see her side of it.

'But I'm doing the best I can, and I feel so upset at these times, that when I go home, I just cry alone in my room.'

Yet some secretaries say that working for a woman is great:

'My first job, after school, was as a filing clerk in an office. It was a small office, with three people, and the most fun I had was going out for coffee at lunchtime. (My salary was so bad, I could only afford coffee.) My boss was a man who rarely laughed.

'There was a woman in the next office to ours, she was running a travel agency. I always liked to look in her door, because the office was bright, with beautiful posters everywhere. Also, she had a big glass door, very wide, you could see in. I never went in, because (like I said) I had no money, certainly I didn't have enough money to take a vacation. One day, guiltily, I did stop anyway – or, I looked in the window, her door, so long that eventually it looked weird if I didn't go in, so I went in and pretended to browse through the brochures.

'She was on the telephone and stopped to apologize for not helping me, but said she was just so overburdened with work, she was all alone there, that could I wait just three minutes? I wondered why she worked all alone, but didn't say anything, I was so nervous. But I felt comfortable there, like she wouldn't be upset if I was "just browsing".

'To make a long story short, after I visited her office a few times, she realized I worked next door, and I started helping her out in her office lunchtimes and after hours. This progressed to full time, as her business got better. This is a really wonderful job, I love it. She pays me exactly the same as I got at the old job, but here I get a super discount on travel, and I can take a vacation every three months! Also, I meet a lot of people, whereas before, I only saw the other two dreary faces, including my boss' dyspeptic countenance. My social life is blooming.

'My boss is a young (well, about 35), dynamic and energetic, fun and pretty woman. She loves living. She has two or three boyfriends, but what she likes best is to work in the travel agency! We have a great time there, putting up new posters, deciding which promotions to feature, talking to customers, booking tickets, and just generally keeping up with all the paperwork, getting new paper for the fax machine, trying to figure out the e-mail, and so forth.

'I like working for her because, though she is the one who decides what we are doing, I get the feeling that my views count, and that what we are doing, we are doing together for a reason: to make a better salary and commission for ourselves! (She sometimes gives me a small part of her commission when she gets a big one, that is very nice – and I bought her champagne once, and flowers another time.) I feel more lively since I've been working there, my social life has blossomed, and I think it's because I'm taking clues from her. I like working in this atmosphere very much.'

The old bargain at work with men was, men give women salaries and promotions, and women give not only work, but also special care-taking, even sex, and an attitude of support, no competition for the man's job. Today, what is the trade-off between women?

Female Bosses' Stories about their Secretaries

The other side of the coin: women executives often say their secretaries seem to act like they would prefer to be working for a man, it would have more social status, glory that would reflect on them... but not always.

Yet one boss says her secretary gives more than her all, including all the side-perks men usually get:

'I have a wonderful secretary. Her name is Jill. One time I worked so hard, I worked 18 hours straight for two days in a row, I started staying on the couch in the office near the computer. She would come during the shift when I wasn't at the computer, and fill in the changes I hadn't finished. Once when I woke up, she had finished all my work and hers early, then cleaned the kitchen in the office, dusted my papers, and made me a beautiful breakfast! She can magically decipher my scribbles on papers and telephone people with the voice of an angel, saying the most charming things to let them know I couldn't get free to call them right then. She is a jewel. Is this what it's like having a great wife??? I wonder!'

Confusion can come about when, after a woman boss makes her assistant's working conditions pleasant, the 'secretary' confuses the relationship with one between 'equals' or girlfriends (anything else challenges her own, perhaps recent, self-esteem):

'I work for a big newspaper in the public relations department. I have worked here for almost 15 years, so I am used to seeing secretaries come and go. In fact, I have two secretaries ! (Yes, my job is important...) I have to keep on top of them all the time. I have to scream at them sometimes, they just don't hop to it like they would if I were a man. They are capable of being efficient, but they start to think I am a sweetie, "just a friend", another woman like them, when I am too nice and "understanding" (one tells me she had her period, the other tells me about her fight with her boyfriend, so she stayed out so she was late for work, and then very inefficient, keeps waiting for the phone to ring, him to call, etc.). I'm supposed to understand all this, or else I'm a bitch! But I wonder if they would expect a male boss to understand any of this??! Of course not! And also, they feel they have more status when they work for a man, "Oh, I work for Mr ___" etc. So I have to just "be a bitch" and let them hate me, it's the only way to get things done right.'

'I can't seem to find a really good secretary. I have a small business, a printing shop, and I need help. I can just afford to pay one person, and she has to be good. I work day and night to keep the business going. But she is ready to quit at the dash of 5.00 – hey it's tea time isn't it?! No matter what is happening. I finally had it out with her, when I am still working, she has to stay and work too, she can't just desert me. (Well, she can, but then I have to find someone else to replace her who is more serious about the job, cares more.) Would she be more involved if I were a man? Would she try harder, take it more seriously?

'Sometimes I think she thinks I am her mother, she is the teenage daughter who can act up, be rebellious and this is cute (though she's five years older than me really). Other times, I think she thinks she is the mother, barely putting up with the tantrums and tensions of her "terrible daughter". I don't like to work with someone around me with these attitudes towards the crises of my business. I think she would think a man was more justified in being tense than she thinks I am. But I am determined to make this business work, and probably most other secretaries would have a lot of the same prejudices. At least she's regular in getting here, loyal.'

Women's expectations of other women are different now after 25 years of 'feminism' and 'post-feminism'.

'My new secretary is working for a woman for the first time. She can be efficient, but she does little things that show a bad attitude, to sabotage me – like, for example, when I have to travel "forgetting" to make the plane reservation until the last minute. Things she does put me at a disadvantage business-wise, but I am so busy with work that I can't stop and always make a big deal out of it. Little things like this mount up – would she neglect to call a travel agent if her boss were a man? Maybe she thinks my business trips are just "girls on an outing" whereas his are "serious sorties into the world"?

Expecting women to stand in 'solidarity' with other women at work could be misguided.

Sometimes, after a series of these "little things", I blow up at her. Then she pretends to pout and act like a girlfriend whose feelings are wounded, and sits, filing her fingernails, waiting for me to apologize! I don't know how much longer I can keep her.'

Sometimes secretaries project an attitude that women are not important – they seem to feel a lack of pride in working for 'just a woman'. This shows in little ways – small remarks, gestures, facial expressions, manner of answering the telephone 'for her', taking (or not taking) messages...

Office Politics: To Be 'Male-identified' or 'Female-identified'?

Women's expectations of other women are different now after 25 years of 'feminism' and 'post-feminism'. Ideas of equality are in the air, hopes for women's advancement. There is a vague feeling that 'women should support each other'. Women no longer think it's 'normal' or acceptable for a woman to treat another woman shabbily – although they fear that women they meet may behave this way, showing 'disloyalty'. They are often wary, suspicious of newcomers.

Yet expecting women to stand in 'solidarity' with other women at work could be misguided. Pressure to have 'solidarity' may feel to a woman like what was expected of mothers and daughters always, i.e. a 'kind and helpful' attitude, 'being a good daughter', 'a good mother', giving unquestioning support. Women don't like being taken for granted. (It never got them anywhere in the past...)

Question: Will it help a woman to play up to male groups at work, and disassociate herself from the women there, to get ahead?

Today women can profit from forming alliances: women can make progress in business by supporting each other. Although Margaret Thatcher's example of 'go-it-alone-in-a-man's-world' is often cited ('look how successful she was'), it is doubtful Thatcher could have become prime minister of the UK without the feminist agitation of the 1970s behind her – and clearly not without the earlier 1910s' female suffragette movement that got women the vote and right to be in Parliament! The situation is the same now: pressure from women's groups allows individual women to progress in their careers, rise further – and hopefully means better pay and working conditions for all women. A women who 'rises' and does not realize the importance of 'paying a bit back', helping groups of women, is using other women in a callous way.

Of course, women need not always agree, or 'be nice' to each other! Male politicians and businessmen argue and disagree on a daily basis, why can't women? Yet women's fights are derogatorily called 'catfights'. There is no similar term for fights between men, men's fights being generally considered serious and important, even heroic (think of England vs Northern Ireland...). Men fight and disagree with each other all the time, and so can women. (Solidarity doesn't mean never disagreeing.)

Fear of being woman-identified
While 'doing it your way', a woman should make sure she is not, deep down, afraid of being 'on women's side', woman-identified.

The definition of a male-identified woman at work is one who trashes other women behind their backs, destroys men's confidence in women colleagues unfairly to gain advantage for herself.

A woman can do this out of fear: 'Women are afraid of men at work. We are afraid that they will hurt us, fire us, say bad things about us.' This fear shows up in small ways at work. Women say they notice that women can be different when men are around, afraid to 'challenge' or openly disagree with men's ideas or even with anti-woman remarks, or they find women afraid to take the lead in conversation, state forcefully their opinions at meetings in the office. Many women are still hesitant to act in a non-subservient manner at work – i.e. 'challenge' male 'dominance', take charge of a meeting, or even offer alternate leadership. (They are afraid, not only that men will scorn and attack them, but that women will not support them, will desert them too.)

Meetings at work with both sexes present can create a tough situation: if a woman speaks 'straight from the hip' as other women might appreciate, she risks alienating the men there, but if she plays the game of being modest, showing her charm, women may be turned off, even afraid to trust her or work closely with her. 'Which side' to play?

One answer to this dilemma for a woman is to get to know the women around her, get her relationships with the women at work straight before meetings take place.

Will Showing 'Solidarity' Help or Hurt a Woman's Career?

Question: Will women be better off in the long run by maintaining solidarity with other women, or going it on their own? In the short run? Will it help a woman to play up to male groups at work, and disassociate herself from the women there, to get ahead?

Whether supporting other women at work will help or hurt a woman's career is a valid question – but it is not PC. As one woman puts it: 'Am I giving up real material gain for my idealism, for my duty and loyalty to other women?'

Women can justifiably be nervous. Everything is changing, economics are very unsure. Although it is now 'against the rules' to be 'unsisterly', many women, deep down, think it's still necessary.

Women can justifiably be nervous. Everything is changing, economics are very unsure. Although it is now 'against the rules' to be 'unsisterly', many women, deep down, think it's still necessary.

As one women explains:

'What did equality get me? Fifteen years ago, my boss offered me a house if I would be his mistress. I laughed and said "Women don't need this shit anymore!" and won awards for producing feminist documentaries on television. Now I think I should have accepted the house, and some diamonds besides! I am poor, age 53

and I have nothing. I have to sell my apartment to survive.'

The bitterness in her remarks is understandable. However, as she probably knows quite well, without 'feminism' she would not have been able to be working as a television producer at all.

Women are better off today, they have the right to work and demand equal pay, because they had solidarity and fought for these rights together. Women have higher old age pension rates than when they started, their own bank accounts (not possible earlier in the century!), plus thousands of other benefits. This is what solidarity, women sticking together for the right goals, has done – and it has helped men too. Many of women's goals remain unfulfilled, still to be won, such as equal pay (!), education for more of the world's women and girls, lack of fear of sexual attack (rape or clitoridectomy), and other urgent needs.

What about in the short run? Of course, there are always situations when you have to go it alone, 'your way'. If so, just don't forget the bigger picture.

New Business Relationships Between Women: Mentors and Protégées

One of the best ways forward in business situations for women now involves creating new categories of relationships – not only 'bosses' and 'secretaries', but also 'mentors' and 'protégées', business and career advisers, etc.

One woman describes with pride her unusual relationship with an older woman in her field, her mentor:

'A woman chose me as her successor as a Symphony Guild president. She spent great amounts of time grooming me for the position, and at the same time she had in me someone with whom to share her frustrations. I continue to feel great warmth towards her and feel that she truly cares about me as an individual. Because she is very busy with her job and with a difficult family situation, we have lunch only a couple of times a year now. Still, I have enormous gratitude towards her for believing I had the potential for leadership at a time I did not know it, and she partly did it by expressing her own self-doubts to me and seeking my advice – treating me as an equal before I actually felt equal.'

'Eventually, she and I and a couple of other women who were equally willing to accept major responsibilities in the volunteer sector (leading to major business positions) became a kind of elite group in our small city. We are not intimate friends but have a great respect for one another and feel a closeness and concern about one another's continued self-realization.'

Some women say they enjoy providing assistance and guidance to younger women, being mentors – they don't resent questions, and enjoy building a relationship of mutual trust:

'Once in a while, young women who see me here at the office (I am in charge of the payouts division of a large corporation) seem surprised to find I am a woman who has the top position. I notice they stare at me as I pass their desks, I think they want to know more about me, how it feels to be me, what it's like to have my job. They are wondering if they would like to have my job someday – or if it's worth it. I can't help smiling to myself – of course it's worth it! I try to get to know their names, and say hello once in a while. This lets them know that they can talk to me. Sometimes they do. They always ask if they can help me! Then while they are helping me, they learn what they need to know, that yes, I have been thriving here, and no, I am not unhappy, and yes, I would do it all over again. That I started out just as a "normal girl" and by working hard, I got here. That, maybe, they can do it too. I hope this helps them.'

'I am a PhD research scientist at a top-notch institution in a man's field. I owe the women's movement the debt of my work life. Therefore I give women more time and support than I might naturally. I give a lot more sometimes when I might rather get on with my own thing, but it's a rewarding feeling.'

Of course, a protégée shouldn't expect too much! For example: 'If she seems too dependent on my approval, always wanting something else, I feel uncomfortable, smothered. And, I don't want to be someone's mother.'

Also, if a mentor expects too much, this creates pressure, makes the woman she wants to help feel restricted, made accountable, and tense.

Alliances for better salaries and business expansion: economic networks

In the 1970s, many women inside large corporations formed 'women's caucuses' to lobby the management for better pay for women, better working conditions, equal policies on advancement to higher positions, and so on. This, naturally, made some corporations angry, and women were sometimes fired. Many of these women then took the companies to court and usually got their jobs back, with compensation. Other companies tried appeasement, so women did increase their salaries and benefits overall.

Women today are again networking inside corporations – for discussion, salary comparison, pushing for equal status within the organization, and exchanging information on sexual harassment situations. Such informal groups[3] often have a weekly sorting out session in which fears and grievances are aired, as well as strategies for advancement. One such group planned a new division inside the corporation, and took their idea to the chairman, proposing to run it themselves. Women from different corporations also meet to discuss goals, find mutual interests and form interlocking women's committees.

There is no law against organizing at work, comparing salaries, or hearing about sexual harassment in the corporation – although it may feel like it!

There is no law against organizing at work, comparing salaries, or hearing about sexual harassment in the corporation – although it may feel like it!

One of the most interesting international phenomena of recent years has been the growth of women-run small businesses, in the US, UK, Europe, India and Africa. These businesses have a high success rate, often with profitable long-term operations. Given the fact that women are used to thinking of owning and running companies as 'something men do', is it hard for women to decide together that they can 'go it alone'? It doesn't seem to be. Networks of women-run businesses are springing up. One such organization in Germany has a newsletter in which members advertise their businesses, so that other women patronize them, and thus keep all their businesses flourishing.

Conclusion: The Future

Women today are on the verge of a breakthrough with each other, despite decaying negative stereotypes about them. Women are successfully changing the atmosphere, along with the social landscape – in just about the most important place they can do it, at work.

This power in business – power to think, act and lead – is the heritage 20th-century women have given to the 21st century, just as 19th-century women 'suffragettes' enabled 20th-century women to gain the vote.

3 Men's networks exist already. Meeting for golf or other sports, not to mention exclusive male clubs, are clearly ways men have of meeting and talking 'off the record', with other men who are not 'friends' but whom they want to know for business reasons.

Brain Software Commands

— SOFTWARE TO DELETE

How is she going to hurt me? How can I get power before she uses it to hurt me?

+ SOFTWARE TO INSTALL

How can this woman potentially help me? How can I help her?

— SOFTWARE TO DELETE

An older woman will give me a hard time (like my mom!). She will resent me.

+ SOFTWARE TO INSTALL

It is a great opportunity to work for a woman boss.

The New Psychology with which Women Regard Other Women: A Loyalty Taboo?

Are women 'born rivals', or is this idea fading? What is women's view of each other today?

If, during the last 25 years, women have changed themselves and their relationships with men, a less noted phenomenon is how this has affected their relationships with women. The changes women have made in their lives are noticeably transforming their relationships with each other.

How often has it been said: 'Women today have power. They have half the votes, they are over half the population. They bring up the children. If they want change, why don't they *use* their power?' Many studies show that women are more likely to vote for a male political candidate than a female candidate, even when the female candidate stands directly for issues the voter agrees with. Women may 'have their rights' but then, why do women not comprise (for example) half the executives of major corporations; why has there not been a female head of Spain, Germany or Japan? People claim this is because women are so busy being rivals that they never stop to 'unify' for larger goals.

Do women need to 'unify' to get ahead? A better way to address this issue is to look at individual relationships: how do women feel about each other?

I have sent several years thinking about relationships between women, as this has been one of the primary areas of my research (1970s–1990s). My conclusions include a theory about affection, esteem and politics between women, as well as identification of a taboo on primary loyalty between women.

Clichés abound – 'a woman will stab another woman in the back over a man', 'a woman will always break a date with a woman as soon as a man comes along', or 'you can't trust a woman in the office' and so on. Other clichés proclaim women are all 'sisters', or 'women stick together no matter what against men'. What is the reality?

Why do men create male-loyalty systems that work (political parties, sports teams, corporations, etc.) whereas women do not?

Although many women have excellent relationships, women often have a lurking suspicion that a dynamic not yet understood lies under the surface of their relationships, making them unstable. For example, many women want to treat women as equals, but when they try gingerly to shift the centre of power to their women colleagues, they can find this shaky ground. Women complain that women don't take them seriously, are 'always late, liable to cancel for any reason, and as a woman, you "should understood"' – and in general, treat you shabbily'. Some women throw up their hands in frustration, concluding: 'The stereotypes are right! Women are born rivals, sneaky and underhanded!' This generalization, of course, is not accurate. What then, causes old clichés and situations to keep being repeated?

The explanation usually accepted for the unsettling hostility women sometimes encounter with each other is that women are 'brainwashed' to prefer men, to compete with each other. This may be true, but I find deeper reasons. (After all, if the explanation offered for twenty years were the only explanation, then more would have changed by now...) This is not to say that in the future 'perfect world' women will always be 'in harmony' with each other – just that women need not fight because the social set-up makes them nervous.

I propose that a major unidentified taboo on loyalty between women exists. Part of this taboo is learned by girls with their mothers at a very early age (ages 1–2); and another art is absorbed by women from repetitive messages in the society around them, warning them that 'putting a woman first' is wrong, silly or stupid, insisting that primarily loyalty between women is 'abnormal' or 'lesbian'.

This hides a political taboo on female alliances. How does this taboo function? In many situations it makes women insecure about their associations, blaming this on 'human nature' or 'female character'.

In meetings or work situations, sometimes women fear siding with another woman 'against the men', and behave nervously, calling it 'modern' not to 'automatically agree with another woman' – although men often agree and work in groups with each other with no self-consciousness or defensiveness. Indeed, men feel proud of their male associations. If the problem were that women have mixed feelings about each other, don't always like each other, then why isn't this a problem for men? Men, too, have mixed feelings about each other, they don't see 'all other men' as equals, but they form successful alliances, corporate boards and sports teams.

Of course, women need not automatically work together, as in some kind of ghetto, but when a woman finds another woman worth supporting, she should not be afraid to throw her full support behind that woman. Many women try to work 'behind the scenes', to avoid this taboo – or wind up not taking action, lamenting: 'The world is unjust, but I can't change it.'

In politics, the trendy knee-jerk reaction to 'How about going to an all-woman meeting? How about joining a feminist political party?' ('What a drag! That's out!') is possibly an example of fear of ridicule (i.e. fear of the hidden taboo). This attitude expresses an underlying fear of rejecting men, of aligning oneself with the taboo group, women. (Not so hip…)

Although generally women are thought to be most vulnerable to men's rejection, praise or blame, in fact – and this was the first key that emerged in my research – women, surprisingly, fear being rejected, dropped by other women. Most women wonder how much other *women* really like them. Women doubt other women will be truly loyal to them, in the long run. Many are terrified that if they take the risk, go against the 'rules' of the system and its hidden taboo on female alliances, pin their hopes on a relationship with another woman (whether in business, politics or in private), in the end, the woman may let them down in favour of a man.

'Would a woman really choose me?', a woman wonders. 'Would she put me first in her life if she had a choice between me and a man? At

work? In private?' Do women lack the self-esteem to believe a woman would willingly do this – or does a hidden taboo make them 'know' their relationship cannot last? But this psychology now is changing.

Consider this: When a woman walks into a room (say, at a business meeting or party), another woman watching her come through the door may automatically think to herself: 'Is she prettier than me? Younger? Better dressed?'

What if a woman were to think instead: 'Here comes a woman. Will she be a good addition to my life? How would I like to relate to her?' If she's 'pretty', the woman could try thinking 'She is very attractive. I'd like to have her for a friend or a companion, or maybe I'd like to touch her hair or hold her hand. I wonder if I'd like talking to her?' She could think: 'She wants to be attractive for *me* so I will like her!' (rather than imagining: 'She has spent time on her appearance to be attractive to the men in this room.') Why shouldn't a woman imagine, when seeing another woman enter a room with a group of people, that the woman is offering her beauty, charm and aliveness to *her* (not only to the men)?

Similarly, while many women have excellent friendships, they do not see each other as potential long-term primary partners. They do not wonder: 'Could I make a life with her? Would I want to buy a home with her?' Would she be a good business partner?' There could be many new kinds of partnerships between women that would be satisfying but women have been blocked from seeing them by the clichés and especially the clichés that express the taboo on primary loyalty between women. A new social institution for women – neither lesbianism nor simple friendship, but a third type of relationship – is a logical way forward for women today. Any woman could now, by taking her relationships with other women more seriously, add a great deal of security and pleasure to her life – as well as creating a new future direction for society.

While many women have excellent friendships, they do not see each other as potential long-term primary partners.

Why is it so hard for us to imagine such ways of life? Perhaps the early years girls spend with their mothers hold a key to understanding. Based on my research, it seems that girls very early learn with their mothers that it is not permitted between women to touch a woman's skin or breasts or lips; for example a daughter cannot touch her mother's vulva or ask to see it. (A boy can easily see his father's penis, or other boys' – but girls cannot see the vulva easily.) Although a girl's young body is very different from her mother's, she soon learns she must control her curiosity, that she cannot ask to look at her mother's body (or touch it) to understand her own development or anatomy, this is forbidden. (Why was Freud so blind to this situation between girls and their mothers?) If mother and daughter speak of sexual parts of their bodies, usually a rather clinical approach is taken, the mother never volunteering to say that touching the sexual part of her feels unusually good, that she likes sexual feelings or has orgasm.

Does the daughter then learn that the proper way to relate to another woman is with 'mind only', to touch only fleetingly in certain spots such as on the cheek or hand? (While girls learn this too about men, they also learn that later it will be 'right and natural' to break through this prohibition with a man they love.) On a deeply unconscious level, women resent this physical (not sexual) taboo, sense it as a rejection, feel irritable. I am not suggesting 'all women must become lesbian', I am saying that women's psychology is affected by the rigid block on sharing physicality between women (for longer than a minute). Physical embracing or sleeping together is one of the most important ways in which humans bond, learn to trust, one of the ways fears are allayed and hope is created.

The taboo on female physical intimacy (mistakenly called 'lesbianism') is merely a symbol of the wider taboo on female loyalty and allegiances of all kinds, not just sexual allegiances. It's even somehow more acceptable for a woman to have sex with another woman ('After all, she can be reformed by a good man!') than it is for a woman to put another woman first on her list of priorities and give her all her loyalty – i.e. it's forbidden for a woman to give her allegiance to another woman unless she can be 'explained' with the label 'lesbian'. It's not only 'lesbianism' (lesbian sexuality) that is taboo, it's all that it stands for: putting a woman first. Women's fear of lesbianism is not so much a fear of touching another woman, as a fear of what it means, i.e. confronting the system. (Sure, it's even OK for women to 'play around sexually together' until they 'meet the right man' – 'what can they really do together anyway?'!)

'Lesbian' is the bogey-word employed to intimidate any woman who might try to form a primary relationship with another woman – in business or buying an apartment with a friend.

Some women may avoid primary long-term alliances with women for financial reasons. As women are perceived as having less money (and less power at work), other women feel less sure they can be 'counted on', and so continue to give men their allegiance.

Yet this is changing: women today form caucuses for equal pay and advancement inside corporations, connect their businesses with networks of other women's businesses (Selbständliche Frauen), and create international financial and political alliances.

Many women now notice there is an imbalance in how they treat men and how they treat women. Although they may feel on shaky ground when they try to relate in new ways to women (sometimes it makes the other woman nervous too), more and more women today are experimenting with new relationships.

Today more and more women do stand up for other women – in public places, such as in corporate board meetings, in supermarkets and in private mixed groups. Sometimes this causes men to feel *they* are on shaky ground! But this is not bad; it could lead to a new and better balance between women and men in the next twenty years.

According to my research, women at this point in history are progressing in interesting ways with each other, changing their perspective on other women and experimenting with new directions in their relationships – ignoring the senseless taboo

Many women now notice there is an imbalance in how they treat men and how they treat women.

on female allegiances, and building economic, personal and political relationships with women they like. Women are resolving the 'I can't find the right man' cul-de-sac by buying homes together and building lives around their friendships, raising children together.

More and more women are re-examining their relationships with the women around them, trying not to be afraid to experiment with their feelings and their communication with other women – reviewing their own attitudes in terms of friendship and emotions. There are many practical steps women today are taking, according to my research, steps now open to them that they previously imagined blocked. These new relationships are of enormous benefit to society.

Why Do Women Fight?

Is it true that women can't work together, they always fight?
While, contrary to stereotype, women don't fight more than men do, let's examine women's reputation for fights more closely: does a lingering idea among women that they are less important than men cause fights to be unresolved – and thus more frequent?

The standard 'explanation' of women's fighting says that women are 'petty, jealous and competitive'. Rivals. Why? Standard answer: because the social structure makes women 'compete for men'.

Although there is some truth to this, there are deeper, more profound reasons. Jealousy is not as much the reason as are signs of disloyalty, subtle references to a woman's 'unimportant' status. Women's disputes with one another are not so much due to fighting over 'men' (although a man or a job can superficially seem to be the object), but signs the other woman does not recognize or accept a woman as a first-rate member of society.

Perhaps this is becoming more true than ever: the question on every woman's mind today: can I play a full part in 'our' world? Are other women 'full players'? How should I relate to them? How seriously should I take them? This is the canvas against which our relationships with each other are now played out.

A second reason fights can erupt today is because women feel they are relating more fully and on more levels, more freely, than before. Ironically, this can be unsettling and unnerving. When questions such as what are the new 'rules' between women at work, how far can or should friendship go, where are the boundaries are unsettled, this causes frayed nerves.

What are the new 'rules' between women at work, how far can or should friendship go, where are the boundaries?

Women's 'bitchiness' is surely exaggerated (men can be 'bitchy' too), but if it is true, women can be edgy and argumentative, testy, with each other. Why? Women may feel confident of their own abilities, but uncertain how others are perceiving them (whether positively or not). Women's doubts about their own self-worth (or their worth in society's eyes) may make them doubt other women's worth too, imagine other women undervalue them – and this leads to fragile relationships, doubts, suspicion and fights.

'Why are women so critical of other women?'
How can we understand women's jealousy and mutual suspicion? Women, like men, may have a gut fear of other women, expecting the worst, even though relationships – especially at work, for instance – may be good on the surface. We can be too quick to bail out when we hear any negative words from a woman, much quicker than when we hear criticism or condescension from a man.

Will other women criticize us, we sometimes fear, like our mothers may have done? After all, for most of us, it was our mother who had the job of supervising, disciplining and teaching us; our mother was more apt to 'criticize' us, as well as encourage us. Mothers are often assigned the role of 'family police'. Criticism from one so powerful as our mother could feel very painful, and seem to limit our ability to be free, create our own identity.

Exclusion and inclusion: acceptance in society

Most fights between women have one common denominator: the issue of exclusion and inclusion.

Most fights between women have one common denominator: the issue of exclusion and inclusion.

Although some fighting is 'part of life', other fighting is part of a system that tries to put women at loggerheads, excluding women from power. It often takes the form of singling out a woman to take the blame (as in Arthur Miller's play *The Crucible,* which was made into a film in 1998) for everything that goes wrong.

If a woman scapegoats another woman, blames her, she is usually doing it (semi-consciously) to align herself with the system and thus stay 'safe'. She may hope to get 'points' for bashing another woman, thus making clear her allegiance (to the system, not to the woman). It puts a woman in a special class if she will 'betray' and publicly bash another woman; it means she is 'OK', you can count on her. But this is cowardly! Getting 'points' for bashing another woman is cowardly, and also short-sighted. Of course, such cowardice and fearful conformity is part of fascism, with its well-known focus on exclusion and inclusion, 'in-groups' and 'out-groups'.

Fights as a battle within oneself about being female

Sad to say, women can have good reason to get angry with other women sometimes, because women too hold prejudices against women!

Women can have good reason to get angry with other women sometimes, because women too hold prejudices against women!

To add insult to injury, women may listen more rationally to ideas or criticisms from men. Points of view or criticisms from other women are often not really 'heard' at all; all that is 'heard' is 'she's complaining', or 'she's speaking a lot'. Women can tend to see other women who want to make a point, and are even angry with them (or with whom they are angry) either as 'bad daughters' who are 'causing scenes' to get attention' – or as 'angry mothers, dominating shrews whom you have to humour ('try to get away as soon as possible'). This is not productive!

Almost everything a woman does can be seen to cause a problem: if a woman is very helpful, she is 'too clinging and wants approval', if she is not helpful, but goes in her own direction, she is 'egotistical and doesn't care about anybody but herself', and so on.

Hidden fear behind jealousy: female prejudices

Jealousy is common: 'My boss is beautiful, rich and powerful. I am insanely jealous, it is just too much! I hate her, I want to be her. But I never let it show, because I know that would make me look like a wimp. I am a wimp! Why can't I get over this? It makes it worse that on top of it all, I like her so much.'

In our culture, sexual rivalry is encouraged between daughters and mothers, younger women and older women. Mothers are seen as 'older women', while their daughters are 'Lolitas' and 'sexpots' – more fun and desirable. Older women are not regarded as beautiful, their power is seen as negative or 'domineering', their self-expression 'demanding'. Thus feelings between the two are very confused, unclear. But to see age and beauty as basic reasons for female fights is extremely superficial.

In our culture, sexual rivalry is encouraged between daughters and mothers, younger women and older women.

Ironically, on some level, interactions between women are tinged with a slight feeling of anger that the other woman is 'just a woman'! Anger that she is not a man! We are subconsciously angry at each other for not being more powerful, for not being 'men', for not having as much status, power and prestige as men.

How often women say, when they compare women and men, that they wish men would 'be as nice as women'. But when women are 'as nice as women', they are often taken for granted. How often do younger women say their mothers were so loving they made them feel guilty? Or, a woman may even say to her friend: 'You're too perfect! Too bad you're not a man, you'd be just right for me!' She may not even perceive the insult she has just made.

Women often hazily feel that other women have a tendency to see them as full of flaws, i.e. 'not men', 'lesser beings' than men. As long as this

prejudice is not examined, no resolution of the relationship is possible.

We should confront our own prejudices directly, work on our minds to remove such attitudes.

Stereotypes insist that a woman must be meek and help others, 'wimps', not be a central protagonist in the world, the 'hero' of the piece. (Characteristics that would be praised in men are condemned in women.) There used to be a lapel button worn by some women that said 'I'm an uppity woman'. This meant 'I will not be docile! Don't take me for granted!'

A classic put-down of a woman says: 'Who does she think she is? The Queen of Sheba??' As a child I wondered who that queen was, and got a bad impression of her. Later, as a history graduate student, I learned that she was a highly interesting ancient ruler of the Sudan. She got a bad name when she fought off the patriarchal armies of surrounding states, as she represented a non-patriarchal woman honouring social order.

A note on the word 'bitch'
Women sometimes enforce the double standard of male privilege/female 'goodness' by making clichéd remarks.

The word supposedly used for the 'worst characteristics' of a woman, 'Bitch!', is used by women as well as men. A 'bitch' is a woman who loves sex, has sex with anybody she wants, not just one man, 'doesn't belong to anybody'. Interestingly, in ancient times, before Classical Greece (in archaic Greece), this was not considered a negative sign: 'not belonging to any man', 'owning oneself', were signs of merit. Today, we have – amazingly – accepted this terminology to mean 'impossible' or 'infuriating'. Secretly, we may even like using this term: it can be fun and releasing to 'hate' women – not take them so seriously. As women are so weighed down with a duty to be 'good and understanding' they need a release, not to be saints. And yet...

Summary

Women have more economic security today, many more women today are self-sufficient (but not rich!). But this new position can make women uneasy, unsure of how to relate to each other. They cannot treat each other the way they did twenty years ago, when a different set of common assumptions and realities was present – but how should they interpret the actions of another woman?

If women are sometimes nervous with each other (they are, increasingly, more likely to be nice) this can be because they feel 1) they should be loyal and 'nice' to women, treat them better, but 2) they don't think they can count on a woman in the long run, and therefore can't really lean on a woman the way they can on a man, take her as seriously.

Therefore, many women feel angry to be caught in an awkward double bind, in an impossible situation – they feel slightly dishonest somehow.

Women feel angry to be caught in an awkward double bind, in an impossible situation – they feel slightly dishonest somehow.

Social whispers don't help, i.e. stereotypes telling women they 'should' be 'bitchy' with each other, informing women obliquely to 'watch out for this', to be on guard against any sign of another woman being 'nasty' or 'starting in with them' – so that any 'sign' of these becomes a focal point, the negative side of any relationship becomes exaggerated.

On top of this, women learn to instinctively fear being tainted with the term 'lesbian'. Thus, ironically, when one woman likes another and works well with her, she may draw back and act hostile.

Today's feuds and fights may not be so much 'classic' signs of women's 'traditional brainwashed role as competitors for men', as of a bittersweet uneasiness women feel in their new identity and social position – a kind of homesickness, wondering how they should deal with each other amid the new realities they themselves have made. Women's testiness – and hope, sense of anticipation – can exist precisely because women know that what they are doing and feeling, saying and thinking, is new. They are experimenting with how to enjoy and appreciate the new relationships between them that are emerging.

This rethinking and experimentation is good!

Many of today's fights and tensions go with the transformation women are making in their relationships and in society. Bringing problems out into the open will enormously speed the process of changing women's position in business.

How can a woman manage other women? It's up to her! Take this book and think creatively!

How can a woman manage other women? It's up to her!

Your Opinion...

What is your opinion and experience? What do you think? What have been *your* experiences of what's been discussed in this chapter?

Please use this space to write your remarks, or alternatively you may e-mail comments to the *Sex and Business* website at www.sexandbusiness.com/myopinion. Naturally, you may express yourself anonymously.

_____

_____

_____

_____

_____

_____

Sexual harassment, like rape, is caused by hostility, a man wanting to prove he is in charge, have another notch on his belt – and the power that comes with having 'bedded' a woman (always more of a feather, traditionally, in a man's cap than a woman's, although women may turn this around), the ability to brag to other men about this, buying the woman's silence. Sexual harassment, like rape, has one objective: humiliating the woman. This is why rape is such a popular tool of war: one side is trying to destroy the morale and self-confidence of the other. Perhaps at work, some men are trying to destroy the morale of the 'new women competitors'.

Sexual harassment:

what it is

and how to avoid it

Sexual Harassment: What It Is and How to Avoid It

The famous cases of Monica Lewinsky and President Clinton (although the sex was declared to be mutual), the lawsuit against Toshiba that wound up costing Toshiba over US$5 million, and the lawsuit by a French mannequin against a corporation that hired her to sponsor their products and then 'fired' her (cancelled her contract), she said, when she did not have sex with the chairman… everyone knows these reports of the new phenomenon, 'sexual harassment in the workplace'. The Michael Douglas film *Disclosure* took a reverse spin on this phenomenon, and portrayed a woman boss harassing a man sexually.

Statistics show that it is mostly women who receive sexual harassment from men (similar to the statistics on rape). *Disclosure* was an attempt at guilt reversal, somewhat like the early attempt by some groups to claim that men are as often raped by women as women are by men – an idea that was relatively quickly denied by the US Surgeon General during the 1980s, going on television with a public health message.

But *why* does sexual harassment occur? It must be easy for anyone to sense when someone else does not really want to be involved sexually or romantically. Why, then, after an initial advance (even if inappropriate at work) does the situation continue until it causes an incident, even a lawsuit? Surely no one is so 'desperate for sex' in today's world, or so unable to be more subtle, that force (whether physical, psychological or financial) really wins the day.

Why does sexual harassment occur?

As one man puts his widely shared opinion:

'I am absolutely not interested in sexually harassing someone. Why would I want to do that? I am not a poor sap who can't get a woman! If I want one, believe me I know where to find them. OK, if you are rejected when you make a pass, it might be a temptation to "get even", but I'm too busy for that kind of thing. I can't be bothered, there are too many exciting things to do. I think of men who do this kind of thing have a problem of some sort.'

Yet, is it so simple?[1]

---

1 Of course, it is not so simple; given society's definition of 'real men', there is, perversely, ego satisfaction for some men in making a woman do something she does not want to do, pressuring and sexually harrassing her, since seeing her squirm makes them feel powerul.

Mini Hite Report: Statistics

Women

Have you ever been involved in a sexually harassing situation, either as the one harassed, or the one doing the harassing?

45% Yes, I have frequently been sexually harassed; not by the same person; not reported
14% Yes, I have been and currently am being, by one person; not reported
17% Yes, but it has only happened once or twice in my life; not reported
8% Yes, and I reported it
16% No, this has not happened to me (or I did not recognize it)

Summary: How many women in this Hite Research sample say that, although they have never reported it, they have been sexually harassed? 76%

Have you participated in sexually harassing another person?

40% I don't know what this means for a woman
13% I don't think so, but who knows? Is asking a guy for a date sexual harassment?
21% Yes, once or twice I flirted with a guy until I know he was turned on, but he didn't really want to go any further, so I stopped
26% Never, this would be beneath me

Summary: Most women are not in senior positions over men; flirtation does not come under the category of harassment, if the man's job is not at stake or affected.

Men

Have you been sexually harassed?

12% Yes, I have often been sexually harassed; not by the same person; not reported
9% Yes, I have been and currently am being, by one person; not reported
23% Yes, but it has only happened once or twice in my life; not reported
3% Yes, and reported it
53% No, this has not happened to me (or I did not recognize it)

But most of these men, although they answered, did not work for women.

Summary: Many men confuse sexual advances in general with the combination of a sexual advance mixed with fear of losing a job, one person's power to give or deny the other work.

Have you ever participated in sexually harassing another person?

31% I don't know what this means exactly; sure I've teased women
12% I don't think so, but who knows? Is asking for a date sexual harassment?
17% Yes, once or twice I kept on making rude suggestions until I know she was turned on, but she didn't really want to go further, so I stopped
19% Her short skirts drove me crazy until one day I decided to show her
21% Never, this would be beneath me.

Have you ever been accused of sexual harassment?

Women:
21% Yes
79% No

Men:
52% Yes
48% No

Experiences of Sexual Harassment

How women describe it

'Sexual harassment? I guess it's just part of life, I accept it as part of life. Men – at least some – are like that, what can you do? When I'm out in the world, including at work, this happens frequently, in thousands of ways, big and small. I guess I've got a lot of practice handling it. But if it ever came to a situation where I might lose my job if I didn't co-operate in a certain way or attitude, I don't know if I'd be smart enough to handle it without coming up on the losing end.'

'I went to my supervisor and told him that Jeff was pestering me, that I would find things like porno magazines in my briefcase when I was packing up to leave the office, then I would find him loitering around near the elevator, waiting for me, expecting to strike up a (hot?) conversation. I told him to stop, that I found this disconcerting, and this was not the way to treat me. He kept it up, not believing me, and even progressed, one evening, to grabbing me in the elevator and kissing me. I started making sure I didn't stay even one minute late at work (I used to like to organize my desk at the close of the day), I would leave in a crowd with the others. I started to develop a defensive mentality and to fear him. This is when I decided to call a halt, and went to see my supervisor.

'Imagine how I felt when, instead of saying he would speak to Jeff or move him to another division or section of the office, at least, he just told me there was nothing he could do unless there was a "real incident" or I suffered some damage! I felt like somebody in a psycho movie

for a few days after that, but then I just made an appointment with the CEO and told him! This unusual step did seem to shake up a few things, it even got my supervisor moved and me a promotion.'

'Yes, who hasn't? I was just out of school, and had my first job as a secretary. The boss, a man older than my father, had hired me after asking for a CV with a photograph, and told me during the interview for the job (that I got) that I was very pretty. His other secretary, older than me, told me that he said, when he was looking at the applications, "That's the one" when he saw my photo (a small back and white machine photo, and I had a scarf on). I felt a bit funny about his comment, knowing I got the job for "that reason", but I knew I was capable, I had a lot of self-confidence and thought I would be a very good secretary (I typed well, my spelling was perfect...) and so I turned out to be. He offered to pay my plane fare to fly over for the interview (a one-hour flight). I spent the entire flight trying to put on some make-up, to be sure I would "make a good impression". My family didn't seem to know or care (didn't want to know) what was going on, they just gave me the equivalent of $10 and said "good luck". Compared to this, my new employer seemed to show genuine caring and tenderness. So, on those occasions when he tried to get me to come over to his apartment, or even (once or twice!) chased me around the desk (sounds cliché, but true), I didn't mind so much. I just worried that he would be insulted because it would be clear that I didn't really like him physically, I felt repulsed when he tried to kiss me, and ran away from him at every opportunity. But I found his remarks tender and attitude genuinely caring, even though (like all secretaries) I was underpaid. The salary wasn't much, but he had me picked up for work with his car. Eventually I went away to university. He still sent me flowers every week, without fail, and tried to get me to come for weekends. Is this sexual harassment?'

'I felt extremely compromised. I was working for a manufacturing company, and my job depended on my boss. He was older than me, and divorced. Once, after work, we went out and got a little drunk. His hands were all over me, but I didn't stop him. I even played with his penis and his hips. He said he loved it, but I didn't (so I stopped). Later, what could I say? That I had been sexually harassed. I had been, I had been sexually intimidated, financially terrified, socially embarrassed (lest anyone at work suspect what had happened and think less of me). Yet I had co-operated, so wasn't it mutual?'

'There is a man at work I have a crush on. He is very young, and he is in the computer toys division of the factory. Sometimes at lunchtime he teases me, when we are standing around the counter waiting for our drinks (coffee, cokes, orange juice etc.) saying I have big knockers (tits and ass), and so on. If I laugh, I look too tough, if I pretend not to notice, they tease me all the more, led by him. So I try to take the initiative now and remark on his body before he starts on mine. So far, this has seemed to clear the air, but it feels like a dangerous game I am playing. I can feel his hostility rising towards me.'

How men speak about it

'I couldn't believe it when she went to see our boss. I mean, she should have talked to me first. I never hurt her, I never touched her. But I sure did catch hell about it from him. I don't believe he really wanted to give me a hard time, I think the company just made him do it. They're scared of lawsuits and having to pay a lot of money. I'm on a sort of probation in the company now. Hope it doesn't hurt my chances for a promotion next year. Who knows, maybe it'll help them!'

'She was adorable, and I saw her and her baby blue eyes every day, I saw her in the morning, I stood by her desk as we wrote texts together, I heard her muffled telephone conversations with friends and boyfriends (I suppose), I saw her cross and uncross her legs at her desk while she looked at her papers, tug her hair thinking, take off for the ladies' lounge. It finally was too much for me, I got turned on so often during those small situations – didn't she feel it too? My eyes were always on her. Did she feel them? If so, she gave no sign of it. No clue. Maybe because she knows I am married, she never even gave me a second look. She was friendly enough in general conversation, but that was it – maddeningly so. One day I decided I had to take some action, so I stood in front of her desk, and told her point blank: "Do you see how you turn me on?" She did a double take, then stood up and told me off.'

'With my secretary, I often pat her shoulder as I pass by, after we have gone over the correspondence together. It's my way of signalling: "Job well done. Now let's get to work." I think she knows that. But in the summer, when her arms are bare, I think twice before patting her, since I might touch her flesh. This could be misinterpreted.'

'There is one girl at my office who is really asking for it. She wears short black tight skirts and tight sweaters. I bet she has a lot of boyfriends. I usually tell her in one way or another that I find her sexy. I think one day we'll go out for an evening together. A night.'

'One of the women in my office approached me for sex. She asked me out to dinner, but I knew what she meant. We went out and she talked about her work, but that was only the pretext. I could feel the magnetism working, and under the table, I put my hand on her knee, under her skirt. She had beautiful stockings and I could feel her squirm under my hand. I asked her if her crotch was wet – because my penis sure was hard! She seemed a little embarrassed, which is normal, and stuttered some kind of response. Things went on like that, and we finished up in bed at her place.'

'I love to tease Martha. Every time she goes to get a coffee or soda, she has to pass in front of us (computer technicians). The more we whistle and make comments (like "Does your mother know you're out?", "Look at those knockers!", "Hey babe, how about a walk on the wild side with me??"), the more she walks with a bounce. This makes her tits and ass jiggle, and so we comment even more. I guess she loves it.'

Test Yourself: Are these Case Histories Sexual Harassment or Not?

'Amanda works for a colleague of mine, as his secretary. He is about 20 years older than I am, but Amanda and I are more or less the same age. I noticed she is not married, she told Lou once that she couldn't work on a Saturday when he asked, because she was going away on a trip with "her friend". So I know she's no fool. I asked her right out if she would like to meet me in the bar of a hotel around the corner, a good one, first class, and then spend the night with me there. Why beat around the bush? This is what I really wanted, so I figured I should come right out and tell her. The trouble was, she freaked. She started shouting at me, half-crying, telling me she wasn't "like that" (whatever that meant) and that I should pick on someone else and leave her in peace. I did, but to this day I don't know whether she really didn't want to go, or just didn't like the way I asked her.'

'When she told me her boyfriend was going to be away for a few days, I thought she was just talking to pass the time. But then when she suggested we go swimming on Saturday, I began to be suspicious. I didn't want to tell her about my girlfriend, because no one in the office knows about our relationship, that fits in with office politics. So I kept cool and just didn't say anything. On Monday, she started again, this time asking me to have a quick drink with her after work at a bar down the street. I said sure, why don't we bring Sally and Jerry along? She looked a little crestfallen, but said OK. When they couldn't come, I drank my drink then made up a story about how I had to buy my mom some flowers for her birthday (I know, pretty lame!) and dashed out. I hope she didn't feel bad.'

'My boss constantly fondles my hair whenever he's passing my desk or dictating a letters. He's about three times as old as I am, really a sweet old guy, so maybe my hair (it's long and brown) reminds him of when he was younger? I don't want to challenge him about it, the way he does it. I would just hate it if anyone saw him doing it though. I would feel compromised.'

'Hannah is my name, and I love to show up at work wearing the most revealing and outrageous thing I can think of. It drives guys wild. Serves them right; they have all the power around work, so why not show mine – the only way I can? Do I delight in telling those guys no when they ask me out? Only one time a guy (he left, he's not here anymore) told me that he could help me at work, get me a job with a regular contract including pension, health benefits, the whole ball game, it would just take a little time and he wanted to go away weekends together, visit his parents, see the theatre – seemed real serious. Too bad I just didn't fancy him. Good-looking, too.'

'I have a supervisor who keeps coming on to me. I work as a sales manager for a cosmetics firm. My district includes all of Western Europe. My supervisor is my link with the board of directors. I'm married and he knows it, he is married too. Sometimes we have attended the same company rallies with our spouses. I have never been unfaithful, and the whole idea seems sordid to me. But I have to be very careful not to offend him completely, because he is unlikely to take a different job, he will probably be my supervisor

for the long term. It's been six years already, and he began his campaign about three years ago, as I remember. I do admit I like him the more he continues, because it shows me that on some level he is quite sincere in his admiration for me. There is something special between us, like he says, but I don't know, I just can't believe it's right to have an affair.'

'I found that I kept calling a man at work "dear", though he didn't like it and it wasn't appropriate, but it kept slipping out. I had known him for years, and I thought he was endearing. It showed, but in the wrong way. I couldn't find the right way to express myself. I think it embarrassed him.'

Another woman at a job where she was 'the executive' recalls an incident of another type:

'I was in charge of overseeing the renovation of a large apartment building. Every day I had to go and check to see if certain work had been completed, was well done, etc. I would arrive on the construction site to usually 99 per cent male crews and it was unbelievable, the scene. They were freaked out to have a woman "checking up on them"! They sure didn't see me as a resource or a friend, to ask to help them out, ordering better supplies or equipment. (My father used to be in this line of work, that's how I got in it and I know a lot of the crews made friends with him.)

'Also, often there would be new construction workers, hired for a short time, and I have to admit, lots of minorities who probably didn't have the right working papers, or fake ones etc. It was best not to inquire too closely! One day, I arrived on a site and, in one of the top floors, I was checking the paint and plaster job that was going on. There were about six men in the area working. Three of them, I noticed, were very young men from some Arab country. As I was writing notes on my clipboard about the paint, I heard, "Lady! Lady!" I turned around and one of the three child workers had his pants down on the floor and was standing there in his underpants! I said, "What are you doing?" His friend said, "He was just changing clothes." But they were all giggling. I looked at him. "Is it normal to change clothes in front of everyone here? Wouldn't it be more normal to go into one of the other rooms where you have more privacy?" "Oh no!, in my culture, I change my clothes wherever I want!" The three were still giggling, ever more nervously now. At this point, one of the older workers came over (probably an uncle of one of the three, or some relative or friend), said something, frowning sternly, in, probably, Arabic, and the boy immediately pulled up his pants and went back to work.

'Was this sexual harassment? I guess it was, yes. Was it understandable? Yes. The most vulnerable and powerless people in the room tried to "fix things" by showing that they could "dominate a woman". Fortunately for me there were others present. I would hate to think what such innocent and understandable young men could do to a woman in another situation. But

When you understand the underlying dynamics that are functioning between the genders, then new behaviours will come naturally to you, without even trying. Take a chance, try it.

still, thinking of it, I have to laugh. It was funny. No, I didn't report it.'

Sexual harassment is widespread. Almost all companies are at risk, no matter what they may think.

Almost all companies are at risk, no matter what they may think.

Unfortunately, executive corporate attitudes such as 'That's a US problem' are unrealistic; anyone who thinks this is especially at risk, in fact, since he or she clearly does not know what sexual harassment is or how commonplace it is. (He or she may also think that it is not possible to have fun with the opposite sex and also maintain a sexual harassment-free workplace – not true!)

The answer is not to act like a frozen robot, the answer is to inform oneself (here). You can be 'charming and gallant', or 'charming and pretty', and not fall into these traps. You don't have to look and act like a machine.

When you understand the underlying dynamics that are functioning between the genders, then new behaviours will come naturally to you, without even trying. Take a chance, try it.

The Classic Definition of Sexual Harassment

Contrary to some beliefs, sexual harassment is a term that refers only to a relationship in the workplace. Basically, it is sexual pressure applied by someone senior to someone junior, whose job or income could be affected by their response.

Maybe it should be called 'sexual bullying', for obvious reasons.

Sexual harassment is a term that refers only to a relationship in the workplace ... Maybe it should be called 'sexual bullying', for obvious reasons.

Not every personal moment between a senior and junior employee, or between equal colleagues, is sexual harassment – even if inappropriate words or gestures take place. There is a thin dividing line, which only lawyers can tread. You need never arrive in that position.

Following are some typical components of sexual harassment:

- **Flirtation**
  Provocative, longing looks.

- **Touching**
  When it is mutual? How do you know?

- **Kissing**
  What about a kiss on the cheek? Is this acceptable as a cultural greeting or parting, a form of politeness, or only appropriate between lovers or special friends?

- **Comments**
  Rude remarks and sexual innuendoes in speech.

Whether or not off-colour jokes told in a group are sexual harassment is a moot point: if they seem to be directed at one person who is the butt of them, even though said in the presence of others, this can be sexual harassment. But if the remarks are of a general nature, not aimed at a particular individual, then it is perfectly possible that these remarks do not constitute sexual harassment – unless you control an individual's job who walks off, and her/his walking off or not laughing could be construed as hostility, leading to dismissal.

How do you decide?
Of course there is a difference between sexual harassment (usually done by a senior to a junior, someone with more power to someone with less power) and mutual attraction–consent.

Of course there is a difference between sexual harassment ... and mutual attraction–consent.

What if you have a crush on someone working next to you? Do you decide to communicate this or not? You don't want to misread the situation, but after trying for several months, you can't shake the feeling that what you feel is real, and that there are signs that your colleague feels something special for you, too.

If you are colleagues on the same level, then things are relatively simple. She or he will tell you relatively quickly whether there is any interest, or you are imagining the whole thing.

If you are the senior of the person in question, you may never be sure. Even if you initiate a relationship and the other person responds, you will never know whether your position was part of the cause of the response, or simply 'yourself'. Do you want this?

If you are the junior of the person in question, it can be even worse – imagine if 'the one you fancy' believes you are just trying to curry favour?! In such a situation, it is very difficult to convince the other person of your sincerity.

Brain Game 7.1

Play out the situations in the last section, based on exchanging the gender (female or male) of the senior and junior in the various situations.

Clichés You May Hear

One of the interviews with a CEO I conducted in France was provocative, interesting and lively, but also full of outrageous clichés.

Can you spot them?

What do you think of the issue of sexual harassment?

Here in France we say sometimes if a woman is attractive, she got her job by 'promotion canapé' [sex]. Also if a man hires a pretty woman, they can say he wants to have sex with her. I would be afraid to have a pretty assistant.

Sometimes women in France say they *like* sexual harassment! [Laughing.]

But surely not when it's compromising their jobs?

It's a question of a man's attitude, his sensitivity. Did you see the commercial for the perfume Égoiste? The women were angry, calling him an egoist, not because he wanted to have sex with them, but because he didn't make the women have orgasm!

That was not my interpretation of the commercial. It seemed to be making fun of women, a joke on women who had been fooled by having sex, then watching the man leave (and so they called him an egoist). Also, the fact that there were so many women – about twelve – and only one man implied the man was certainly getting around, the women were not so 'successful'…

No, the joke was on him.

Do you think that to run a successful corporation, one of the secrets is to make sure people do not have love affairs inside a corporation? To keep private life outside of work?

It is not possible to have a corporation without personal life, since each person comes to work every day with that personal life inside their mind. But it is very important to hope that no other employee has an affair or falls in love, or lives with or marries any other employee. This blocks communication with all the others at work, and creates fiefdoms, small kingdoms inside the company.

Why are women having such a hard time arriving at top positions in companies?

I've seen a lot of unfairness in various places where I worked. Women usually work for men. But men blame women for things that go wrong. Women are not confident with men, because they are used to being trapped in this system. The boss will never say something is her success – but if something goes wrong, it is her fault. Men at work are cowards; they usually blame women.

Women are not confident with men, because they are used to being trapped in this system.

I don't know how this works in businesses like steel, cars, etc. where you have few women working, but in firms where there are starting to be more women, you see these dynamics happening all over the place.

Casting Couches in the Office

Probably every 'attractive' woman at an office has had it said about her that she 'probably got her job you-know-how'. It's unfair, but the clichés are very strong, and though we are in a time of change, many still believe the stereotypes. We are neither beyond the clichés, free of them, nor do we really believe them – but we still live with them.

Mini Hite Report: Statistics

Question: If you have ever had sex or given sexual favours to a man because it could help your job or career, did it pay off?

31% I'm not sure
14% Yes, he kept his promises
17% He helped my career, but not as much as I had hoped
9% Yes, but looking back, I think I would rather just have been given money
29% No, he didn't help me anyway

Women's experiences with this vary enormously:

'We didn't have a clear-cut agreement, but my career seemed to go OK, especially during the time I was seeing him. Maybe it wouldn't have otherwise. I'll never know. Maybe I would not have made as much money as I did by contracts with the firm, but we never spoke about this. I don't know if he was super-discreet and smart, or if my own work would have paid off anyway. By the way, it's hard for me to admit to you that I even did this. I sound cheap and stupid – but I'm really intelligent and ethical most of the time.'

'Does playing ball with the boys really get women ahead? I'm not sure. Did women ever get ahead this way, or is the efficiency of the "casting couch" only a legend? I have to admit that I've tried using sex to get help at work, and I'm still waiting to see results (real results). I have to admit it's interesting though, and after all, you do have to sleep with someone, don't you? It's entertaining to me, to seduce a man at work, I mean, I like the game of seduction involved in negotiating with a man. It's challenging, a little like being a big game hunter.'

Whether or not a man will help a woman's career because there is or has been sexual intimacy may depend, according to my research into male psychology during love and sex, on his own sexual and emotional identity.

According to findings in *The Hite Report on Male Sexuality,* many men are ambivalent about *being* in love with a woman, or being sexually attracted. This ambivalence – Is she a nice girl? Worthy of my love? Does she have too much power over me? – creates confusion, conflict and doubt that can make some men exclude a woman they love from promotion, no matter how much her work proves she deserves it. A man may want to punish her rather than reward and include her in business.

In some cases, a man – after a sexual encounter or relationship – will simply drop a woman rather than help her (one thinks of Monica Lewinsky and the famous attempt of Vernon Jordan to help her find another job…) – but maybe not always for the 'obvious' reason, i.e. 'he's a cad'. Rather, he can be filled with doubt and guilt about being in love or turned on: 'A mere woman should not have too much power over me!' Alternatively, on the surface it might appear that a man is afraid that others would say he is playing sexual favourites, but in fact, some men would like it if other men thought they were having a sexual affair, and had to promote a woman as payment.

According to my research into male psychology, it seems that a man's ambivalence about whether, being in love or drawn to a woman who is 'sexy', he can still be a full 'man', in total power and control over his own life, or whether he is foolishly 'bewitched' by a 'female who will soon turn on him' – this confusion creates such inner emotional turmoil and doubt inside many men that they wind up excluding the very women they love from any help whatsoever.

This is hard for women to understand, because men seem to have so much power. Why can't they trust? Why can't they help? The answer has to do with men's complex fears about 'being in love', 'being a man', and 'in a woman's clutches'. (See Chapters 4 and 5.)

Deeper Causes of Sexual Harassment

What is going on psychologically in cases of sexual harassment? Obviously, if the issue were simply one of manners, such things would never happen.

What is going on psychologically in cases of sexual harassment? Obviously, if the issue were simply one of manners, such things would never happen.

Since it is usually clear fairly quickly if another person is interested and responding, or not, how do things get to this stage?

Sometimes the situation arises out of confusion: a man may not have any sexual interest in a woman, and still make a pass at her. Why? Because historically, two issues have come into play. First, men were told that 'real men' always want to make passes at 'young women' – so not doing so means you are 'not a real man'. It is 'expected'. Second, if a man likes a woman, although he may not be interested sexually, the culture has only given him one or two scenarios in which to make his feeling of 'liking' fit: a relationship with a woman can only evolve, two people of the opposite sex can only hang out together, if they are dating and have 'a relationship' (sexual or emotional) or if they are related (sister and brother, father and daughter). There is no such thing as socially condoned 'friendship' between a man and a woman (although, of course, such friendships do exist). A great deal of suspicion surrounds relationships between men and women that are not sexual. Men and women, of course, sometimes rise above social mores in order to have friendships.

Here we are trying to construct new ways of directing positive energy between people at work. There can be new kinds of relationships between the sexes, kinds that may never have existed before – or at least, not in historical memory. Just because they may not have existed in the past does not mean we cannot construct them now. These new relationships – which we might call 'teammates' – can unlock an enormous amount of energy that can be channelled into working together, projects and plans; these new relationships can bring pleasure to the most mundane parts of our jobs and inspire us – harmlessly.

However, sexual harassment can be caused by something more than simple confusion. It can be a sign of a desperate hostility, a kind of taunting of women that is similar to the taunting boys endured on the school ground in the days (at puberty) when they were bullied into 'being a man': 'Can you take it?' Many men feel that the reward for all that brutality that they endured (the so-called 'initiation rites') is the special status they should be rewarded with as a 'man', i.e. work is a man's private preserve, no women should be there, etc. Such men, especially those who feel that

they are not getting enough appreciation or rewards in life, may strike out and do to others what was done to them, and, especially, try through sexual intimidation and taunts to harass women into leaving. This in fact has been successful in some cases that have come to light in the US military, as well as the training school West Point, where women students (the few who tried to enter) were taunted and harassed until some left.

Sexual harassment, like rape, is caused by hostility, a man wanting to prove he is in charge, have another notch on his belt – and the power that comes with having 'bedded' a woman (always more of a feather, traditionally, in a man's cap than a woman's, although women may turn this around), the ability to brag to other men about this, buying the woman's silence. Sexual harassment, like rape, has one objective: humiliating the woman. This is why rape is such a popular tool of war: one side is trying to destroy the morale and self-confidence of the other. Perhaps at work, some men are trying to destroy the morale of the 'new women competitors'.

Sexual harassment, like rape, is caused by hostility.

Sexual harassment, especially unreported, can be dangerous to women. Even if a man doesn't have sex with a woman, the fact that he is seen to be sexually harassing her, making remarks about her clothing, teasing her in front of others, can begin to marginalize her from the others, sideline her.

Is sexual harassment one-sided? Is the person doing the harassing the only one involved?

Should a 'victim' of sexual harassment feel guilty if she (he) co-operated with the situation? As one comments:

'Sometimes a woman can be really confused. On the one hand, she feels she is not really sexually attracted to this man who is coming on to her. But, on the other, it would be fun to go on his sailboat, meet important people, have glamorous dinners with champagne. And – it can't hurt on the job front! These are the things she is thinking, while he is coming on and she is trying to decide what to do. It works like that. It's not all, hey, I'm a good girl, why are you being like that!'

Flirtation can reach a certain level that is pleasant for both people, such as admiration in the eyes, a sympathetic remark, courtesy at an important moment. Flirtation is not the same thing as harassment. (Flirtation is not the stereotype of Carmen, a woman with a low-cut bodice smoking a cigarette; this is a kind of sexual exhibition, a different statement.) Harassment is the pointing out of one person by another, focusing on the sexuality of that person, asking for a sexual entrée, in a context in which power is exerted by the initiator. Whether or not the person being asked for a sexual response really wants to give one or not will never be clear in such a situation, either to the person asking or the person giving. Both people will be left feeling somewhat uncertain and betrayed. Yet since many find such situations sexually exciting, it is almost useless to use logic to deter people; the only effective way to make sure this does not happen inside a company is to have clear company rules and guidelines.

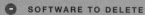

Brain Software Commands

SOFTWARE TO DELETE

Any sexual flirtation is sexual harassment.

SOFTWARE TO INSTALL

Sexual pressure is sexual harassment if it affects one person's job.

Is Sexual Harassment about Sex – or Power?

A note about male sexuality

What is male sexuality?

Is it in men's 'sexual nature' always 'to try to get some'?

'Sexual harassment' is a socially constructed problem, not an inevitable problem of 'biology' ('put a man and a woman in a room together alone, and you are playing with fire...'). Men are not behaving in response to a 'biological imperative' so much as in response to a social software package that tells them 'real men make passes at women, no man is monogamous by nature!'

'Sexual harassment' is a socially constructed problem, not an inevitable problem of 'biology'.

People generally think they know what male sexuality is: a drive for penetration, a drive to reproduce, a drive to 'get it on' with an attractive women. Be James Bond, Darth Vader (with genitals).

However, I believe that what we know as 'male sexuality' is a socially constructed set of behaviours, a way society has had of channelling what men feel into one (reproductive) scenario. When I asked over 7,000 men thier sexual experiences, a picture of much more diversity than could have been expected emerged, implying that what we do with our bodies sexually is something we design with our minds. In fact, the places we aim our 'lust', the fantasies we have, many of our sexual dreams are in part guided by society's programming – much as we would like not to believe this.

The key question is: Do corporations have the will to re-tune male psycho-sexual identity so that men do not feel it is 'natural' to sexually harass women? Executives may fear that such a training programme would not be terribly popular. But, of course, such a training programme could be very, very popular!

'Real Men' and Viagra

The drug Viagra was very much in fashion in the late 1990s, a 'miracle pill' that meant a man could have an erection 'on demand'. Benefits for men? One the one hand, relaxation, no fear of whether or not erection will happen. On the other hand, many news reports seemed to reinforce in men a harmful idea: that erection is necessary for a 'real man to have sex'.

For reasons of historical divisions of 'body and soul', we have learned that erection is mechanical; many men do not seem to feel that their erection has something to do with their emotional condition. If they do not have erections, there may be a problem in their relationship, not in their penis. Although emotions and erection are connected, many men would rather believe anything else, i.e. 'Well, I guess when you get middle aged, this is bound to happen.'

This implies that the penis is not connected to feelings, that the penis is connected to a more or less self-generating set of hormones or body mechanisms, that should operate no matter what a man is (or is not) experiencing in his life. People have often made fun of the 'toys-for-boys', 'erection set' idea of masculinity – wooden blocks boys place together in various ways to form buildings, atoms, etc. – do you use a wooden kit to build 'the erection' too? Others point to skyscrapers and pointed objects, saying these are artists' representations of the penis.

Yet all this talk, silly remarks, make boys get the impression when they are growing up that they have a foreign object between their legs – that the flesh on their body called 'the penis' is not part of the overall 'being', not their self but just 'a rude piece of meat', 'down there'. The epithet 'He thinks with his penis' is further damaging, since it implies that when men have erections and desire sexual connection, they are not thinking but being 'stupid' or 'animalistic'. He's a 'jerk' is an epithet coming from 'jerk off', meaning someone who masturbates, i.e. someone who 'plays with himself'.

The truth is that the penis is a delicate part of the male being, one that responds with exquisite sensitivity to every nuance of emotion a man can feel.

However, since the society has not accepted this form of masculinity (the sensitive version), it has tried to insist that 'a real man' should 'get hard' at will, whenever he decides (in his brain?) it is 'appropriate'. But it is impossible to will an erection into being. Trying to do this has caused a great deal of psychological pain and self-hate in many men – and often in their partners too, as both took lack of erection as a sign of lack of desire, lack of love.

Erection or sexual desire is something in a man or a woman that comes out of the depths of feeling – whether that feeling is for another person, for an enthusiasm about the beauty of the day or a beautiful colour in a dress, or for a perversion one has just seen in a sex video. (The causes of this type of arousal are fascinating, but too complex to dissect here.)

The five Hite Reports have been stating for several years now that, in fact, a man can enjoy 'sex' without even having an erection. How? In two ways. First, as women have had sex for centuries without always having an orgasm themselves, but enjoying helping a man have an orgasm, just so men could enjoy helping a woman have an orgasm via clitoral stimulation, being excited with her, together, without having an orgasm themselves. Second, the definition of sex should change. It has been focused on the reproductive act, i.e. coitus, because we have evolved from a culture that wanted to increase reproduction. Now, however, most of us use birth control while 'performing sex' in the reproductive scenario we learned.

Yet sex could be more interesting if it was not always focused on one scenario, the high point being penetration or insertion (coitus); sex could be a varied individual language of ways to touch, fondle and excite oneself and another person – whether that means stimulation by hand of both people, whether sharing the excitement of a sexual fantasy or oral sex. For none of these activities is an erection necessary.

Finally, erections come and go in men – during sex and during sleep. A man who is kissing a loved one may stop, worrying: 'I can't get an erection now, so I'd better not keep on with this.' But in fact, he may or may not get an erection, yet could continue being deeply involved physically with his partner. Many men do stimulate themselves during sex, masturbate for a minute or two, to make sure their penis is hard at the very time they want it to be. This is the best approach, the one that works better than any other. No man should ever fear lack of erection, as he has nothing to do but reach down and touch himself, while continuing to embrace and love his partner.

Sexual Submission – The Point of Harassment?

Of course, sexual harassment is usually not so simple as 'somebody wanting sex with somebody else'.

Sexual harassment is usually not so simple as 'somebody wanting sex with somebody else'.

Why can it be exciting for many men to 'make a woman submit sexually'?

The answer to this important question is one of the most vital keys to understanding sexuality – not only male sexuality. (See 'Boys' Sexual Identity' in Chapter 5 (pages 124–126), for a deeper understanding.)

Lipstick and Short Skirts at Work

Is looking for deep causes of sexual harassment, hidden motivations, overly complicated?

The common wisdom, as expressed by one person:

'After all, lots of women dress smartly at work, wearing all the latest trends in fashion seen in the magazines, sexy clothes and lipstick, short skirts and tight-breasted tops… aren't they asking for it? Aren't they creating situations, the same situations ("sexual harassment"), they complain about?'

This view scapegoats women, were it to be adopted as 'the whole truth'. In the past, it was believed that women who were raped often caused the rape because of what they were wearing. However, Western courts have now ruled that the culprit, no matter what a women is wearing, is the rapist and not the person aggressed on. Rape in marriage has also been declared illegal.

Interestingly, in unreported sexual harassment cases (85 per cent), it is usually the harasser who keeps his job and the woman harassed who loses hers or leaves.

Connections between pay discrimination and sexual harassment

There is a hidden issue here: discrimination in salary and promotion. Seemingly unrelated, it has everything to do with the increasing number of sexual harassment lawsuits.

There is a hidden issue here: discrimination in salary and promotion. Seemingly unrelated, it has everything to do with the increasing number of sexual harassment lawsuits.

Texaco, Merrill Lynch, Ford Motors – today, discrimination against women, sexually or in pay, is costing corporations millions of dollars in back pay and damages, usually through class action group lawsuits.

Women are sometimes popular with firms because, as Alan Greenspan quipped a few years ago, 'they cost less and they do more'. A company that has squeezed a profit margin out of underpaying women workers may find itself dragged into court by a coalition of these women, justly demanding back pay, damages and compensation. So far, most of these court cases have been successful. Corporations should devise new ways of using the energy and special skills that women provide, without risking financial loss later. This way is to integrate women and men in the workplace in fair ways, giving promotion to those who deserve it. This serves as an example to others, showing that working hard leads to success, not relying on hanging out with the right employees in the bar, etc. Yet...

Situations inside a company that tend to breed sexual harassment and lawsuits include:

❶ Bullying of women or arrogant behaviours by male colleagues and bosses.

❷ A feeling that women are not equally promoted or spotted, not given credit for the value they produce.

❸ Lack of equal pay.

Sexual harassment can happen anywhere, but it is less likely to happen or lead to a lawsuit if the women inside a company are empowered, feeling confident that their work will propel them forwards, without having to take 'extra steps' in hidden ways, use 'special help' from someone.

Would sexual harassment be such an issue if women received equal pay and equal promotions? Perhaps not. But this is a non-question, since sexual harassment, by definition, means that someone who is more powerful than another asks that person to perform sexually or offer sexual-emotional services, physical affection, etc. If women and men were more often equal in corporations, women would feel a thousand times more able to deal with individual sexual and emotional situations as they came up. As it is, women feel that this symbol of their powerlessness in the face of the massive male, boys-together power of the corporation is humiliating and insulting – and deserves to be taken public.

Would sexual harassment be such an issue if women received equal pay and equal promotions? Perhaps not.

What can make women even angrier about sexual harassment on the job than the situation itself is that it points out their secondary status. For example, when the young man took his pants down 'on the job' of constructing a wall inside an apartment for a woman, what he was trying to say was that his status as a man was higher than her status as 'employer' because she was a woman.

Many men are horrified at such stories, and honestly want things to change. It is up to these men, as well as women, to put in motion wheels of change.

Such change should take place, of course, in people's brain software, not simply in legislation. An atmosphere should be created in which men can rethink, explore their ideas about what a valid 'male sexual expression' is – and whether or not they really believe or want to continue the old game of 'my cock is bigger than your cock'. ('He who can't get an errection is impotent...' etc.)

Is Neutering the Office the Solution?

Some executives say, simplistically, that the way to avoid any whiff of sexual harassment is to declare the workplace off limits to any acknowledgement of the gender of the opposite sex, and especially, off limits to dating or forming sexually intimate relationships.

Is this a realistic solution? No, and imagining that a simple policy like this will 'solve the problem' and mean there is no sexual harassment taking place in the corporation is only a recipe for disaster. Blindly naïve, at best.

There is a fundamental difference between sexual attraction and sexual harassment (see Chapter 8); attraction is something that can be expressed in a thousand ways, harassment is something an individual knows very well is intimidating to the other person but carries on doing anyway, because it is somehow sexually and psychologically pleasurable to humiliate the other person. It is done to 'prove a point', i.e. to prove that one person can get another person to accept their will.

Companies that try to block the problem of inter-gender sexual harassment or problems by placing a ban on 'love' only heighten the pleasure for the harasser: the sexual 'pass' is doubly illicit. The ban will only succeed in making employees lonely, causing them to feel alienated about the company they work for; this is especially true, of course, for single employees – an increasing number of today's workforce (nearing 50 per cent).

Companies that try to block the problem of inter-gender sexual harassment or problems by placing a ban on 'love' only heighten the pleasure for the harasser: the sexual 'pass' is doubly illicit.

Information from Hite Research:
Why Do Women sometimes Co-operate with Sexual Harassment?

Flirtation with fathers for special treatment
'My mother accused me of being flirtatious with my father. I was really very close with him, but that's not the same thing. Didn't I have the right to be close to him? I loved him, and he loved me, he understood me like no one else in that family.'

Girls' feelings when they are their father's 'favourite' can be quite hard for them to deal with: the girl can feel she is betraying the mother, as the mother is supposed to be the loved one, not the daughter;

the daughter may also feel shame for the hidden sexual implications, whether she feels sexual or not. Even smiles exchanged with the father sometimes become guilt-laden.

The daughter can wonder: 'Am I being flirtatious? or am I just irresistibly lovable, superior to my mother?'

Is it possible that girls could desire, in their heart of hearts to 'seduce' the father, emotionally at least, because this would mean having more power in the family, more power than the mother *or* the father? This would take a girl out of the hated category of the powerless, the 'child'. Thus, an impulse in this direction might be natural. However, to interpret this as perversity on the part of girls would be to make the mistake Freud did when he interpreted girls' desire for the rights of men in society as 'penis envy'.

To understand what is going on, we must not neglect to take into consideration the gender and ageist power constructions enmeshed in the structure of the 'traditional family'. These feelings and behaviours on the part of family members certainly do not imply that there is a 'natural heterosexual attraction' or urge between father and daughter. The society is busy obliquely whispering to the father and daughter that they 'might' feel this sexual attraction, but without this social suggestion or tension, would the thoughts occur so easily? Without it, fathers and daughters could have much better relationships. They could be friends.

The family system as we know it is set up for trouble because, due to the way that the social order is constructed, most girls soon learn that their one basic power is their sexuality (whereas boys' might be sports, athletic prowess or good grades or being group leaders of boys, etc.).

The family system as we know it is set up for trouble because, due to the way that the social order is constructed, most girls soon learn that their one basic power is their sexuality.

Some girls think they are 'guilty' of having sexual feelings for their fathers when they are not. For example a girl who receives gifts from her father – money, dresses, shoes etc. – could naturally feel pleasure and excitement, which might cause her body, including her genitals, to flush with a heated, happy feeling. This flush could be confused with, or interpreted as, guilty 'sexual arousal'.

It can also be interpreted as general emotional arousal, happiness. That is how it probably would be interpreted if the gift were coming from the mother. However, standing behind every interchange between a father and daughter is a big sign: 'Danger: Heterosexuality Here.' There is 'always' a possibility of sexual attraction between opposite genders.

This self-consciousness about 'the meaning of it all' or 'fear of looking the wrong way' lends a sexual atmosphere even where there is none. Films such as *Lolita* and *Gigi* make this idea, especially between older men and young girls, socially very widely known. Further, there are very few models of men and women being 'just friends' in our society; usually 'friends' are of the same gender, and so all opposite gender contacts are presumed to be sexual.

The situation for a girl, in a family like this, is similar to the emotional dynamics experienced in date rape. In a typical date rape scenario, the man says: 'Don't you want it too... Really?' and because her body may be turned on and stimulated by the situation, the girl feels she can't honestly say 'no'. In other words, girls often are not sure why they may enjoy sex, when they really do mean 'no'. However, this doesn't mean that *emotionally* she 'really wants it'.

The division between an emotional and a psychological response is one that can be very confusing to a girl. It is this confusion which is exploited by fathers or older male relatives in cases of sexual abuse.

Why girls learn that 'female sexuality' is power, their only real power/weapon, has to do with our society's construction of 'a woman's place', not with girls themselves, or with whether a girl is a 'good girl' or a 'bad girl'. When one has so little of it, it is a natural temptation to use power. This does not 'prove' anything about 'heterosexual impulses between father and daughter being natural'; it merely proves that fathers have power in the hierarchical family, and that girls see that one way to get to that power and approval is through sexual flirtatiousness, cuteness or 'innocence'.

Women in careers can watch their software to make sure they don't repeat any of these scenarios with the chiefs (or 'daddies') all around them.

How Do CEO 'Fathers' Feel about their 'Daughter Employees'' Sexuality?

Are some CEOs like fathers who don't like 'their daughters' having sex or falling in love with another man?

Their policies towards young (married or unmarried) women who become pregnant (vs 'younger' single women) would seem to indicate 'yes'!

Do some corporations have a problem with 'pregnant women working' because they don't like visible signs of female sexual activity? Simply because a pregnant stomach is a visible sexual reference that (supposedly) 'the woman has enjoyed it'?

There is still, in most of our mental softwares, the old archetype of the 'good woman' being someone like Maria, the pure, asexual woman and mother ... and an archetype of 'the bad woman' being a 'sexual temptress', an Eve who is sexually wicked and deserves to fall.

In paternalistic management style, the father is like God or Moses, and a woman or 'daughter' should be like Maria (before she had Christ). If she has sex or gets pregnant, she becomes the 'bad girl', Eve, who had to be banished from the Garden of Eden. Thus, pregnant women must be banished from all corporate gardens...

Do some corporations have a problem with 'pregnant women working' because they don't like visible signs of female sexual activity?

Fathers and Daughters: The Need for Friendship

In the Holy Family model of 'family' that we have in the West,[2] there is no type of relationship which men have with women that is not based on gender. The model is one which stresses sexuality and gender as forming the basis of all relationships: sons and mothers, fathers and daughters, wives and husbands – friendship is not even hinted at, it is nowhere on the map. So perhaps it is no wonder that many fathers have a hard time figuring out how to relate to their daughters.

Perhaps it is no wonder that many fathers have a hard time figuring out how to relate to their daughters.

The sexual archetypes stored in most fathers' software, according to my research, can cause harsh words when a daughter arrives at puberty and her body flowers sexually.

There is a moment at which some fathers 'accuse' their daughters of being sexual, lamenting: 'You used to be so nice, so sweet, when you were little. What happened? You've changed.'

As one young woman describes:

'My father freaked out every time I as much as mentioned such things as lipstick or dates or dancing. Once my mother and I went shopping and I bought a beautiful purple velvet cape at a sale. I showed my father the cape and he called me a prostitute ("street girl" was the expression he used; I think what he had in mind was the Biblical "harlot"). The next day I gave the cape to the Salvation Army.'

Sometimes, without fully realizing what they are doing, fathers respond to their daughters' new sexuality with misogynist double-standard ideas:

'Don't wear that lipstick! You look like a prostitute.'

'You used to be my sweet little girl, What happened?' (On being 'confronted' with a daughter with breasts and/or a boyfriend, etc.)

Or, daughters report instances of their fathers not respecting them:

'My father was very abusive. I grew to hate and fear him. He always thought of me as a whore. I was pretty and friendly, and in his psychotic mind that meant slut. Now he has stopped drinking and is more amiable, but he is still ungiving.'

Girls are usually stunned when such things are said to them. Most girls think this is not their 'real father' speaking and hope he will change back to his nicer self, the 'real him', and stop this 'scary behaviour'. Unfortunately, most fathers never find a way to acknowledge positively (or even negatively) the onset of girls' menstruation, or build other bridges of communication.

Many fathers feel genuinely confused about their own feelings. Are their feelings 'sexual'? Or OK, just affectionate? If a man has grown up and seen nothing but patriarchal attitudes to women, and likes his own daughter, he may wonder if his feelings are 'OK'.

How can he express his feelings of friendship and admiration – even 'attraction' – and not be 'politically incorrect'? Men have few models for friendship with women and girls – but they always have presented to them, by the culture, the 'fact' that a 'real man' should be leering and feel lascivious about 'younger females'. And this may not be what the father is feeling at all.

Can he talk this over with the girl's mother?

2 Since this reproductive model of the family (the one seen on Christmas cards and in department store windows) is actually less than 2,000 years old, it is obviously not 'human nature'.

How Can Fathers 'See' and Accept their Daughters' Sexuality?

There must be a way for fathers to speak with daughters about sexuality that is more direct and not coquettish; to express a comradely and affectionate notice that she is growing up, that he sees her 'femaleness', and indicates that he is trying to find a way to relate to this new aspect of her with respect. Could they work it out together?

Mothers, grandmothers and other relatives frequently point out or make references to a boys' masculinity or sexuality with pride and/or awe – or a feeling of 'That's his, there's nothing I can do about it, it's part of the male world, which is stronger than I am, and it's his self-identity, it's pretty great, huh! Yeah, he'll be a man, have a penis, have all the macho and rights of a man!'

Fathers, however, in their sexual references to their daughters, too often shame girls about their sexuality – why? Perhaps they know no other language (except the language of love and that is even more negative in the context)? It is time to change all this, and for fathers to congratulate girls and become their friends, to give them pride! This would be the best protection (if any were needed in the kind of a world we hope to build) from any degradation or exploitation she could be exposed to from other men during her life.

Many fathers don't know how to relate to their daughter after she becomes more 'female' since there is little room in the society for male-female friendships. Most girls reported things like: 'My father spent time with me going to museums, reading. We talked a lot about everything except sex (he is so prudish!). I wish he had felt free to talk to me about man/woman relations but for those things I was shuffled off to my mother.'

A father can respectfully recognize his daughter's new sexuality, say that she looks female and bright and attractive, focusing on her good points. Express not a leering encouragement to have sex copying men or a 'dominatrix' model – but a happy, positive explorative yet self-contained identity which makes its own individual sexual signature, with pride.

Solutions and Practical Ways to Handle Situations at Work

Not every other person's mind can be changed, enlightenment brought, so what to do?

Not every other person's mind can be changed, enlightenment brought, so what to do?

How to discuss the problem of sexual harassment

❶ If you think you might have said or done the wrong thing, seemed to be harassing and employee or colleague (if you're the harasser...) which of the following three responses should you make?

    ⓐ ignore what happened and never do it again

    ⓑ apologize and never do it again

    ⓒ sit down together and talk it over.

How do you avoid sexual harassment lawsuits in your firm?

2 If you're the harassed, should you:

a report the situation immediately

b think it over overnight and speak to your best friend about it

By giving sexual energy and attraction, sparks, another place or places to go – an even more attractive place than a short-lived sexual encounter or a hidden affair.

c punch the offender

d other.

3 If a staff member or colleague complains to you she's being harassed, turns to you for understanding or help, should you:

a report the situation immediately

b talk it over with her over dinner

c confront the offender with her

d other.

How can problems of 'sexual harassment' be avoided?

- By understanding the dynamics that cause it.

- By memorizing the simple guidelines here.

The Bottom Line

How do you avoid sexual harassment lawsuits in your firm? How can this looming problem be eliminated from corporate culture?

By giving sexual energy and attraction, sparks, another place or places to go – an even more attractive place than a short-lived sexual encounter or a hidden affair.

Where is that? New kinds of exciting work relationships, relationships that do not proceed to sex, but that develop a new kind of collegiality, especially as teammates.

What are the rules of such teammates and other new relationships?

1 You can go out to dinner.

2 You cannot stay overnight, make love or kiss on the lips.

3 You can go places together, people at work can know that you work especially well together, are a team.

4 This team does not exclude your forming another team with someone else and you should not be jealous if your teammate does so.

5 The focus on your relationship should be primarily on work and projects you are doing together.

This is a new kind of relationship.

To avoid gender discrimination lawsuits, for sexual harassment or for back pay, a company must think about and revise its hiring and promotion policies towards women. This does not mean only the hiring of young recruits, but also hiring female executives at the executive level. More and more corporations find that the trend is not only to promote executives from inside the company, but also to bring in executives from elsewhere (even to bring in CEOs) to guide the company in a new way. There is no reason why executive women cannot be found, there are many today in the professions and universities, as well as in government executive positions. (Where quota systems were in force, more executive women now exist).

A company should look at pay levels, as the British government did in 1999. Although the findings of any study a company undertakes may not make for easy reading, at least there will be a place to begin, and the insider think tank can go to work on the problem: lower some men's salaries? Raise the women's to the level of men's? Change the company's pay and reward structure altogether? These are questions that each corporation will want to answer for itself, but questions that are urgent to address: the longer they are left to smoulder, the more likely that the board of directors will suddenly be surprised by the kind of lawsuits Merrill Lynch and Texaco, among others, have faced.

Rethinking these policies will make people proud of their company.

Your Opinion...

What is your opinion and experience? What do you think? What have been *your* experiences of what's been discussed in this chapter?

Please use this space to write your remarks, or alternatively you may e-mail comments to the *Sex and Business* website at www.sexandbusiness.com/myopinion. Naturally, you may express yourself anonymously.

_____

_____

_____

_____

_____

_____

It is natural for men and women to become attracted and fall in love at work. Today, most people with serious careers have very little time to 'go out and meet someone'; it is natural to form relationships with people one sees every day and shares interests with. (This is not to say every relationship ends perfectly, or happily...!) A study once showed that most people marry someone who lives within a five-mile radius of them. Why? Because seeing someone who lives further away is too irregular. Just so, people at work, who see each other often, and learn to know each other in various conditions (tired, bright-eyed, happy, sad), find that their feelings grow.

Are love and romance

off bounds

at work?

Are Love and Romance Off Bounds at Work?

Many corporations have a policy[1] – official or unofficial – that 'love' should not take place at work. Flirtation is banned from the office. Yet half of today's employees are single and many have very little 'free time' outside the office to 'look for someone':

'Every morning we take the taxi to work together, from our apartment to the office, but before we get there, about a block away, she gets out and I continue on, so no one at work suspects we come in together or live together or sleep together...'

Forty-two per cent of people at the corporations surveyed by Hite Research are now in relationships with someone else at work; 35 per cent are hiding that relationship from others at their offices.

There is no case to be made that women and men can't work together in corporations.

Flirtation is banned from the office.

Although some executives 'rationalize' or justify the policy by saying this avoids sexual harassment lawsuits, this is simplistic. To declare the workplace off limits to dating or intimate relationships will not 'save' a corporation, merely temporarily push the situation under the rug.

The way to avoid sexual harassment lawsuits is to change attitudes, implement the guidelines indicated in this book and hold training sessions on the topics of how to get along in a new way with 'the other sex' at work (indicated in these chapters), as well as holding seminars and discussion groups for executives and personnel on 'issues of masculinity', the new corporate manners, 'basics of female psychology', 'male psycho-sexual identity'. (Please contact the author for a list of suitable consultancies.)

Boys and girls go to school together all over the world and do well. University performance by males and females shows that students are not 'too distracted' to do their work, yet dating and love affairs take place on a regular basis. There is no case to be made that women and men can't work together in corporations.

Love Stories

What happens when people in gender-neuter offices (where sex and love are banned) fall in love or start dating?

What happens when people in gender-neuter offices (where sex and love are banned) fall in love or start dating?

---

1 Recently there is discussion of a new 'love contract' for employees: in this contract, an employee promises to inform the company of any personal (sexual – romantic) involvement with another employee. This is clearly a misguided policy.

'I was 30 when I met John. I almost thought I would never want to get married, it just didn't interest me, and the men I met were hardly people I would want to share a flat with let alone take home to mom. He was wonderful. When I met him, I couldn't believe it. His hair, his eyes, his build! He was always sensitive and caring (we met at work), when I had a work problem he would help me – but he never showed any special sexual interest in me, he just "behaved normal". I had no clue he was interested. He told me later he used to go home and fantasize about me. I thought about him a lot but I kept telling myself that he was someone I worked with, that sexual affairs at work don't work, and that was it, period. Finally, one day we both found ourselves at work on a day when everyone else was off, a bank holiday. We both came in to catch up on some work. Outside the doors to the bathrooms (I know, I know!), we fell into each others' arms. It was the most wonderful embrace of my life. We began living together, and six months later, we were married. Yes, we both still work at the same place, and yes we told everybody (we invited them to the wedding) and it doesn't seem to have caused a problem at work.

'They say that if everybody knows that two people live together, then that forms a sort of Mafia at work, and the others feel closed out, they can't co-operate as well as they need to with you as an individual. But this assumes a really super-neutral workplace where nobody knows anybody, and nobody knows who is whose friend, etc. We all always knew which of the guys were friends, who went out for drinks after work or at lunch together, who had lunch in each other's offices, etc. It would make work a terribly lonely and sad place if everybody had to stay away from having friends. I once worked in a place like that, and I got stomach ulcers. I think knowing that John and I love each other makes not only my life better, but the lives of those around me. Loving him makes my life so much better, it cannot have anything but a positive effect on others. It lets people there know that love is OK.'

Can You Fall in Love at Work – Without Disaster?

'Sexual affairs at work don't work'

Is this commonly accepted idea true? According to Hite Research statistics, love affairs between co-workers continue happily just as often as affairs and dating relationships outside work, with a slightly higher (5 per cent higher) success rate.

Office relationships may or may not 'reach a happy landing'.

As most dating relationships have ups and downs, and many may not work out at all for one reason or another, so office relationships may or may not 'reach a happy landing'.

Yes, emotional upsets between a couple can be brought to work, but then, emotional upsets between a couple outside work will still affect work, i.e. one employee will be upset anyway – and desperately trying to use the telephone all day, in most cases.

If half of the office staff is single[2]

Today, half the population of the world's large cities is 'single', and also, about half of the employees of most firms are single.[3]

If half of the office staff (of various ages) is single in today's offices, is this acceptable to corporations – or do corporations expect people to be 'stable and married', especially after a certain level? If CEOs 'should be married with children' (see Chapter 3), shouldn't all other employees? Yet romance between employees is considered 'inappropriate'; therefore logically, corporations expect that their employees, managers and executives be married to someone who doesn't work at the firm – or if single, keep dating firmly outside the office, with no telephone calls, no visits to the office, no photographs on the desk, etc.

These are the unspoken rules intended when corporate chiefs say confidently: 'The way to avoid sexual harassment lawsuits is to say that sex and love are off bounds at work.' Yet they are impractical and harsh in terms of people's quality of life.

Companies' policy, usually unwritten, against 'relationships' at work, flies directly in the face of many employees' needs, i.e. most working people do not have a lot of time to search around outside work for people to get to know, like and love. It is more human to develop interests and understanding with other people at work.

It is more human to develop interests and understanding with other people at work.

Corporate attitudes announcing that romance at work is 'inappropriate' don't work – and reflect hidden assumptions – software that needs updating and replacing.

Fear of Sex...

Question: Are some CEOs like fathers who don't like 'their daughters' having sex or falling in love with other men?

It is natural for men and women to become attracted and fall in love at work. Today, most people with serious careers have very little time to 'go out and meet someone'; it is natural to form relationships with people one sees every day and shares interests with. (This is not to say every relationship ends perfectly, or happily...!) A study once showed that most people marry someone who lives within a five-mile radius of them. Why? Because seeing someone who lives further away is too irregular. Just so, people at work, who see each other often, and learn to know each other in various conditions (tired, bright-eyed, happy, sad), find that their feelings grow.

Many corporate executives, managers and employees work twelve hours a day, sometimes

2 Although this is declared to be 'a disaster' reflecting the 'collapse of civilization', such exaggerations are untrue, see page 51, Democratization of the Family.

3 What if most of the workforce is 'single'? It is often assumed that 'lots of singles and divorced people' represent a non-stable work pool, yet this is not true. The revolt against the 'traditional family' (statistics showing 50% of the population lives single) does not mean that 'civilization' or business is collapsing, but rather that a process of democratization and revaluation of personal relationships is taking place. This change heralds the birth of a more moral and satisfying private life, a more 'complete' identity inside oneself, as well as a readjustment of work's place in life.

longer. Even if an executive 'meets someone' outside the office, there is still the daily schedule to maintain, plus booking in 'quality time' for the relationship. How much more logical it is, many people find, to share some of the work time and have a reason to stay in touch (work, in addition to desire), so that what the other 'does all day' is not a mystery, causing needless conflict.

Others argue that an acknowledged 'couple' at work creates a fiefdom, leading to power blocks at work, etc. But wouldn't this be true in any case, don't some employees create power fiefdoms?

In the future, as more and more women work at all levels in corporations, people will find partners mostly at work, developing feelings for each other through the heady experience of working together. It's a well-kept secret: the fascinating bonding energy of shared work and shared projects leads to very good partnerships. Corporations would do better to develop new points of view toward the existence of 'private feelings' inside the office, than to insist 'there is no sex or private life at work'.

Corporations would do better to develop new points of view toward the existence of 'private feelings' inside the office.

The Bumpy Road to Love: What if You Fall in Love with Someone at Work?

Is making lovers hide behind the scenes good for a company's productivity and morale? The ban on sex and love in the office means that many couples hide their relationships from colleagues. The tensions thus created ('it's our secret') can sometimes be fun, but over the long run, harm the relationship when there is no seeming end to the dilemma:

'I have been having a torrid affair with Stuart. He's a bloke at work, I truly adore him. But he hasn't got the courage to tell anybody at work about us, so I'm beginning to disrespect him. I think he's being a wimp in this respect. How seriously can I take him, if we have to hide all the time?'

As the CEO of Spanish Telecom (see Chapter 3), himself young and single, commented in 1999:

'It is not good for an employee to have to search every night to decide who to have dinner with, etc. so if they have a partner, we try to help them both have jobs here, we believe in relationships, wherever they meet. This is good for the company.'

Negative corporate policy can fray relationships. What happens when the company has one of those annual or regular parties in which people are encouraged to bring their spouse or date? This leaves those not in 'sanctified relationships' to fight it out in private:

Negative corporate policy can fray relationships.

'Tony and I almost broke up once when there was a company boat ride, and we couldn't go together on it – even though at that point we had been living together for over a year. We went to work together every morning, but we were always careful never to enter work together. I told him that if he went on the boat ride without me, this would be tantamount to giving me my freedom, and I would feel free to do as I pleased, even though I was living with him – since he seemed to feel he could do as he pleased, never mind my feelings. So if he went, I would start going out with my friends and even dating others, even though I "lived with" him. It would remain "our secret". Guess what? He told everybody at work he married me! We went to the boat ride together, and so far everything's OK at work.'

There is no reason for banning love from the office. This doesn't mean that couples should hold hands in meetings: it simply means that basic rules of office behaviour should be followed inside the office – but it's still OK to develop a relationship with a co-worker outside the office. If it works out, they can tell the office later.

There is no reason for banning love from the office.

Some US military has had various negative incidents because of its policies about women at work. Men in the military have an unfortunate record of sexual harassment of women in the military; in fact Top Brass have made it plain that they prefer not to have women 'on board' in the military – at all. Corporate policies that want to deny that women are there (by making even discreet cases of falling in love 'inappropriate') seem to mirror these it's-better-not-to-have-women attitudes (they interfere with

'men's serious work') – but if you have to have them, try to make them be invisible...

Some US military... Top Brass have made it plain that they prefer not to have women 'on board' in the military – at all.

The Neutered Office (!)

Some executives say that corporations should make *all* behaviour at work gender-neuter: there should be no acknowledgement of gender (especially women's) whatsoever. For example, if a man and a woman pass through a doorway, the man should not hold the door for a woman; the junior employee should hold the door for the senior-in-rank employee (see Chapter 3). Potentially, this scheme could bar women from the workplace, as men (nervous about women as competition?) could say they 'cannot work with women' because they feel 'distracted' – although any feelings of distraction would be created by the company's big-brother ban on 'thoughts in that direction', not by the 'sexual temptation supposedly offered by women'.

'There's no sex in this house!': hidden reasons for the ban on love at work

Saying private life should be 'left at the office door' is suspiciously like the approach many parents took/take, i.e. 'There's no sex in this house!' Just as parents know that their teenage children are interested in sex (maybe even 'out somewhere' having sex), as long as their kids don't 'bring it home', have sex at home, it's OK. In other words, neither 'the kids' nor the parents 'have sex' at home, it would seem: parents almost never kiss passionately or mention having sex together to their children,[4] leaving sons and daughters to conclude that 'there is no sex in this house'.

Corporate CEOs and other 'executive daddies' may be projecting a little bit of this attitude onto the workplace. Do some corporate chieftains feel jealous of their daughters and sons having sex, is this a reason why they like the 'no sex and love' policy?

Such hidden attitudes could also explain corporations' strange policies towards women and pregnancy. Most corporate heads questioned in this research felt that 'the problem for women advancing their careers is getting married and having children'. Yet the corporations themselves carry out a punitive policy towards women in this regard, blocking their careers. This is not to say that 'corporations should grant more maternity and paternity leaves' (that is another issue), but to point out that corporations don't want to see pregnant women at work. They don't want to see the evidence that 'one of their daughters' has been having sex with someone ('been fucking', put plainly). This part of a woman's life must be kept hidden, far away from inside a corporation's walls, similar to the biblical story of Mary giving birth to Jesus: there is no round stomach (none of the famous depictions shows her this way), no blood or opening of her legs during birth, no 'messy' after-birth liquids – no, the conception and birth were 'immaculate'. Corporations are, comically,

imposing the same model of reproduction on women today inside corporations!

Think about it.

What would another kind of corporate landscape look like? Could people design something more dignified yet more real inside new relationships in the workplace?

Could people design something more dignified yet more real inside new relationships in the workplace?

Lovers or Friends?

How can you know in advance if it is friendship or sexual romance?
Many people feel uneasy beginning a new kind of relationship with a member of the opposite sex, wondering where it's going:

'I'm afraid he wants more out of our relationship than I can give. He says he just wants to be my friend, that it's ridiculous – what do I imagine? That he wants to drag me kicking and screaming into his bedroom? I guess even his saying that seems to me like he is thinking about that. Of course, such verbal remarks excite my imagination, and make me wonder about that side of him – while at the same time reassuring me too. Part of me thinks he meant it, that he just wants to be my friend. He says that real friendship between the sexes can exist,

---

4 Can you imagine a mother, cooking breakfast for her children, telling them, 'Oh I'm tired this morning! Your father and I stayed up late last night, making love...' (see *The Hite Report on the Family*).

and what he will get out of it is a friend who is interesting and interested in him too. But do I want only that? Maybe I want him to be attracted to me, maybe I want to tell myself "yes, we'll be friends" because this way I can allow the chance for him to make a pass at me, become my "adoring fan" and prop up my ego, in a way a woman friend wouldn't do? I guess it's too complicated to think about; I'd rather just not try to be friends with a man I work with.'

Brain Software Commands

SOFTWARE TO DELETE

If I have an important relationship with someone of the opposite sex, there will always be a sexual undercurrent there; if I stop and think about it I will recognize it.

SOFTWARE TO INSTALL

I have new choices today, a bigger world is available to me, I can have relationships with the opposite sex that do not involve sex, relationships that do not interfere with my love relationship (any more than a same-sex friendship would), but are nevertheless close and sharing. These relationships will make it possible for me to experience life more fully and expand as a person.

A New Spectrum of Emotions: New Friendships at Work

Of course, every relationship at work between a woman and a man does not have to lead to the bedroom. You say 'I know that!' But do you really believe it? That life can be fulfilling and rewarding without even having a sex life!?

It is the thesis of this book that more relationships than need to go down the road of 'we're attracted, we like each other, we're of the opposite sex, so sex must be what we're after'. Many people feel a spark of attraction for another person that is not really best expressed by having sex. (What do you do after? If one of you doesn't really want to do it again, will the other person be angry, accusing the first of 'only wanting a one night stand'?) It is better to have a wider choice of directions to take a budding relationship; the relationships trying to happen can happen perhaps best in terms of work and friendship.

Today, when people at work feel a warm attraction, they can use this energy in a variety of directions. They need not conclude that the only way to be 'close' (declare a gender truce and feel safe??) is to throw themselves into each others' arms. Suppose both are married and do not want a big change, they are happy – but feel 'it seems a shame just to stop here, let it go at that'. At this point, it would be nice to see that there are two or three other types of more or less long-term relationships that can be enjoyed.

Society would be better off with more flexible choices of ways for women and men to relate.

Society would be better off with more flexible choices of ways for women and men to relate, than only one focused on the possibility of reproduction ('sex', i.e. coitus).

A diversity of possible relationships is appropriate and will benefit everyone.

A diversity of possible relationships is appropriate and will benefit everyone.

Friends or a new kind of colleagues?

Should office relationships be friendships or some new form of colleagues?

Do people at work perform best when they stick with being colleagues, and don't become friends? Whether a work relationship should grow and develop more in the style of friendship or collegiality depends on several factors.

Friendship at work, especially with someone of the opposite sex, is often hidden; the tendency is to downplay it.

It seems that friendships between men and women at work are taboo, in the same way that they are taboo in society in general:

It seems that friendships between men and women at work are taboo, in the same way that they are taboo in society in general.

'I started to have fun at the pub with Sally after work. It was harmless, just our way to relax. I noticed, however, that neither of us acted like we were friends when we were at the office and we always left the building separately. It was an unspoken understanding, our "guilty secret".'

Friendships are considered 'normal' between people of the same sex – men hang out with their male friends, women hang out with 'the girls' – but if a man hangs out with a woman, it is considered peculiar ('unless he is after something'), or they are having sex or heading for sex.

This situation is further complicated if one or the other is on a higher level; not only is it complicated for the people involved (see Chapter 7), but also outsiders will think things they would not think if two men, a junior and a senior, hung out together.

Brain Game 8.1

Consider the differences

Situation one:

Noticing two men tend to hang out together, one senior, one junior, colleagues comment: 'Hmmm, they get on well together. I guess Mr _____ is grooming "Jim" for a better position.' 'Jim wants to get on in the company, so he's lucky that he and Mr ____ hit it off.'

Situation two:

Colleagues notice a man and woman hang out together, one a senior, one a junior: 'I wonder who's using who? I bet one of them wants sex, the other wants a promotion! Good luck to them!' 'If she thinks she'll get anywhere that way, she has a lot to learn.'

There is a clear difference in perception when two colleagues of the opposite sex become friends. This is a difference we must work to eradicate from our minds, in the interest of all of our mental health and future intelligent life on the planet.

In fact, the situations described may not depict people who are friends, but who are a team (what I also call Stage 2 collegiality, that is deeper collegiality). In Stage 2 collegiality, the focus of the friendship is work, with more personal remarks and personal observations allowed than in Stage 1 collegiality. Stage 1 is best maintained with others one is not easily attuned to work with, those with whom formality and polite etiquette work best. Yet there is a difference between being friends and being a team (Stage 2 colleagues).

We really should change our tendency to badmouth friendships between women and men, since many people find that these friendships do exist and are excellent.

Brain Software Commands

⊖ SOFTWARE TO DELETE

Between a man and a woman, there is no such thing as 'only friends'; anyone who thinks so is a fool, just kidding him or herself.

⊕ SOFTWARE TO INSTALL

Friendships between women and men (of every age and financial status) are helpful and part of a society that functions more fully, part of the future.

I have the right to be friends with members of the opposite sex; who would I like to become friends with?

The Sexual Future

It is not always easy to see one's way forward in creating a friendship or serious work collegiality (being teammates) with someone at work, as this woman explains:

It is not always easy to see one's way forward in creating a friendship or serious work collegiality (being teammates) with someone at work.

'I really liked one of my colleagues. I kept on wanting to invite him places, take him along when a group of us were getting together, etc. It was so easy to talk to him, and I didn't want to limit our working relationship by being so formal all the time. It even seemed to help the work if we could get into fun, relaxed conversations, it had a good influence on our work. But at the same time, I didn't invite him anyplace, because I worried that though the situation would work at first, it might backfire somehow, and cause a problem later. What problem? I don't know, maybe a colleague's jealousy if we got on too well together, or tensions between us ("what next?", you know the feeling!), or perhaps an inability to accept another male-female relationship that one of us might have... Anyway, was this a chance missed for a good friendship? Did I do the right thing and save the project? I don't know, I'll never know.'

Men may hesitate even more than women to initiate friendly elements in a working relationship, especially with a senior or junior staff person, someone not on their level:

'It was tough. I kept seeing Sally and stopping myself from drifting over to her desk to talk to her. It felt completely natural, it always got me thinking when I could chat with her, it helped me. But I questioned myself about this: was my real motivation that I was becoming sexually attracted to her? What would she think? She would probably think I was coming on to her, I became self-conscious around her, and even thinking of stopping to talk to her became a problem. This irritated me, and I was glad to see her go when she moved to another branch – even though I had originally liked her and hoped she would stay with us. Illogical, isn't it?'

People today at work have a much larger canvas of choices for designing relationships with the opposite sex than they previously had in private life.

In trying to change work relationships, women and men can break new barriers and form creative, stable friendships that continue for years, never feeling a need to 'progress to the inevitable climax'. This does not mean we are creating a 'neuter world' at the office; it means we are creating a more diverse world, with a more appropriate range of choices between men and women.

In trying to change work relationships, women and men can break new barriers and form creative, stable friendships that continue for years.

Friendships at Work – Leading towards New Kinds of Relationships Between Women and Men

The workplace today offers a great opportunity for people to break old patterns of relationships and create new ones – and, thereby, to create a new type of society.

The workplace today offers a great opportunity for people to break old patterns of relationships and create new ones – and, thereby, to create a new type of society.

In the past, the main area where people of the opposite sex met was in 'private life'. The danger now is that we will unwittingly apply old ideas from this pre-existing software in our heads to situations at work – and miss our opportunity: 'If it's a woman, she must be like my mom, my sister or my lover'; 'If it's a man, he must be like my dad, my brother, my boyfriend or husband.' This is illogical, but many people are thinking just this without realizing it.

People at work today have a much larger canvas of choices for designing relationships with each other than they previously had, or than is usually available in 'private life'.

It is now a question of transforming relationships in a way we have never done before. To achieve this, we must believe in ourselves, get to know ourselves as distinct from our software programming – see through our own eyes, not through the outdated clichés or software programs jammed into our heads. Reaching out to others, after looking into ourselves with genuinely new questions and software, we will create these relationships.

It is now a question of transforming relationships in a way we have never done before.

A great assignment.

Your Opinion...

What is your opinion and experience?
What do you think? What have been *your*
experiences of what's been discussed in this
chapter?

Please use this page to write your remarks, or you
may e-mail them to the *Sex and Business* website
at www.sexandbusiness.com/myopinion. Naturally,
you may express yourself anonymously.

_____

_____

_____

_____

_____

Final Software Blowout

These exercises are for those still stuck in their ruts...

(a) Name ten hidden reasons for the ban on love at work.

(b) Give three examples of entrenched male I-must-show-you-my-dominance attitudes.

(c) Give three examples of female fear in the face of (corporate) male power.

(d) What do you most deeply desire to have changed in your office?

(e) Who would you like to get rid of in your office, and why?

(f) Have you changed anything about yourself since reading this book? What?

(g) What is sexual harassment, and why is it an issue?

(h) Can an individual find meaning in the corporation?

(i) Do you want to be CEO in ten years? Why, or why not?

(j) Are you in love with someone in your office? How is it going?

Please mail your answers (anonymously, don't sign them) to: S. Hite, Pearson Education, 128 Long Acre, London WC2E 9AN, UK, or e-mail to s.hite@hite-research.com.